SOCIAL CONNECTION IN EVERYDAY SPACES

Edited by
Milovan Savic,
Roger Patulny and Jane Farmer

First published in Great Britain in 2025 by

Bristol University Press
University of Bristol
1–9 Old Park Hill
Bristol
BS2 8BB
UK
t: +44 (0)117 374 6645
e: bup-info@bristol.ac.uk

Details of international sales and distribution partners are available at bristoluniversitypress.co.uk

Editorial selection and matter © the editors; individual chapters © their respective authors 2025

The digital PDF and ePub versions of this title are available open access and distributed under the terms of the Creative Commons Attribution-NonCommercial-NoDerivatives 4.0 International licence (https://creativecommons.org/licenses/by-nc-nd/4.0/) which permits reproduction and distribution for non-commercial use without further permission provided the original work is attributed.

DOI: 10.51952/9781529246735

British Library Cataloguing in Publication Data
A catalogue record for this book is available from the British Library

ISBN 978-1-5292-4671-1 paperback
ISBN 978-1-5292-4672-8 ePub
ISBN 978-1-5292-4673-5 ePdf

The right of Milovan Savic, Roger Patulny and Jane Farmer to be identified as editors of this work has been asserted by them in accordance with the Copyright, Designs and Patents Act 1988.

All rights reserved: no part of this publication may be reproduced, stored in a retrieval system, or transmitted in any form or by any means, electronic, mechanical, photocopying, recording, or otherwise without the prior permission of Bristol University Press.

Every reasonable effort has been made to obtain permission to reproduce copyrighted material. If, however, anyone knows of an oversight, please contact the publisher.

The statements and opinions contained within this publication are solely those of the editors and contributors and not of the University of Bristol or Bristol University Press. The University of Bristol and Bristol University Press disclaim responsibility for any injury to persons or property resulting from any material published in this publication.

Bristol University Press works to counter discrimination on grounds of gender, race, disability, age and sexuality.

Cover design: Andrew Corbett
Front cover image: Stocksy/The Laundry Room

Contents

List of Figures and Tables		v
Notes on Contributors		vii
Acknowledgements		xiii
1	More than Loneliness: The Quest to Understand Social Connection *Milovan Savic, Roger Patulny and Jane Farmer*	1

PART I Personal Spaces

2	Male Friendships and Social Connections: Privileges and Pitfalls *Roger Patulny*	23
3	Older Filipina Australians' Local and Transnational Connective Care Practices *Earvin Charles Cabalquinto*	42
4	Social Connection by Design: Finnish Approaches to Long-Term Care *Jasmine Knox and Hannele Komu*	57
5	Companionship in Times of Uncertainty: The Role of Pets for Families with Children during COVID-19 *Shannon K. Bennetts, Sharinne B. Crawford, Tiffani J. Howell, Fiona C. Giles and Kylie Burke*	71

PART II Physical Spaces

6	Can Our Housing Environments Impact Loneliness? A Tale of Two Studies *Marlee Bower, Caitlin Buckle, Jennifer Kent, Lily Teesson, Roger Patulny, Laura McGrath and Emily Rugel*	89
7	Urban–Rural Disparities in Social Network Profiles Among Older Koreans at the Early Stage of the Pandemic *Pildoo Sung*	102
8	The Rise of Parkrun: Collective Positivity, Rituals and Episodic Togetherness in an Age of Loneliness *Nicholas Hookway and Zack Dwyer*	118

| 9 | United by Insects? Insects' Control and Development of Social Connections in a Large City
Oksana Zaporozhets and Olga Brednikova | 130 |

PART III Community Spaces

| 10 | Nature-Based Social Prescribing with LGBTQIA+ Asylum Seekers and Refugees: A Feasibility Study Using 'Friends in Nature'
Nerkez Opacin, Nicholas Hill, Sarah Bekessy, Ian Seal, Jill Litt and Katherine Johnson | 145 |
| 11 | Social Connectedness in Pandemic Times: A Case Study of Australia's Italian-Background Community
Simone Battiston and Damon Alexander | 159 |
| 12 | Local Place-Based Social Connection in Urban Fringe Areas: Learning from Resident Experiences
Jane Farmer, Tracy De Cotta, Annette Kroen and Andrew Butt | 174 |

PART IV Digital Spaces

| 13 | From Disruption to Digital Adaptation: Young Women's Social Connection During Lockdowns
Jessica Franks | 191 |
| 14 | Technological Bridges and Digital Ambivalences: The Role of Technology in Tackling Loneliness in Later Life
Barbara Barbosa Neves | 205 |
| 15 | Digital Pathways to Social Connection and Mental Health on the Urban Fringe
Milovan Savic and Anthony McCosker | 219 |
| 16 | Improving Social Connection in Everyday Spaces: Some Guidelines for Everyday Policy and Practice
Roger Patulny, Milovan Savic and Jane Farmer | 232 |

Index 247

List of Figures and Tables

Figures

1.1	Social connection circles and dimensions	13
2.1	Gender differences in norms and attitudes to social interactions, AUSSA 2007–2022	27
2.2	Gender differences in social networks and support, AUSSA 2007–2022	30
2.3	Gender differences in social practices, interactions and activities, AUSSA 2007–2022	32
2.4	Gender differences in socially oriented feelings, AUSSA 2007–2022	34
3.1	The YouTube video on exercising (left) and the Apple watch (right)	47
3.2	The video of Doc Willie Ong	48
3.3	The Facebook page (left) and the chicken feet recipe (right)	49
3.4	The photos of Rachel's grandchild learning to swim	50
4.1	The 'cat nook' in a long-term care facility in Finland	66
5.1	Social benefits (normal text) and challenges (italic) raised by parents regarding the role of pets for family wellbeing during the COVID-19 pandemic	78
7.1	Characteristics of six social network profiles among urban respondents	108
7.2	Characteristics of four social network profiles among rural respondents	110
10.1	A participant shared a photo of two galahs feeding in a grassy field at Darebin Parklands in a WhatsApp group, expressing gratitude for a lovely day	153
14.1	Kathleen's handwritten diary entry reflecting on feelings of loneliness in the evening	212

Tables

5.1	Characteristics of survey respondents	75
5.2	Pet-related activities ordered by frequency	76

7.1	Study variables	107
7.2	Linear regression of social network profiles on depressive symptoms	111
11.1	Participant characteristics	164
11.2	Self-reported impact of COVID-19 across life fields	165
11.3	Self-reported impact of COVID-19 on social connection	166
11.4	Respondent provision and access of support measures during COVID-19	166
11.5	Support network composition by support type: relationship to ego	167

Notes on Contributors

Damon Alexander is Senior Lecturer in Politics and Public Policy at Swinburne University of Technology. His interdisciplinary research spans public policy, civic and political engagement, and social network analysis. Recent works include 'Should we change the way we think about market performance when it comes to quasi-markets? A new framework for evaluating public service markets' (*Public Administration Review*, 2022).

Barbara Barbosa Neves is an award-winning sociologist specializing in technology and ageing. An international expert on social health and digital inequalities, she holds a prestigious Horizon Fellowship on AI at the University of Sydney's Centre for Healthy Societies. Her research has shaped technology and policy design, cited by the United Nations, Organization for Economic Co-operation and Development, and governments across 13 countries. With US$6 million in funding, 28 awards and 90+ publications amassing over 4,000 citations, she is also a sought-after media commentator whose insights have reached over three million people globally through outlets such as ABC, *The Guardian*, SBC and CBC.

Simone Battiston is Senior Lecturer in History and Politics at Swinburne University of Technology. His research focuses on postwar Italian emigration, particularly in the Australian context. Key publications include *Cittadini oltre confine: Storia, opinioni e rappresentanza degli italiani all'estero* (il Mulino, 2022) and *Italy and Australia: Redefining Bilateral Relations for the Twenty-First Century* (Palgrave Macmillan, 2023).

Sarah Bekessy leads the ICON Science research group at RMIT University, which uses interdisciplinary approaches to solve complex biodiversity conservation problems. She is particularly interested in understanding human behaviour's role in conservation, designing cities to encourage 'everyday nature' experiences and defining and measuring 'nature positive' development.

Shannon K. Bennetts is Senior Research Fellow at La Trobe University. Her research primarily focuses on parenting, child development and parent/

child mental health. She has a passion for cats and dogs and a keen interest in understanding human–animal interactions and the role of companion animals in family wellbeing.

Marlee Bower is Senior Research Fellow at the Matilda Centre for Research in Mental Health and Substance Use. Marlee's research explores the broader social determinants of mental health, particularly in understanding loneliness and isolation among marginalized individuals and how this relates to the built environment.

Olga Brednikova is Senior Researcher at the Sociological Institute of the Russian Academy of Sciences. Her research explores migration, borders, everyday life, urban neighbourhoods and qualitative methodology. She has published over 40 articles and co-edited four books. From 2022 to 2024, she served as editor-in-chief for the *Journal of Social Policy Research*.

Caitlin Buckle is Lecturer in City Planning with a background in human geography and environmental science. Caitlin's research focuses on regional housing and migration policy, city equity health and wellbeing, and informal housing market change. Her research interests lie in exploring people's connection to 'place' and 'home', and how this can be expressed through migration decision-making and housing choice.

Kylie Burke is Honorary Associate Professor with the School of Psychology, the University of Queensland and is Director of Research Strategy and Evaluation Metro North Mental Health Queensland. Kylie's work focuses on supporting parents and children experiencing adversity, including parenting adolescents, supporting parents of children with life-threatening childhood illnesses, the intergenerational effects of social disadvantage and on the systems and impacts of mental health services.

Andrew Butt is Professor of Urban Planning at RMIT's Centre for Urban Research. With over 30 years in planning practice, research and teaching, his work focuses on land use change, regional development and peri-urban planning. He has co-authored *The Future of the Fringe: The Crisis in Peri-urban Planning* (CSIRO Publishing, 2020) and *Local Government Co-ordination: Metropolitan Governance in Twenty-first Century Australia* (AHHURI, 2021).

Earvin Charles Cabalquinto is Australian Research Council (ARC) DECRA Research Fellow and Senior Lecturer in the School of Media, Film and Journalism at Monash University. His expertise lies in the intersecting fields of digital media, migration, mobilities and ageing research. He is the author of *(Im)mobile Homes: Family Life at a Distance in the Age of Mobile Media*

(Oxford University Press, 2022). His research focuses on the dynamics and impacts of digital inclusion and exclusion among migrants and their networks in a digital, global society. Learn more at www.ecabalquinto.com.

Sharinne B. Crawford is Senior Research Fellow in the SPHERE Centre for Research Excellence, Department of General Practice at Monash University. Sharinne is a public health researcher focusing on women's sexual and reproductive health, parenting and children's health, social media and ethics in public health research.

Tracy De Cotta is Research Associate at Swinburne University's Social Innovation Research Institute and the ARC Centre of Excellence for Automated Decision-Making & Society. Her research explores human geography, community mental health and wellbeing, social connection and public space. She has published in a broad range of journals including the *Journal of Sociology*, *Area*, *Health & Place* and *Information, Communication & Society*.

Zack Dwyer is a PhD candidate in sociology at the University of Tasmania. His research focuses on the role of sport, leisure and identity in contemporary life. He currently works as a policy advisor for the Tasmanian government.

Jane Farmer is Professor of Health and Innovation at Swinburne University of Technology. Her research focuses on social connection, community engagement and digital innovation, with extensive experience in collaborative, place-based research.

Jessica Franks is a PhD candidate at the University of Melbourne and Manager of Co-design and Engagement at Western Victoria Primary Health Network, where she leads the Social Prescribing portfolio. Her research focuses on social connections, best-practice engagement, lived experience and person-centred health. Her work has been published in prestigious outlets including *Social Media + Society* and *Convergence*.

Fiona C. Giles is Research Fellow at the Safer Families Centre of Research Excellence, the University of Melbourne and an Adjunct Lecturer at the La Trobe Rural Health School. Fiona's work focuses on improving health system responses to domestic and family violence, and rural health inequalities.

Nicholas Hill is a community-engaged researcher working in the areas of LGBTQIA+ mental health and suicide and supported decision-making. He specializes in participatory methods and co-producing innovative resources for individuals accessing mental health support, service providers and policy makers.

Nicholas Hookway is Senior Lecturer in Sociology at the University of Tasmania. His research focuses on emotions, identity and social connection with a growing interest in the sociology of sport. Nick has published in top international sociology journals and his book *Everyday Morality: Doing it Ourselves in an Age of Uncertainty* (Routledge, 2019) was awarded the 2020 Stephen Crook Memorial Prize from the Australian Sociological Association, a biennial prize for the best authored book in Australian sociology.

Tiffani J. Howell is Senior Research Fellow within La Trobe University's Anthrozoology Research Group. Her research explores various aspects of human–animal relationships, animal behaviour and cognition, animal welfare, and assistance animals.

Katherine Johnson is Dean of the School of Global, Urban and Social Studies at RMIT University. Her research focuses on improving the health and mental health of LGBTQIA+ communities through policy and practice transformations. Funded by ARC, EU Horizon 2020, NHMRC and others, her current projects address sexuality, religion in schools and nature-based social prescribing. She is series editor of Routledge's *Transforming LGBTQ+ Lives* and serves on multiple editorial boards.

Jennifer Kent is Senior Research Fellow and Urbanism Research Lead at the University of Sydney School of Architecture, Design and Planning. Jennifer's research interests are at the intersections between transport, urbanism and human health and she is a leading authority on the use of qualitative methods in this space.

Jasmine Knox is a social researcher and PhD candidate at Swinburne University of Technology, Australia. Her research focuses on social connection, wellbeing among older adults and broader aspects of positive ageing.

Hannele Komu is a nurse and Doctor of Health Sciences with extensive experience in elderly care, organizational culture, and the comparison of public and private care services. Her expertise is reflected in her 2016 dissertation, *Organizational Culture in Care Homes: A Comparison of Public and Private Care Homes from Environmental and Personnel Perspectives* (University of Eastern Finland). She continues to contribute to the field through ongoing research in gerontology.

Annette Kroen is Senior Research Fellow at the RMIT's Centre for Urban Research, specializing in urban and regional planning. Her research focuses on suburban growth, integrated land use and transport planning, social connectedness and urban resilience. She works closely with government and industry partners on projects addressing planning policy, disaster risk reduction and the long-term impacts of place-making. Key publications include 'Neighbourhood essentials: the importance of local shops and services in new suburbs' (in *The Next Australian City: The Suburban Evolution*, Connor Court Publishing, 2024) and 'Precinct planning for active and public transport in growth suburbs' (*Australian Planner*, 2021).

Jill Litt is Professor of Environmental Studies at the University of Colorado Boulder, an Adjunct Professor at the Colorado School of Public Health and Senior Researcher at ISGlobal in Barcelona. With a PhD from Johns Hopkins University, her research explores the intersection of neighbourhoods, nearby nature, food-producing landscapes and health. She focuses on environmental and policy approaches to promote healthy eating, active living and mental wellbeing in equitable and just ways.

Anthony McCosker is Professor of Media and Communication at Swinburne University of Technology. He is the Director of the Social Innovation Research Institute and Chief Investigator in the ARC Centre of Excellence in Automated Decision Making and Society (ADM+S). His research focuses on digital inclusion, inequalities in technology adoption, and the social impacts of automation and artificial intelligence. He is the author or co-author of *Everyday Data Cultures* (Polity, 2022), *Automating Vision* (Routledge, 2020), *Intensive Media* (Palgrave Macmillan, 2013), and co-editor of *Negotiating Digital Citizenship* (Rowman & Littlefield, 2016).

Laura McGrath is Senior Lecturer in Psychosocial Mental Health at the Open University. Laura's research focuses on the ways in which people's material environments influence their psychological experiences, including mental health, loneliness and wellbeing. Her work is influenced by community and social psychology, human geography and sociology.

Nerkez Opacin is Research Fellow at RMIT University, focusing on community engagement, nature-based solutions, social connections and post-conflict recovery. His work integrates programme development, social research and project evaluation. As part of the RECETAS project, he investigates nature-based social prescribing for at-risk populations. Using participatory methods like ethnography and co-design, Nerkez collaborates with communities and organizations to produce research that informs practice, shapes policy and fosters resilience in vulnerable communities.

Roger Patulny is Professor of Sociology at Hong Kong Baptist University. His research spans emotions, loneliness, social isolation and wellbeing, with extensive publications, grants and influential works on emotions in modern society.

Emily Rugel is an environmental epidemiologist whose research explores health-promoting community design across the lifespan, with a particular focus on roles for urban nature in improving mental health, supporting social ties and increasing pro-environmental behaviour. Throughout her work, she aims to develop evidence that can be embedded in sustainability plans and integrated in policies that advance equity.

Milovan Savic is Research Fellow at Swinburne University. His work explores the intersection of artificial intelligence, digital technologies and human connection, advancing ethical technology governance and digital inclusion while making knowledge accessible beyond academic confines.

Ian Seal is Executive Director of Many Coloured Sky, the Queer Development Agency. Ian has worked in community development and capacity building for over three decades in Australia, Asia Pacific and East Africa.

Pildoo Sung is Assistant Professor of Sociology at Hanyang University. As a quantitative sociologist, he investigates the interplay between social relationships and health and wellbeing. His research addresses three main themes: (1) the complexity and dynamics of social networks in later life and their health implications; (2) stress, coping and mental wellbeing among family caregivers; and (3) social capital and health in a comparative perspective.

Lily Teesson is Research Assistant at the Matilda Centre, University of Sydney. She is interested in how we acquire evidence for the social determinants of health. Lily has published on the impact of the built environment on mental health, youth mental health and the impact of COVID-19 on mental health.

Oksana Zaporozhets is Researcher at the Georg Simmel Center for Urban Studies, Humboldt University of Berlin. Her work focuses on urbanization, neighbouring in new urban areas, digitalization of urban life and citizen-led digital infrastructures. She has co-edited *Microurbanism: City in Details* (2014) and *Nets of the City: Citizens, Technologies, Governance* (2021), with articles published in *City* and the *Journal of Cultural Geography*.

Acknowledgements

We acknowledge the Traditional Owners of the unceded lands on which this work was conceived and developed. We pay our respects to their Elders past, present and emerging, and recognize their continuing connection to land, waters and culture.

This edited collection emerged from a symposium hosted by Swinburne University in 2023, which brought together 15 presentations on social connection. While the book grew beyond the initial symposium presentations to include additional international perspectives and contributors, that gathering provided the foundation for this comprehensive collection.

This work was supported by the Australian Research Council Linkage Project (LP200301335) and our industry partners – Australian Red Cross, Neami National, City of Casey, City of Whittlesea, City of Wyndham and Today Design. Their collaborative commitment has enabled us to make this work freely accessible through open-access publication. This aligns with our goal of making research available to the broadest possible audience.

We are grateful for the contributions of all authors who have shared their expertise and insights in this collection.

1

More than Loneliness: The Quest to Understand Social Connection

Milovan Savic, Roger Patulny and Jane Farmer

At 18, Emma lives alone in an outer Melbourne suburb where rent is affordable, but social connection is costly. Juggling two part-time jobs to make ends meet, her free time and transport options are scarce. While her therapist offers coping strategies for loneliness, the real barriers to belonging lie beyond individualized interventions. Without a car, each social opportunity requires complex calculations of time, transport logistics and work schedules. Though social media helps her keep up with old friends, the physical landscape of her suburb – designed for families with cars – leaves young people like her with few places to just hang out.[1]

Stories like Emma's highlight how social connection is shaped by many things, including housing affordability, employment opportunities, transport infrastructure, urban planning and digital access – structural realities that individual-focused interventions cannot address. Recently, social connection has gained unprecedented policy attention. The World Health Organization established a Commission on Social Connection (World Health Organization, 2024), while the US Surgeon General warned that addressing social disconnection is a public health priority, perhaps more significant than combatting diabetes and obesity (Murthy, 2023). Several nations have introduced policies to address loneliness, with the UK and Japan appointing dedicated ministerial positions.

While the problem is acknowledged, its conceptualization, root causes and solutions remain contested. Much public discourse reduces social disconnection to an individual 'pathology' requiring health intervention, neglecting how structural, cultural, political and institutional factors influence relationship formation. This suggests the need for a more comprehensive framework that can integrate multiple perspectives and levels of analysis.

Recent thinking has seen a shift towards understanding social connection as more than just the absence of loneliness or the presence of interactions. Studies identify multiple dimensions affecting how individuals and communities build relationships (OECD, 2024), including structural patterning, functional roles, quality of interactions, and broader community and neighbourhood connections as key to social connection (Cheshire, 2022; Holt-Lunstad, 2022; Bower et al, 2024; Verhagen et al, 2025).

The conceptualization of social connection spans diverse perspectives. Psychology-led studies often focus on individual-level changes and measurable indicators of connections. At the same time, interdisciplinary approaches examine how social connection is shaped by economic inequality, changes in built environments, eroding social infrastructure and technological shifts (Neves et al, 2019; Patulny and Bower, 2022; Bower et al, 2024). These alternative perspectives critique how current policy and research often overlook fundamental interactions between people, society, politics and environments. The diversity of these approaches, while valuable, points to the need for a more comprehensive conceptualization that can synthesize multiple theoretical perspectives to better understand the complex nature of the social connection.

In this introductory chapter, we examine social connection's complexity beyond prevailing loneliness discourses. We review frameworks for understanding social connection across disciplines, emphasizing how it operates across different *everyday spaces* – personal, physical, community and digital – and how broader social, cultural and structural conditions shape interactions in these spaces.

Drawing from the chapters in this collection and previous evidence synthesis (Farmer et al, 2021; 2025), we have identified eight key perspectives through which to consider social connection across the personal, physical, community and digital spaces:

1. *dimensions* of structural, functional, and quality aspects;
2. *network qualities* of strong and weak ties;
3. *relational dynamics* between structure and agency;
4. *social capital* resource components;
5. *community development* activities;
6. *(inter)-cultural perspectives*;
7. *temporal trajectories*; and
8. *synthesized perspectives* – how these different theoretical approaches and evidence bases work together to advance understanding of social connection across spatial settings.

While each perspective offers valuable insights, this final synthesized approach provides the most comprehensive and practically applicable framework for understanding and improving social connection.

The chapter concludes with a roadmap of the other chapter contributions.

Reconsidering loneliness: from individual-centred to structural understandings

The dominant approach to social connection largely frames it as solving loneliness – a personal (mental health) condition requiring medical intervention (Hickin et al, 2021). While quantitative experiments and large survey datasets have drawn attention to the phenomenon's importance, they often neglect how societal structures enable or inhibit meaningful relationships.

Survey-based research, while valuable, has inherent limitations: it captures single time points, often uses atypical populations, constrains responses to pre-ordained questions, and struggles to identify complex processes of change and influences over time (Coleman, 1958; Wilkinson et al, 2017). This approach potentially misses important causal and contextual factors. Understanding social connection requires exploring its manifestations across diverse everyday spaces, examining both individual-oriented and structural factors and tensions between these perspectives.

Personal connections and structural constraints

Personal connections, while experienced through intimate interactions with family and friends, reveal the complex interplay between individual agency and structural constraints. Dominant approaches often frame social connection as primarily a matter of individual choice and action – suggesting people simply need the right tools or guidance to connect. However, factors traditionally framed as matters of individual agency – how age groups socialize, gender-based interaction patterns, employment-related networking and health-related isolation – are deeply embedded in broader structural conditions.

For instance, older adults' loneliness experiences typically reflect not just individual choices but systematic constraints: reduced mobility, limited income, inadequate community facilities and societal devaluation of ageing (Neves et al, 2019; Gardiner et al, 2020; Hawkley, 2022). Similarly, higher loneliness rates among marginalized groups reflect not a lack of individual effort to connect but rather systematic barriers, including social exclusion, stigma and restricted access to community participation (Weiss, 1973; Bower et al, 2024). Economic inequality fundamentally shapes the scope of individual agency – financial hardship restricts not just resources for social activities but access and confidence for participation.

Physical-structural constraints

The built environment and social infrastructure also shape the parameters within which individual agency operates. While individuals may seek connection opportunities, their capacity to act is enabled or constrained by environmental features and socioeconomic conditions (Roof and Oleru, 2008; Bower et al, 2024). Well-maintained public spaces, green areas and community facilities do not just provide venues for social interactions – they create the conditions that make meaningful connections possible. Yet, these resources remain unequally distributed, with fewer available in economically disadvantaged areas.

The decline of 'third spaces' – locations where people gather outside home and work (Oldenburg, 1989) – illustrates how structural changes limit individual capacity for connection. Social infrastructure encompasses not just physical gathering places like libraries, parks and community centres but the integrated system of transport, digital networks and local services that enable or inhibit connection possibilities (Bower et al, 2024). While individuals might desire to maintain relationships across distances, their ability to do so depends on transport accessibility and digital infrastructure. The erosion of social infrastructure through funding cuts or privatization disproportionately affects disadvantaged communities where market alternatives are unaffordable, creating concentrated zones of restricted social connection opportunities.

Community connections and structural policy issues

Policy responses focusing solely on enhancing individual capacity for connection – such as social prescribing (where health practitioners link clients to local activities) or psychological interventions – often overlook how structural conditions shape the possibility of sustained connection. While these approaches may provide short-term individual support (Reinhardt et al, 2021), they cannot address the fundamental inequalities and systemic barriers that inhibit the development of self-sustaining socially connected communities. Individual-centred interventions may help people identify connection opportunities, but their effectiveness depends on the existence of accessible, well-resourced community spaces and networks. The COVID-19 pandemic highlighted this dynamic, as existing structural inequalities amplified the impact of isolation measures across different population groups (Patulny and Bower, 2022).

Digital social connection and structural issues

Digital technologies further reshape the landscape of individual agency in social connection, while simultaneously reflecting and sometimes amplifying existing structural inequalities. While individuals might exercise agency in choosing how to connect online, their choices operate within platforms designed and controlled by commercial interests (van Dijck, 2013; Zuboff, 2019). The apparent democratization of connection through digital means masks the ability to leverage these tools effectively and remains structurally patterned.

Digital divides persist not only as matters of individual choice or capability but as manifestations of broader social inequalities. Beyond basic access, digital connection requires specific forms of literacy, skills and resources – capabilities shaped by educational opportunity, economic status and cultural capital (Helsper, 2021). Marginalized groups face compounded barriers: limited access to devices and reliable internet compounds existing social exclusion (Baum et al, 2014). The COVID-19 pandemic's shift towards digital-by-default services revealed how technological infrastructure and digital capabilities have become fundamental structural determinants of social connection possibility (Patulny and Bower, 2022).

Moving beyond individually focused approaches requires recognizing how economic, social, cultural and political structures create varying possibilities for social connection across population groups. While individuals navigate these structures with varying degrees of agency, their capacity to form and maintain enduring relationships is fundamentally shaped by structural conditions (Farmer et al, 2021). Rather than focusing solely on individual capacity to overcome loneliness, a comprehensive understanding of social connection must examine the complex interplay between individual action and the broader system of structural influences operating across different contexts and scales.

Ways of understanding social connection

1. Dimensions of social connection

Recent Organization for Economic Co-operation and Development analysis identified four key dimensions that shape both individual capacity and structural opportunity for social connection: structure, function, quality and community/societal connectedness (OECD, 2024). The (i) *structural* dimension describes observable features of social relationships – how networks form and operate within given constraints (see also Chapter 2, this volume). While individuals may initiate connections, these patterns reflect broader social organization and resource distribution. These are amenable to objective measurement of contact frequency and group activity participation.

The (ii) *functional* dimension addresses the role or function of relationships – that is, what outcomes they produce for people, such as wellbeing, satisfaction and prosperity (Chapter 3 and Chapter 15, this volume). Beyond individual support, this dimension reveals how social networks channel resources – often reinforcing existing structural advantages as Bourdieu (1986) observed in how social capital leverages economic capital.

The (iii) *quality* dimension refers to relationship depth and trust, shaped by both individual interaction choices and broader cultural norms and institutional contexts. While individuals cultivate relationship quality through personal investment, their capacity to do so is enabled or constrained by time resources, spatial proximity and cultural frameworks (Weiss, 1973; Cacioppo and Cacioppo, 2014).

(iv) *Community/societal connectedness* links an individual's belonging to broader social structures and collective identities (Verhagen et al, 2025). This dimension reveals how personal connection practices are embedded within and shaped by institutional arrangements, cultural movements and power relations. It highlights how individual agency in building connections operates within collectively produced possibilities for inclusion and cultural expression.

These dimensions manifest differently across everyday spaces. In personal spaces, structural patterns shape intimate relationships, while functional support operates through emotional care. Physical spaces configure structural opportunities for interaction through built environment features, while community spaces illustrate how quality emerges through shared values and trust-building activities. Digital spaces increasingly mediate all dimensions, enabling hybrid forms of social connection from private messaging to public forums, though access to and benefits from these spaces remain structurally patterned.

The interaction between these dimensions reveals how individual and structural factors shape social connection. Different relationship structures, emerging from both personal choice and structural opportunity, enable varying functions and qualities of connection. Resilient communities often emerge where individual network-building capacity aligns with supportive structural conditions (Neves et al, 2019; Farmer et al, 2021; 2025).

2. Social network perspectives

Social network theory describes how relationship structures and resource flows operate across different social contexts. The distinction between strong ties (close relationships with frequent interaction and emotional intensity) and weak ties (casual or distant connections) (Granovetter, 1983) is important and manifest distinctly across space. Close, personal spaces nurture strong ties through family and intimate friendships; physical spaces enable both strong ties through recurring community participation and weak ties through casual encounters; and community spaces bridge between tie types through organized activities.

That being said, ties that transcend spaces also reveal important dynamics. Ryan (2016) notes from studies of Polish migrants in the UK that tie strength and ethnic composition of networks are less important than social distance and willingness to share resources. She argues that strong ties can serve as 'vertical' ladders to assist migrants in improving their prospects, while 'horizontal' ties that are too weak lack the trust required for sharing. Digital platforms also create unique opportunities for maintaining diverse tie strengths across distances. Digital platforms particularly facilitate what Reyes Acosta (2016) calls 'latent and flexible ties' – connections that can be engaged or disengaged with relative ease, requiring less emotional investment than traditional relationships while still contributing to social capital in distinctive ways.

Social network analysis can examine networks either 'ego-centrically' through individual survey samples (investigating friends and acquaintances and their associated benefits; for example, Ramia et al, 2017 or through 'small world' analysis of whole network structures. Core network characteristics – density (interconnectedness between members), reciprocity, diversity and composition (for example, gender diversity or kin versus non-kin proportions) – affect how people mobilize support across different contexts (Hurlbert et al, 2000). Denser networks, where members maintain interconnections, offer advantages for resilience and support, facilitating crisis communication and community preparedness (Losee et al, 2021).

3. Relational approaches to social connection

A relational approach emerged from sociological traditions examining the interplay between structure and agency (Archer, 1995; Emirbayer, 1997). Rather than viewing social connection as either individually determined or structurally imposed, this approach examines how connection practices develop through ongoing interactions between societal structures and individual capacities.

Following Stones' theoretical framework (2005; see also Chapter 2, this volume), external and internal structures shape connection possibilities. External structures encompass institutional arrangements, material conditions and geographic factors independent of individual actors. These include workplace organizations, economic conditions, built environments and technological infrastructures that create or constrain social interaction opportunities. Cultural institutions and social norms also establish expectations about appropriate forms of connection across different contexts (Emirbayer and Mische, 1998).

Internal structures comprise the internalized patterns, skills and dispositions individuals develop through social experiences. These include not only beliefs and attitudes about social relationships but also practical knowledge about navigating different social situations, cultural competencies for engaging with diverse groups and embodied habits of interaction. These internal structures shape how individuals interpret connection opportunities and mobilize relationship-building resources (Crossley, 2011).

A relational perspective manifests differently across everyday spaces. In *personal spaces*, family arrangements and housing conditions interact with emotional competencies to shape how relationships develop and are maintained (Patulny and Petrolo, 2024). *Physical spaces* demonstrate how built environments create conditions people navigate based on internalized social norms and spatial practices (Crossley, 2011). *Community spaces* reveal how collective practices emerge through institutional structures and shared cultural resources, enabling different groups to develop distinct patterns of connection while navigating broader social contexts.

The interaction between external and internal structures becomes particularly visible in *digital spaces*. Here, technological platforms create new conditions that individuals must interpret and navigate using their digital literacy, cultural understanding and internalized norms about appropriate online interaction (van Dijck, 2013). For example, social media platforms offer particular affordances for connection, but their use depends on both technical skills and cultural knowledge.

The methodological implications suggest combining methods that can capture both structural contexts and individual navigation of these contexts (Emirbayer and Mische, 1998). This might include network analysis alongside qualitative investigations of how people interpret and act upon connection opportunities across different spatial settings.

4. Social capital: resources, relations and critical perspectives

Social capital theory examines how socially connected people generate and distribute resources. The theory identifies distinct forms of connection: bonding social capital (emotional support and group identity through close relationships), bridging social capital (access to diverse resources across different social groups) and linking social capital (connections to institutions and formal structures) (Putnam, 2000; Aldrich, 2012).

Bourdieu's (1986) critical perspective reveals how social capital often reproduces existing inequalities by accruing benefits for exclusive groups. Access to and ability to mobilize social capital depends heavily on one's position within broader social structures and possession of other forms of capital – economic, cultural, symbolic and emotional. This critical lens shows how seemingly neutral social connections actually operate within and often reinforce existing power relations and social hierarchies.

These forms of social capital manifest differently across everyday spaces. Personal spaces facilitate bonding capital through intimate relationships and family networks. Physical spaces enable both bonding and bridging capital through community facilities and public spaces, though access remains unequally distributed (Bower et al, 2024). Community spaces particularly facilitate bridging and linking capital through organized activities and institutional connections (Farmer et al, 2021), while digital platforms create new possibilities for all forms of social capital. However, leveraging these benefits depends on social position and digital literacy (Baum et al, 2014).

Access to and mobilization of social capital varies significantly across social groups. Socioeconomic status, education, gender and cultural background shape both the available resources and mobilization capacity. While working-class communities often demonstrate strong bonding capital, they may face barriers to developing bridging and linking capital that could provide economic opportunities. Digital technologies have transformed these dynamics in complex ways – online platforms enable flexible engagement with diverse networks (Reyes Acosta, 2016) and potentially broader access to resources; this flexibility can lead to more superficial connections. While digital platforms may lower initial networking barriers, connection quality depends on pre-existing social and cultural capital. The flexibility of online ties is double-edged – enabling easier access while potentially fostering 'dark side' social capital through online communities where misinformation and intolerance thrive (Roberts and Wescott, 2024).

5. *Community development perspectives on social connection*

Community development approaches examine and facilitate social connection at collective levels. Rooted in social planning and community development traditions (Rothman, 1968), these approaches focus explicitly on place-based connections. They analyse how local communities function, and seek to develop interventions to strengthen neighbourhood ties. While Asset-Based Community Development theory emphasizes building on existing community strengths (Kretzmann and McKnight, 1993), critics note how this approach may reinforce existing power dynamics (DeFilippis, 2001).

The place-based focus of community development faces particular challenges in contemporary contexts (Magre et al, 2016). Contemporary neighbourliness can involve 'a range of contradictory experiences, narrative and social expectations' (Cheshire, 2022: 3). Many neighbourhoods lack traditional connective infrastructure – from community centres to corner shops – while residents often face structural barriers to local engagement, including long work hours, extended commutes from affordable suburbs to employment centres, and the disappearance of local gathering spaces. Digital technologies create new possibilities to develop connections between people in and with place (for example, community groups on Facebook, Good Karma Networks) but can potentially detract from local engagement. For instance, a young retail worker might find traditional community activities inaccessible due to irregular work schedules and transport limitations, turning instead to online neighbourhood groups or interest-based digital communities that better accommodate their circumstances.

Effective community development now requires understanding this interplay between physical and digital connections. While online platforms cannot replace local infrastructure, they can complement place-based approaches by providing flexible engagement options that work around structural constraints. This suggests the need for hybrid approaches that recognize both the value of local physical connection and the practical reality of how people navigate connection opportunities within their daily circumstances.

6. Cultural dimensions of social connection

Cultural frameworks expose how social connection is understood, valued and practised differently across societies. While Western approaches favour individualistic forms of connection, other cultural traditions emphasize collective and relational aspects of social life (Hall, 1976; Hofstede, 2001). Cultures differ in how people seek and provide social support. While some cultures encourage direct requests for help, others emphasize reading social cues and offering support without explicit asking (Kim et al, 2008). These differences reflect deeper cultural values about individual autonomy versus group harmony and interdependence (Markus and Kitayama, 1991).

For example, Chinese *guanxi* networks operate through distinct cultural dynamics of status, face and long-term reciprocity (*renqing*). While sharing some features with Western social capital, *guanxi* networks are more fluid, with less distinction between public and private relations (Feng and Patulny, 2021).

Digital technologies challenge and transform these cultural patterns of connection. While online platforms might appear to standardize social interaction globally, research reveals how cultural values significantly influence digital connection practices (Hjorth and Kim, 2011). Societies adapt their use of digital technologies in culturally specific ways, from varying preferences for public versus private communication to alternate norms about appropriate online relationship maintenance (Miller et al, 2016).

These cultural norms of connection are not static but evolve over time, shaped by technological change, generational shifts and cross-cultural exchange. Understanding this dynamic nature of cultural practices is important for examining how social connection operates in increasingly diverse and mediated societies.

7. Temporal dimensions of social connection

Life course theory suggests that relationships develop and transform according to life stage, presenting challenges and opportunities for connection (Elder et al, 2003). The 'social convoy' model describes how individuals maintain different circles of relationships throughout their lives, with some connections remaining stable while others shift with major life transitions such as moving cities, changing jobs, starting families or experiencing health changes (Antonucci et al, 2014).

Hall's (2019) research reveals the significant time investment required for relationship formation – around 40–60 hours of interaction for casual friendships, 80–100 hours for close friendships and over 200 hours for best friendships. These time requirements reflect the gradual process of building trust and mutual understanding. In subsequent research, Hall (2020) found that while digital interactions can help maintain relationships, they do not generate the same emotional resonance or depth as face-to-face encounters, suggesting that physical co-presence remains crucial for developing deeper connections.

Digital technologies affect these temporal patterns in complex ways. While online platforms enable more frequent interaction by reducing the practical barriers to face-to-face connection like travel or scheduling (Savic et al, 2025), they do not necessarily accelerate the development of close relationships. Instead, they create patterns of 'relating through technology' (Hall, 2020), where relationship development combines mediated and face-to-face interaction.

Different generations integrate digital connection into their relationship practices in varying ways. While younger people might maintain continuous contact through messaging apps (Johns et al, 2024), and older adults might use digital tools primarily to arrange face-to-face meetings, both groups typically combine online and offline interaction to maintain meaningful relationships (Neves et al, 2019; Savic et al, 2025).

While these perspectives offer valuable insights, separating them into distinct theoretical domains limits their practical application. What is needed is an approach that can integrate these various dimensions of social connection while remaining practically applicable for policy and intervention. The synthesized model that follows addresses this need.

8. 'Pragmatic' synthesized models of social connection

As public and policy interest in improving social connection has increased, alongside the need for whole-of-system and whole-of-organization approaches, there has grown a need to synthesize evidence across disciplines to understand and 'capture' social connection pragmatically, on the ground, and in everyday spaces. Such an approach requires drawing together evidence and theory from different knowledge domains (aligning with perspectives 1–7 presented here) to inform evaluation of interventions. To design, implement and evaluate policy or practice interventions effectively, a grounded pragmatic model is needed that adequately 'defines' social connection, encompasses factors affecting its status and enables measurement of change in everday contexts.

One such synthesized conceptualization emerged from a seven-year programme funded by the Australian Red Cross (Farmer et al, 2021). The model stemmed from a practical need to understand progress and collect data about social connection improvement across different programmes – from community resilience initiatives building social capital to programmes addressing youth and older people's loneliness and supporting migrants' friendship-building. While the Red Cross knew these programmes all targeted social connection, they lacked a holistic model to unify their data collection.

Such a model requires recognizing various internal subjective states of feeling supported and connected, and external situations that cut across, support and undermine such states. An individual's subjective sense of being connected involves evaluation of their relationship structures, access to resources and support, relationship quality, and feelings of connection (Verhagen et al, 2025). This state emerges through different relationship types identified in evolutionary psychology and sociological research. Dunbar's (1998) social brain hypothesis identifies universal patterns of human relationships across cultures and history, while Pahl's (2000) work reveals how people categorize friendships into circles of varying intimacy serving different functions.

As illustrated in Figure 1.1, the model identifies four concentric circles of social connection: close connections at the core, surrounded by social allies, group connections and wider community belonging. Unlike approaches focusing solely on individual relationships, these circles capture how personal connections exist within broader social structures. For instance, a migrant's close family connections might be maintained across distances. At the same time, their local allies provide practical support, community groups offer cultural belonging and wider community engagement enables civic participation. Importantly, such 'embeddedness' does not come as a 'static achieve state', but a dynamic, structural and relational process that is continually renegotiated over time (Grzymala-Kazlowska and Ryan, 2022).

The model recognizes four key dimensions that cut across these circles, addressing both individual and structural aspects of connection. The quality of connections dimension assesses subjective experiences – from intimate bonds with close connections to casual interactions in wider community settings. Structural aspects capture observable features like numbers of contacts and interaction patterns, revealing how different circles require varying time investments and maintenance practices. Two types of outcomes are measured: affective outcomes reflecting people's internal feelings of connection across these circles and social support outcomes indicating how different relationship types provide varied forms of support.

Figure 1.1: Social connection circles and dimensions

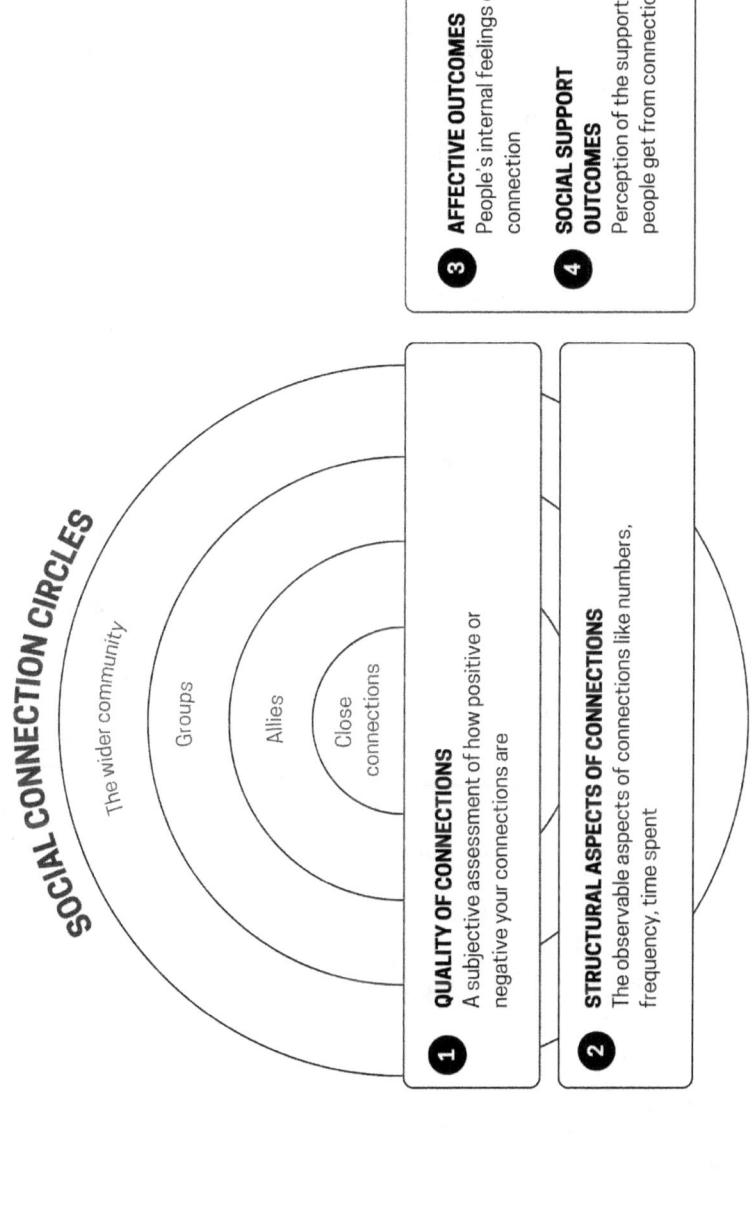

Source: Adapted from SocPET (De Cotta et al, 2024)

This measurement framework moves beyond simple counts of relationships or individual interventions. Aligned with contemporary approaches (Holt-Lunstad et al, 2017; OECD, 2024), it enables the evaluation of both personal connection experiences and the structural conditions that shape them. Through iterations of co-design with community practitioners and applications for research and routine data collection, the model has been validated as an effective tool for 'capturing' social connection status.

The synthesized model's practical utility lies in its ability to unite diverse theoretical perspectives while remaining operationally relevant. While such 'bricolage' approaches might be considered theoretically 'impure', their value lies in their ability to bridge theory and practice. The model provides a framework that can unite efforts across different societal roles – from health practitioners and urban planners to community developers and voluntary groups – in working to improve social connection. By offering a common language and measurement approach across policy, practice and community contexts, it enables coordinated action towards enhancing social connection at both individual and strucutural level.

Roadmap for the book

The theoretical conceptualizations identified inform analyses in this collection. Social capital theory guides examinations of community resource mobilization, relational approaches frame digital–physical environment interactions, and cultural frameworks illuminate connections across diverse populations and contexts. These aspects of social connection emerge and evolve through everyday spaces where people live, work and interact. These spaces should not be thought of as physical locations; rather, they are dynamic contexts where relationships form, transform and adapt to changing circumstances.

The chapters that follow examine how connection manifest across personal, physical, community and digital spaces. While organized around these distinct domains, the book recognizes their interconnected nature, particularly how digital technologies permeate all other spaces, reflecting how people navigate social connection fluidly across multiple contexts in their daily lives. In our concluding chapter, we examine how each contribution incorporates and advances this comprehensive conceptualization of social connection.

Part I: Personal Spaces

The first section comprises studies of social connection within personal and intimate spaces, showing how individual circumstances interact with social structures and everyday practices. Patulny (Chapter 2) explores how masculinity and gender norms influence men's capacity for meaningful connection. Cabalquinto (Chapter 3) investigates how older Filipina Australians navigate transnational connections through digital technologies, revealing the intersection of cultural, personal and familial relationships. Knox and Komu (Chapter 4) examine how the intentional design of Finnish long-term care facilities creates environments that nurture social connection among older adults. Bennetts and colleagues (Chapter 5) extend the understanding of personal connections to include human–animal relationships, revealing how pets provided crucial emotional support and facilitated social connections during times of crisis.

Part II: Physical Spaces

The chapters in this section expose how built environments shape social connection opportunities, from housing design to community spaces. Bower and colleagues (Chapter 6) demonstrate how housing environments fundamentally impact experiences of loneliness. Sung (Chapter 7) examines urban–rural disparities in South Korean social networks during the COVID-19 pandemic, revealing geographic influences on mental health outcomes. Hookway and Dwyer (Chapter 8) analyse 'parkrun' as an innovative platform for creating 'episodic togetherness' through shared rituals and activities, while Zaporozhets and Brednikova (Chapter 9) explore how common urban challenges – that is, insect infestations in St. Petersburg – can unite or divide neighbours.

Part III: Community Spaces

This section examines interventions and initiatives that foster social connection among diverse communities. Opacin and colleagues (Chapter 10) evaluate nature-based social prescribing for LGBTQIA+ refugee and asylum-seeker communities, showing how tailored approaches enhance connectedness. Battiston and Alexander (Chapter 11) explore the Italian-Australian community's mobilization of social networks during the COVID-19 pandemic, revealing how bonding and bridging ties maintain community resilience. Farmer and colleagues (Chapter 12) investigate social connection in rapidly growing urban fringe communities, highlighting how social infrastructure and thoughtful community engagement support meaningful interactions.

Part IV: Digital Spaces

The final section examines the ways in which digital technologies reshape contemporary social connection practices. Franks (Chapter 13) maps young women's evolving social networks through different stages of the COVID-19 pandemic, revealing both challenges and resilience in digital connection maintenance. Barbosa Neves (Chapter 14) examines technology's role in addressing loneliness among older adults, weighing digital solutions against face-to-face interactions. Savic and McCosker (Chapter 15) explore how young people in Melbourne's urban fringe adapt digital platforms like Discord and Facebook to foster connections while managing mental health challenges, highlighting the critical role of digital literacy.

Conclusion

The chapters in this collection examine social connection as it occurs across everyday spaces – from intimate personal settings to broader community contexts. Through studies of personal intimacies, physical environments, community initiatives and digital practices, this collection shows how social connection emerges through the interplay of individual agency, social structures and environmental conditions.

Our comprehensive review of theoretical approaches – from social capital and network perspectives to cultural and temporal frameworks – reveals both the complexity of social connection and the limitations of single-perspective approaches. In response, we offer a synthesized model that integrates these diverse insights while remaining practically applicable. This model, validated through extensive field testing and co-design with practitioners, provides a robust framework for understanding, measuring and improving social connection across different contexts and populations.

By uniting diverse perspectives and experiences while offering a practical framework for intervention, this book contributes both theoretical insight and actionable knowledge for fostering social connection in an increasingly complex world. We encourage researchers, practitioners and policy makers to utilize this synthesized approach in their efforts to enhance social connection across communities.

Note
[1] This narrative is a composite, fictionalized account based on interviews with young residents of Melbourne's outer metropolitan suburbs conducted as part of Australian Research Council funded project LP200301335.

References
Aldrich, D.P. (2012) *Building Resilience: Social Capital in Post-Disaster Recovery*, University of Chicago Press.

Antonucci, T.C., Ajrouch, K.J. and Birditt, K.S. (2014) 'The convoy model: explaining social relations from a multidisciplinary perspective', *The Gerontologist*, 54(1), 82–92.

Archer, M.S. (1995) *Realist Social Theory: The Morphogenetic Approach*, Cambridge University Press.

Baum, F., Newman, L. and Biedrzycki, K. (2014) 'Vicious cycles: digital technologies and determinants of health in Australia', *Health Promotion International*, 29(2), 349–360. doi: 10.1093/heapro/das062.

Bourdieu, P. (1986) 'The forms of capital', in J.G. Richardson (ed) *Handbook of Theory and Research for the Sociology of Education*, Greenwood Press, pp 241–258.

Bower, M., Smout, S., Johnson, S., Costello, A., Andres, L., Donohoe-Bales, A. et al (2024). *Placing Social Connection at the Heart of Public Policy in the United Kingdom and Australia*, London and Sydney: UCL Policy Lab and The Matilda Centre, University of Sydney.

Cacioppo, J.T. and Cacioppo, S. (2014) 'Social relationships and health: the toxic effects of perceived social isolation', *Social and Personality Psychology Compass*, 8(2), 58–72.

Cheshire, L. (2022) *Neighbours around the World: An International Look at the People Next Door*, Emerald Publishing.

Coleman, J.S. (1958) 'Relational analysis: the study of social organizations with survey methods', *Human Organization*, 17, 28–36.

Crossley, N. (2011) *Towards Relational Sociology*, Routledge.

De Cotta, T., Verhagen, J., Farmer, J., Karg, A., Sivasubramaniam, D., Savic, M., et al (2024) *Social Connection Program Evaluation Toolkit*, Swinburne University of Technology. https://doi.org/10.25916/ztks-bd62

DeFilippis, J. (2001) 'The myth of social capital in community development', *Housing Policy Debate*, 12(4), 781–806. doi: 10.1080/10511482.2001.9521429.

Dunbar, R. (1998) 'The social brain hypothesis', *Evolutionary Anthropology: Issues, News, and Reviews*, 6(5), 178–190.

Elder, G.H., Johnson, M.K. and Crosnoe, R. (2003) 'The emergence and development of life course theory', in J. Mortimer and M. Shanahan (eds) *Handbook of the Life Course*, Springer, pp 3–19.

Emirbayer, M. (1997) 'Manifesto for a relational sociology', *American Journal of Sociology*, 103(2), 281–317.

Emirbayer, M. and Mische, A. (1998) 'What is agency?', *American Journal of Sociology*, 103(4), 962–1023.

Farmer, J., De Cotta, T., Hartung, C., et al (2021) *Social Connection 101* [guide], Social Innovation Research Institute.

Farmer, J., De Cotta, T., Savic, M., Rowe, C., Verhagen, J., Sivasubramaniam, D., Karg, A., McCosker, A., Butt, A., Kroen, A., Shaw, B. and Knox, J. (2025) *Social Connection 101* (Revised edition), Swinburne University of Technology. https://doi.org/10.25916/sut.28415261

Feng, Z. and Patulny, R. (2021) 'Should I use my "weak" social capital or "strong" "guanxi"? Reviewing and critiquing two theories in the context of Western-Chinese migration', *Journal of Sociology*, 57(2), 464–482.

Gardiner, C., Laud, P., Heaton, T. and Gott, M. (2020) 'What is the prevalence of loneliness amongst older people living in residential and nursing care homes? A systematic review and meta-analysis', *Age and Ageing*, 49(5), 748–757.

Granovetter, M.S. (1983) 'The strength of weak ties: a network theory revisited', *Sociological Theory*, 1, 201–233.

Grzymala-Kazlowska, A. and Ryan, L. (2022) Bringing anchoring and embedding together: theorising migrants' lives over-time, *Comparative Migration Studies*, 10, Article 46.

Hall, E.T. (1976) *Beyond Culture*, New York.

Hall, J.A. (2019) 'How many hours does it take to make a friend?', *Journal of Social and Personal Relationships*, 36(4), 1278–1296.

Hall, J.A. (2020) *Relating Through Technology: Everyday Social Interaction Through Digital Media*, Cambridge University Press.

Hawkley, L.C. (2022) 'Loneliness and health', *Nature Reviews Disease Primers*, 8(1), 1–2.

Helsper, E. (2021) *The Digital Disconnect*, SAGE.

Hickin, N., Käll, A., Shafran, R., Sutcliffe, S., Manzotti, G. and Langan, D. (2021) 'The effectiveness of psychological interventions for loneliness: A systematic review and meta-analysis', *Clinical Psychology Review*, 88, 102066. doi: 10.1016/j.cpr.2021.102066

Hjorth, L. and Kim, K.H.Y. (2011) 'The mourning after: a case study of social media in the 3.11 earthquake disaster in Japan', *Television & New Media*, 12(6), 552–559.

Hofstede, G. (2001) *Culture's Consequences: Comparing Values, Behaviors, Institutions, and Organizations Across Nations*, 2nd edition, SAGE.

Holt-Lunstad, J. (2022) 'Social connection as a public health issue: the evidence and a public health framework for action', *Annual Review of Public Health*, 43, 433–459.

Holt-Lunstad, J., Robles, T.F. and Sbarra, D.A. (2017) 'Advancing social connection as a public health priority in the United States', *American Psychologist*, 72(6), 517.

Hurlbert, J.S., Haines, V.A. and Beggs, J.J. (2000) 'Core networks and tie activation: what kinds of routine networks allocate resources in nonroutine situations?', *American Sociological Review*, 65, 598–618.

Johns, A., Matamoros-Fernández, A. and Baulch, E. (2024) *WhatsApp: From a One-to-One Messaging App to a Global Communication Platform*, Polity Press.

Kim, H.S., Sherman, D.K. and Taylor, S.E. (2008) 'Culture and social support', *American Psychologist*, 63(6), 518–526.

Kretzmann, J.P. and McKnight, J.L. (1993) *Building Communities from the Inside Out: A Path Toward Finding and Mobilizing a Community's Assets*, ACTA Publications.

Losee, J.E., Webster, G.D. and McCarty, C. (2021) 'Social network connections and increased preparation intentions for a disaster', *Journal of Environmental Psychology*, 79, 101726.

Magre, J., Vallbé, J.-J. and Tomàs, M. (2016) 'Moving to suburbia? Effects of residential mobility on community engagement', *Urban Studies*, 53(1), 17–39.

Markus, H.R. and Kitayama, S. (1991) 'Culture and the self: implications for cognition, emotion, and motivation', *Psychological Review*, 98(2), 224–253.

Miller, D., Costa, E., Haynes, N., McDonald, T., Nicolescu, R., Sinanan, J., et al (2016) *How the World Changed Social Media*, UCL Press.

Murthy, V. (2023) *Our Epidemic of Loneliness and Isolation: The U.S. Surgeon General's Advisory on the Healing Effects of Social Connection and Community*, U.S. Department of Health and Human Services. Available at: https://www.hhs.gov/sites/default/files/surgeon-general-social-connection-advisory.pdf (Accessed 20 November 2024).

Neves, B.B., Sanders, A. and Kokanović, R. (2019) '"It's the worst bloody feeling in the world": experiences of loneliness and social isolation among older people living in care homes', *Journal of Aging Studies*, 49, 74–84.

OECD (Organization for Economic Co-operation and Development) (2024) 'Measuring social connectedness in OECD countries: a scoping review', *OECD Papers on Well-being and Inequalities*, No. 28, OECD Publishing. doi: 10.1787/f758bd20-en

Oldenburg, R. (1989) *The Great Good Place: Cafes, Coffee Shops, Bookstores, Bars, Hair Salons, and Other Hangouts at the Heart of a Community*, Paragon House.

Pahl, R. (2000) *On Friendship*, Polity Press.

Patulny, R. and Bower, M. (2022) 'Beware the "loneliness gap"? Examining emerging inequalities and long-term risks of loneliness and isolation emerging from COVID-19', *Australian Journal of Social Issues*, 57(3), 562–583.

Patulny, R. and Petrolo, B. (2024) 'Are we softly constructing more inclusive males? An examination of men's interpersonal emotion work for children and partners', *Emotions and Society*. https://doi.org/10.1332/26316897Y2024D000000047

Putnam, R.D. (2000) *Bowling Alone: The Collapse and Revival of American Community*, Simon & Schuster.

Ramia, G., Patulny, R., Marston, G. and Cassells, K. (2017) 'The relationship between governance networks and social networks: progress, problems and prospects', *Political Studies Review*, 16(4), 331–341. doi: 10.1177/1478929917713952

Reinhardt, G., Vidovic, D. and Hammerton, C. (2021) 'Understanding loneliness: a systematic review of the impact of social prescribing initiatives on loneliness', *Perspectives in Public Health*, 141(4), 204–213. doi: 10.1177/1757913920967040

Reyes Acosta, C. (2016) *Digitally Mediated Social Ties and Achieving Recognition in the Field of Creative and Cultural Production: Unravelling the Online Social Networking Mystery*. PhD thesis, London School of Economics and Political Science.

Roberts, S. and Wescott, S. (2024) '"Manfluencers", masculinities and the practice of misogyny in educational settings: critical analyses, theoretical advances, and potential solutions for addressing a pernicious problem for gender equality', *Gender and Education*, 36(7), 817–818.

Roof, K. and Oleru, N. (2008) 'Public health: Seattle and King County's push for the built environment', *Journal of Environmental Health*, 71, 24–27.

Rothman, J. (1968) 'Three models of community organization practice', *Social Work Practice*, National Conference on Social Welfare, Columbia University Press, New York.

Ryan, L. (2016) 'Looking for weak ties: using a mixed methods approach to capture elusive connections', *The Sociological Review*, 64(4), 951–969. https://doi.org/10.1111/1467-954X.12395

Savic, M., McCosker, A. and Farmer, J. (2025) 'Navigating isolation: mobilising a digital social connection ecosystem on the urban fringe', *Information, Communication & Society*. https://doi.org/10.1080/1369118X

Stones, R. (2005) *Structuration Theory*, Macmillan.

van Dijck, J. (2013) *The Culture of Connectivity: A Critical History of Social Media*, Oxford University Press.

Verhagen, J., Karg, A., Sivasubramaniam, D., Yeomans, C. and Farmer, J. (2025) 'Affective judgement of a sense of social connection: a scale refinement process', *Social Indicators Research*. https://doi.org/10.1007/s11205-025-03610-0

Weiss, R.S. (1973) *Loneliness: The Experience of Emotional and Social Isolation*, MIT Press.

Wilkinson, L.R., Ferraro, K.F. and Kemp, B.R. (2017) 'Contextualization of survey data: what do we gain and does it matter?', *Research in Human Development*, 14, 234–252.

World Health Organization (2024) *Commission on Social Connection*. Available at: https://www.who.int/groups/commission-on-social-connection (Accessed 20 November 2024).

Zuboff, S. (2019) *The Age of Surveillance Capitalism: The Fight for a Human Future at the New Frontier of Power*, Profile Books.

PART I

Personal Spaces

2

Male Friendships and Social Connections: Privileges and Pitfalls

Roger Patulny

Introduction

Amidst the great welter of concern over social isolation and loneliness in the post-COVID-19 era, the role of gender and masculinity in shaping disconnection has been side-lined. This issue is timely and deserves more attention. Loneliness and social isolation are linked to negative health outcomes, with the former predicting early mortality (Holt-Lundstad et al, 2015), reduced mental and physical health, reduced wellbeing (Lim, 2018) and increased suicide risks (Kidd, 2004), and the latter linked to increased risk of mortality and poor physical health conditions and behaviours (for example, smoking, inactivity poor sleep, alcohol usage, and so on [Holt-Lunstad et al, 2015; Ratcliffe et al, 2024]).

Furthermore, an array of evidence suggests that men are often lonelier (for exampe, Flood, 2005; Franklin, 2009; Hysinga et al, 2020; Barretoa, 2021) and usually more isolated (for example, Goodman et al, 2015; Relationships Australia, 2018; Bonsaksen et al, 2021) than women. However, we still lack a full picture of male social connectivity. Many existing studies risk pathologizing loneliness as an individualized affliction best treated by individualized, medicalized, therapeutic techniques (Jeste et al, 2020). These rarely pay sufficient attention to the *social structures* that underpin the emotional experience of loneliness; such as the structures of gender and masculinity that shape men's interactions with others.

The understanding that social structural qualities shape the experiences of loneliness is expressed in the relational approach to social connection proposed by authors in this collection (Chapter 14, this volume). I seek to build on this perspective by utilizing Rob Stones' (2005) distinction between 'external' and 'internal' structures in shaping active agency and outcomes.[1] *External* structures refer to those social factors that clearly sit outside individual agents but still constrain their actions. They include institutional, material and geographic factors that are conceptually separate but nonetheless impact social interaction. For men being social, these might include social institutions such as culture and family (Franklin et al, 2019); economic constraints around work and retirement (Patulny, 2009); digital communication constraints (see Chapter 15, this volume); constraints from the physical/urban environment (see Chapter 6, this volume), or the decline in traditional institutions of male interaction – clubs, societies, unions – long-noted by Robert Putnam (2000).

Internal structures refer to internalized social patterns and skills that operate 'in-situ' to shape behaviours and feelings, that is, beliefs, attitudes, norms, habits, and socially ascribed resources and affordances. They are potentially more complex, but help us constitute a more complete, multidimensional understanding of social connection, and they are the focus of this chapter. I have identified several distinct elements relevant to social connection in prior work developing a multidimensional conceptualization of social capital (Patulny and Svendsen, 2007). I have argued that such connectivity is not simply interacting with others but is also necessarily enabled by cooperative social norms that motivate and facilitate interaction (for example, trust and reciprocity with others), which drive and constrain 'appropriate' male interaction in the present. Connectivity is also realized through *social networks*, the conduits that allow social resources to be brought to bear and steer people towards or away from certain types of other people/alters (for example, males, females, families, colleagues, and so on).

Therefore, social connection is neither a feeling (that is, of loneliness) nor action (that is, social interaction or isolation), but a *process* where external and internal structures influence individual actions. Internal structural processes necessarily include normative motivations and network facilitations, which are then realized in social interaction (active agency) and experienced and managed as feelings of loneliness (outcomes). In a prior study (Patulny, 2021), building on the work of James Grossman and Christian Von Scheve, I have developed a similar theoretical 'process model' to describe how emotions in the workplace are experienced and managed under structural pressures (for example, norms, networks, resources, capital), which then in turn shape those structural factors through a process of structuration. I utilize this prior work to conceive of social connection as: *a process influenced by external structures and realized through internal structures that include: (a) socially derived norms and perceptions of appropriate connectivity; (b) social networks and sources of support; which lead to (c) social activities and interactions (that is, active agency); and (d) ultimately result in the experience and management of feelings of quality connection or their absence (that is, loneliness outcomes).*

There is no scope in this chapter to empirically examine this 'process' in full and determine all the relevant causal pathways between these components. Future attempts to do so should recognize that any process involving external and internal structures will be more probabilistic than deterministic (Heaney, 2023) and should not seek to 'over-determine' individual actions and feelings (thus erasing agency). Nonetheless, examining a wide array of indicators pertaining to these components will help us identify key internal structures of masculine connectivity and serve as a precursor to future causal studies. I will, therefore, examine indicators in this chapter pertaining to men's connections in these four areas: norms, networks, interactions and feelings.

Methods

In order to further illuminate these issues, I will analyse a range of indicators of men's social connections in Australia in this chapter. The analysis draws on data from several Australian Social Attitudes Survey (AUSSA) iterations. These surveys utilize randomized samples of the Australian population, recruited via physical mail-out of the survey each wave to a randomized sample of 5,000 Australian adults selected from the Australian Electoral Roll (conducted through the calendar year of May to May). Four waves of the AUSSA will be used, containing a range of indicators about male social interaction in Australia:

- 2011–2012 (n=1,926): questions on the importance of and practices of kindness to others, particularly family, and whether social networks are gender homogeneous/heterogeneous.
- 2015–2016 (n=1,211): questions on the type of closest friend, support from the closest friend, and care/love emotions experienced.
- 2017–2018 (n=1,317): questions on who deserves kindness, being kind and receiving kindness from others, using and reciprocating friendships, regularity of contact with family and friends, and feeling isolated.
- 2022–2023 (n=924): questions on performing interpersonal emotion management, including emotion work for male and female family and friends.

I discuss the findings by looking at data on gendered support norms, networks, interactions and feelings. Population proportions by gender are provided in the four figures, designed to capture as many aspects of socializing as possible available from the surveys. In describing the results, I refer to 'men' and 'women' as those respondents who self-identify as cisgender males and females. All indicators have been coded into binaries, and significant gender differences have been identified for every indicator through a series of logistic regressions. Each indicator has been predicted based on gender (that is, male) and controlling for age (younger: less than 35 years, or older, greater than 55 years) and parental status (partnered no kids, single no kids, single with kids), to allow for the important impact of external structures around the life course and generational change, and family partnership. Significant gender differences are indicated in each figure by stars[2] or 'ns' labels at the end of each bar.

Male and masculine norms and attitudes to social interaction

Masculinity norms refer to the sociocultural gender beliefs inculcated in men through upbringing, socialization and interaction that motivate and drive their attitudes, goals and perceptions of appropriate behaviour. Traditional *hegemonic* masculine accounts (Connell and Messerschmidt, 2005) see males exercising more authority than empathy. If such norms encourage confident involvement in public and civic life, they may support men's social trust and social capital (Patulny and Svendsen, 2007). They may also improve men's sense of 'belongingness' in the public domain (Franklin et al, 2019), though male suspicions about the 'correctness' of other men's behaviour may undermine public male-to-male connections (Ratcliffe et al, 2023). Hegemonic attitudes may also undermine social connections through intolerance, by promoting hierarchical, heteronormative male-dominated forms of interaction that disparage those who do not fit appropriate normative patterns (for example, LGBTQIA+ men, single parents, and so on) (Willis and Vickery, 2022). Ratcliffe et al's (2023) qualitative study identifies a reluctant complicity among men who see socially obstructive masculinity norms as 'beyond their control', even as they ascribe to perceptions and values around male independence and invulnerability.

My findings here provide some evidence of changing gendered norms around socializing (Figure 2.1). Men were more likely to think most people could be trusted in 2011, though the gap was only minorly significant (p<0.1), and disappeared when controlling for being young or not working. This gap then disappeared by 2022, mostly because of a reduction in the proportion of men saying most people could be trusted. Gendered attitudes to kindness also changed. Men were less likely to think it was important to be kind or that most Australians were kind in 2011, but the gap in the latter disappeared by 2017 as more men came to believe that most people are kind.

This gender equivalizing in trust and kindness may be indicative of a loss of male privilege, authority and control in civic and social situations (that is, decreasing their sense of broad social trust), but also an increase in emotional connection and sympathy to others (that is, greater perceptions of kindness).

Figure 2.1: Gender differences in norms and attitudes to social interactions, AUSSA 2007–2022

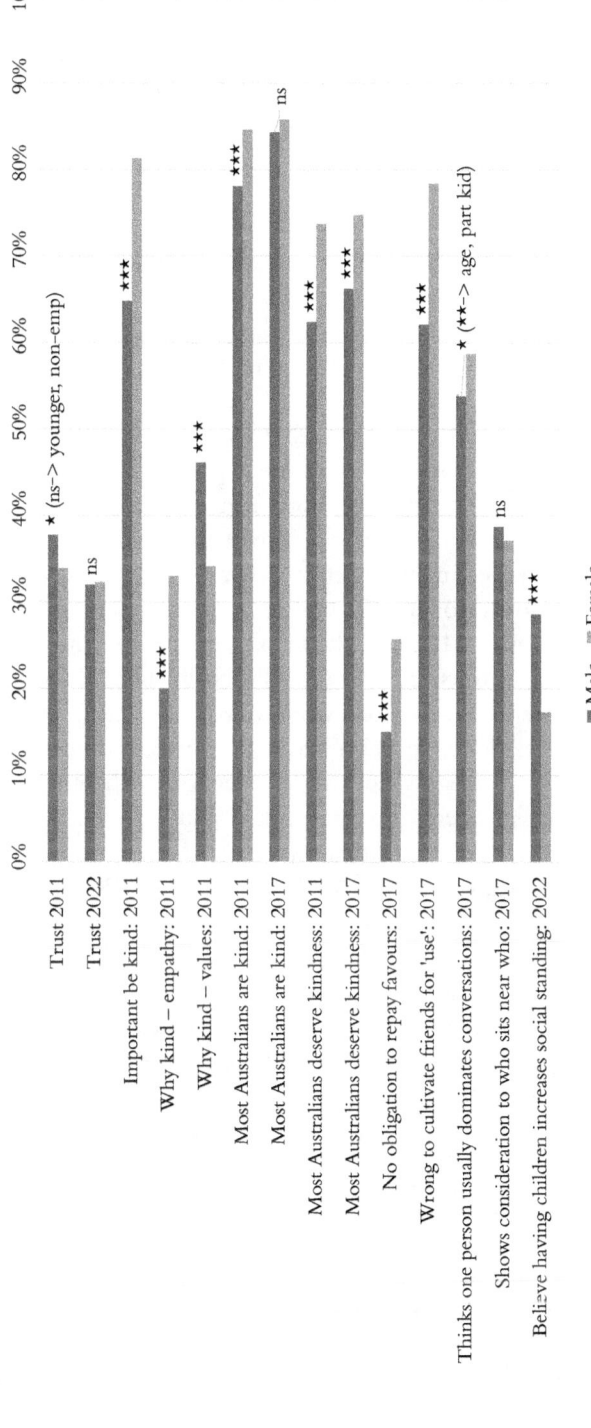

Note: NS = non-significant difference; * = $p < 0.1$, ** = $p < 0.05$, *** = $p < 0.01$
Source: Author's calculations based on Australian Social Attitudes Survey, various waves

Other indicators suggest some gender equivalence in 'social manners', with men as likely as women (as of 2017) to show consideration for things such as 'who sits next to who' at social events. Taken together, these indicators and interpretations support the tentative emergence of more *inclusive* masculinity (Anderson and McCormack, 2016), where men may be adopting more inclusive ideas and skills around emotional expression, intimacy, care and social engagement, resulting in more flexible and progressive norms around men's socializing and connection.[3]

However, claims that men are developing less hegemonic and more inclusive socializing must contend with other evidence pointing to the retention of many traditional, gender-conservative norms of socializing and connection. My findings show that men in 2011 were more likely to be kind because they wanted to 'live up to their values' and less likely to do so from empathic feelings that they 'just can't help responding to the needs of others'. While these findings accord with studies finding that men still adhere to masculinity norms around being moral, polite and chivalrous (Wong et al, 2020), it also demonstrates a more instrumental-rational (Willis and Vickery, 2022) rather than an emotional-empathic approach to socializing and emotionally connecting with others. Men in 2017 clearly demonstrated transactional relational norms. They were more likely to say it was fine to cultivate friendships just because they could be 'of use' and that they felt obligated to repay favours. They were also less likely to think one person regularly dominated conversations when out socializing (possibly because they were the ones doing the dominating).[4] These findings paint men as more individualist socializers, seeking connection with others to gain an advantage, avoiding longer-term obligations,[5] and less aware (or caring less) about being inclusive in social situations.

Furthermore, the most recent AUSSA data (2022–2023) revealed that Australian men were more likely than women to believe that having children increased their social standing. This supports heteronormative beliefs about the importance and centrality of the heterosexual nuclear family for men in general (Totby, 2022) and aligns with other studies showing that nuclear family roles played a prevalent and problematic role in men's forming of social connections (Ratcliffe et al, 2023).

Men's social networks and support

It is important to distinguish networks from norms because while norms motivate and guide social interaction, networks enable and channel those interactions. Norms may provide the cultural, social and educational references to connect us to a particular group (that is, the cultural capital that underpins social capital [Patulny and Svendsen, 2007]). Still, the group, scale, orientation, support potential, and available and cultivated networks often determine *the quality* of the connections. This is why loneliness and social isolation should not be conflated. Men can be lonely in a crowd or socially fulfilled when spending time alone, depending upon the *quality* of the networks they usually surround themselves with. There is evidence that high-quality connections are likely to be gendered, with men lacking emotionally high-quality relationships critical for alleviating loneliness.

Ratcliffe et al (2023) find that men's ability to form social connections is constrained by others' perceptions of appropriate masculinity norms. They found that men's own and perceived-other prejudices impacted their opportunities to form and maintain connections with others, including other men, as men who did not share masculine interests experienced greater difficulties in forming connections. This, in turn, led to a greater reliance on women in their networks for support, with whom they opened up about intimate/emotional issues more than they did with men. Spouses were seen as particularly helpful in positively shaping men's social connections. Some referred to their father's relationship with their mother as creating a sense of reliance on women for social support.

The data (Figure 2.2) reveals similar support for men's normative veneration of the family, with men more likely to centre their networks and support sources around nuclear family bonds, heteronormative partnerships and women in general. The 2011 data reveal that men were less likely to have friends of the same gender and more likely to have friends of mixed gender, compared to women, while the 2015 data reveals that significantly more men see their female partner as their closest friend than women do their male partner. Furthermore, the 2022 data show that men are more likely than women to rely on family over friends for support and believe that family is more important than friends.

The data also reveals the potential toll on emotional support that men experience from having more restricted social networks. The 2015 data revealed that a significantly greater proportion of men reported receiving no support from their closest friends.[6] It also showed that men were less likely to receive emotional support from their closest friends and more likely to receive fun, good times, and practical advice and support instead. Data from 2017 showed men were less likely to turn to anyone – whether close or more distant family or friends – for support with emotional difficulties, sickness or care. It is important to point out that while other forms of support are important and useful, emotional support is the form most likely to be linked to high-quality friendships and, consequently, reduced loneliness for men.[7]

Men were more likely to receive non-emotional support from more distant sources than women. Men were less likely to receive kindness from others in general but more likely to receive it from strangers, which is likely a reflection of men being less involved in the day-to-day give-and-take of kind actions in the known community (that is, schools, neighbours, community groups),

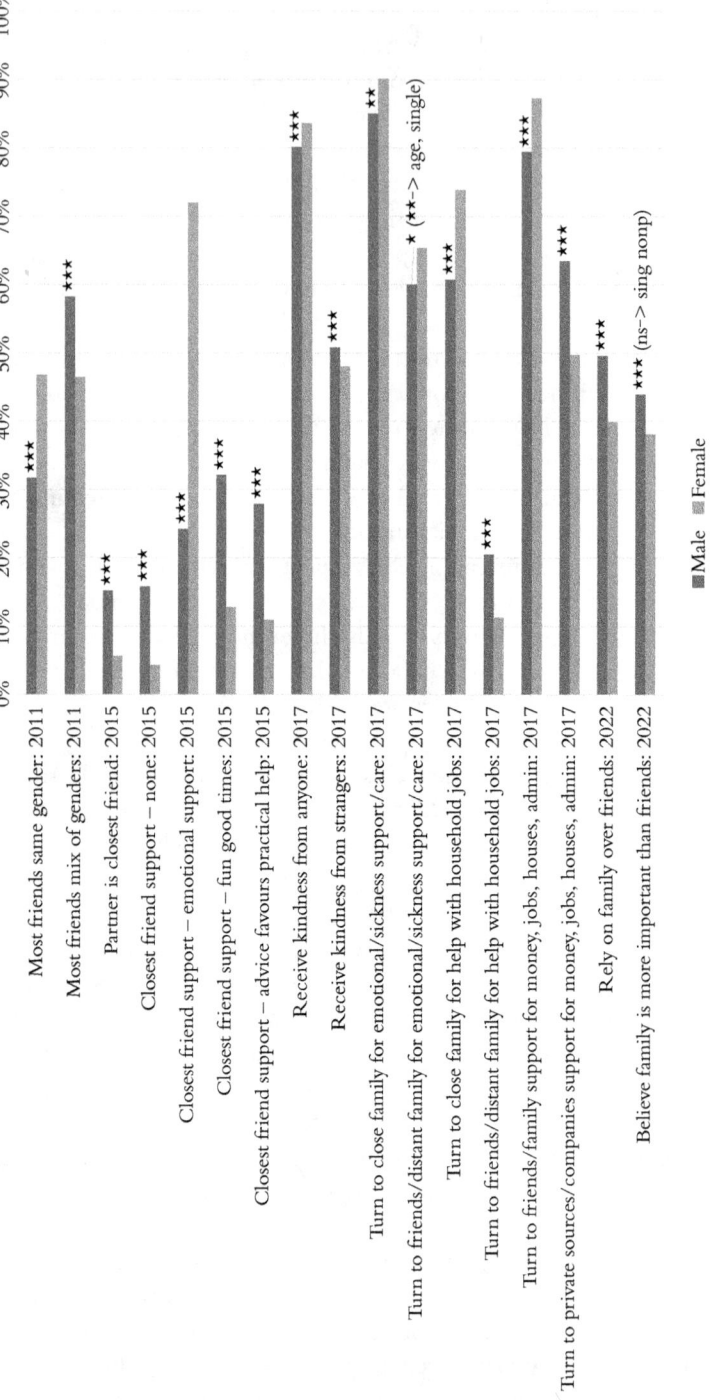

Figure 2.2: Gender differences in social networks and support, AUSSA 2007–2022

Note: NS = non-significant difference; * = p < 0.1, ** = p < 0.05, *** = p < 0.01
Source: Author's calculations based on Australian Social Attitudes Survey, various waves

but more able to interact with distant strangers (that is, most likely because they feel relatively safer interacting with strangers, and more familiar with transactional relationships). Men were also more likely to choose distant family or friends, rather than close family, for help with household jobs. In seeking more practical forms of support, men were less likely to seek support for money, jobs, houses and admin from family and friends and more likely to seek it from private sources and companies, presumably using financial resources and bridging social capital.

Men's social practices, interactions and activities

Networks cannot be realized unless they are activated (Putnam, 2000). There is little value in having widespread connections that one never uses; practices and interactions are required for social connection to materialize. Ratcliffe et al (2023) find that reliable social interactions are often helpful for men, despite not always providing 'intimate' connections, and that there was a positive benefit to men from being 'positively occupied'.

Looking at men's social practices, interactions and activities, I find that gendered kindness activities have changed (Figure 2.3). Men were significantly less likely to be kind both to others and strangers in 2011. Still, this gender gap disappeared for both indicators by 2017,[8] with the latter gap disappearance due to an increase in men being kind to strangers. These (slightly) promising improvements in male socializing practices are also accompanied by men being on par (that is, no significant differences) with women in having contact with less than ten people in a week; socializing with a friendship group at least once per week; making new friends or acquaintances when going out; seeing most contacts face to face; or having weekly contact with a brother or sister, or other family member.[9] These indicators further support the emergence of more open and inclusive masculine socializing practices.

However, some important gender differences were evident in more distant (that is, non-nuclear) family-oriented socializing. Men were significantly less likely to have contact with an adult child, and they were significantly less likely to have weekly contact with a parent after controlling for age and retirement status. Men were also *far* less likely than women to plan or organize social and family activities all or most of the time, by a difference of almost 50 percentage points. Such findings suggest that while men prioritize 'the family' as their locus of social interaction, this does not translate to a relatively large amount of social activity spent with either children or parents outside the home (compared to women) and absolutely does not translate to men taking the initiative in planning and organizing the social events that keep families connected to the community.

Men were also significantly less likely to have contact with a close friend after controlling for age and retirement, in keeping with the findings about

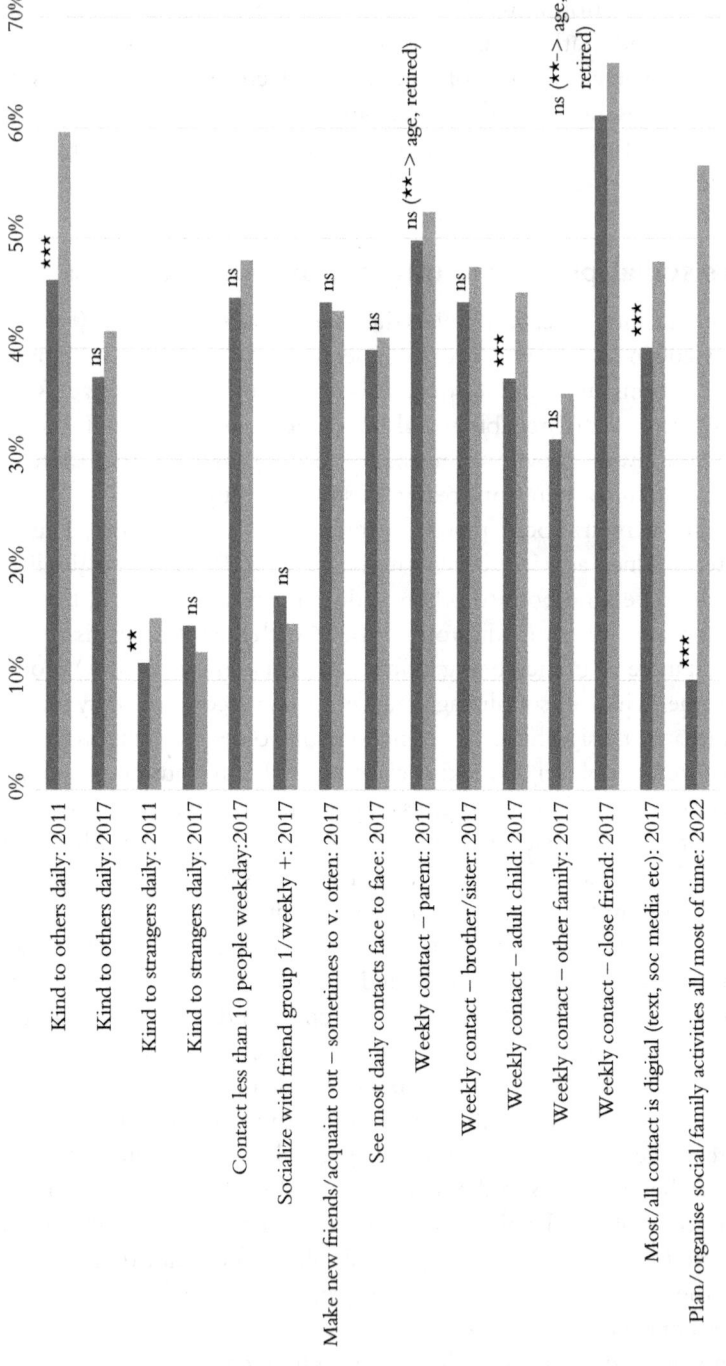

Figure 2.3: Gender differences in social practices, interactions and activities, AUSSA 2007–2022

Note: NS = non-significant difference; * = p < 0.1, ** = p < 0.05, *** = p < 0.01
Source: Author's calculations based on Australian Social Attitudes Survey, various waves

poorer male network connections with close friends. Men were also less likely to report that most or all their contact with other people was digital, suggesting that they may be missing out on the great array of social contact enabled by modern digital mechanisms.[10]

Men seem more open to engaging with strangers and enjoy a reasonable 'general' social life. However, the evidence suggests that the time and energy they devote to social practices with family and friends beyond their households may be lacking.

Men's socially oriented feelings

Finally, it is important to examine men's feelings. While some studies show men to be more lonely (Hysinga et al, 2020; Barretoa et al, 2021) and some less lonely (Ratcliffe et al, 2024) than women, it is important to realize that men underreport loneliness, particularly when survey questions explicitly use the term 'lonely' (Ratcliffe et al, 2024). Men are more likely to hide their feelings of loneliness not only because of the impact on their feelings of self-worth from admitting to the vulnerability inherent in being lonely (Ratcliffe et al, 2023), but also because of the stigma for men in talking about and displaying emotions in general (Patulny et al, 2017; Wong et al, 2020).

The data (Figure 2.4) shows that men do face emotional challenges in experiencing and managing feelings of connection to others. In 2015, men were less likely than women to 'feel close' to their closest friend and were less likely to say that the most common emotion they experienced in the last week was love.[11] In 2017, men were also more likely to say that they felt isolated in the last four weeks and that they felt pressured by (and thus potentially distant from) their families about the way they organized their social lives. Also, when asked in 2022 about whether they helped other people manage difficult emotions, men were significantly less likely than women to report helping their children, helping other friends or family, or even helping anyone else (other than their partner) manage their emotions.

This is not to say that men feel completely disconnected, particularly from family. In keeping with previous findings that men do regularly exhibit feelings of care towards others (Patluny et al, 2017), men in 2015 were as likely as women to say that the most common emotion they experienced in the last week was a feeling of care and sympathy. Men in 2017 were also no less likely than women to say that they lacked companionship or felt left out of social events in the last four weeks. Critically, men were also significantly *more* likely than women to report helping their partners manage their emotions. Such findings confirm that Australian men's social orientation is squarely centred on their family, most particularly on their partners' networks and feelings.

Figure 2.4: Gender differences in socially oriented feelings, AUSSA 2007–2022

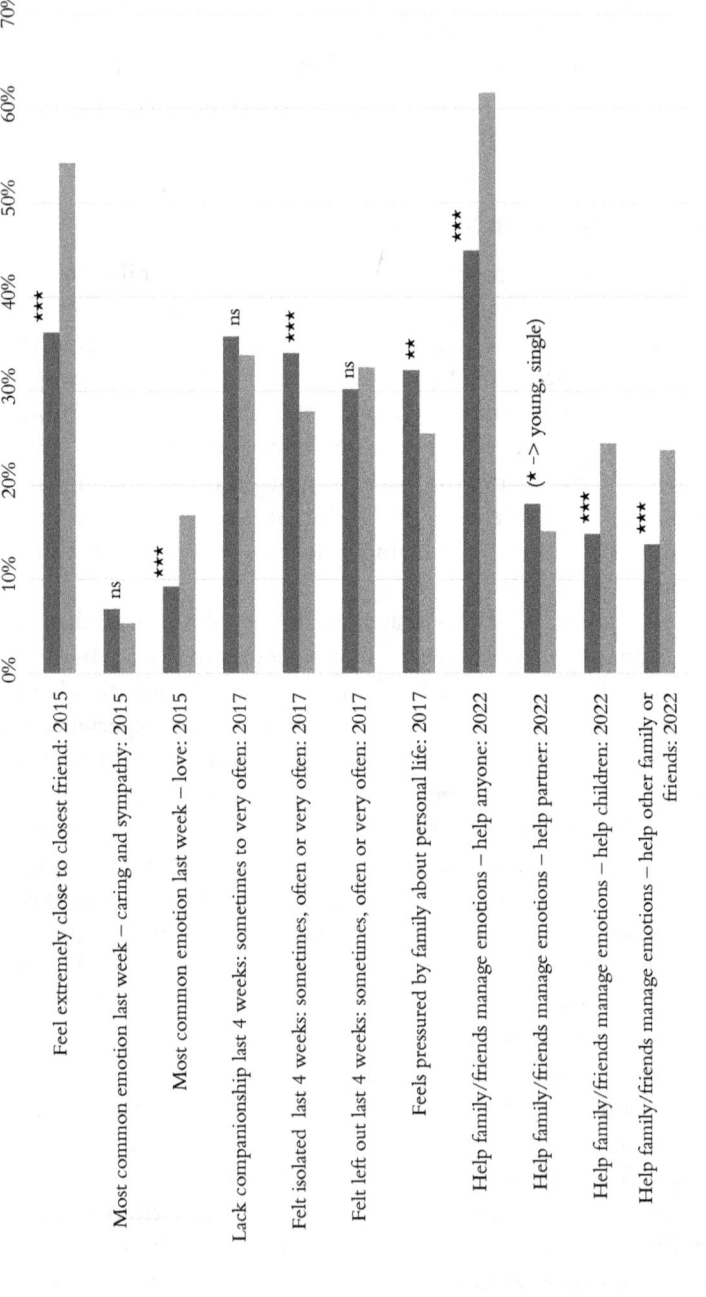

Note: NS = non-significant difference; * = p < 0.1, ** = p < 0.05, *** = p < 0.01
Source: Author's calculations based on Australian Social Attitudes Survey, various waves

Discussion and conclusion: 'happy wives, happy "social" lives'?

Contrary to conventional depictions of socially confident, publicly engaged 'civic' males (Franklin et al, 2019), my findings show that men are more likely to be socially disconnected than women according to many indicators. A significantly greater proportion of men reported receiving no support from their closest friend, receiving practical over emotional support, having less contact with a close friend, not having anyone for emotional support, not feeling 'very close' to their closest friend, or not feeling 'love' as their most common emotion. There is some evidence of more 'inclusive' masculine connections (Anderson and McCormack, 2016), with men more likely (than they used to be) to think others are kind and to be kind to strangers. Men are also (now) just as likely as women to trust others; report care and sympathy as their most commonly experienced emotion (Patulny et al, 2017); have contact with others; socialize with friendship groups; make new friends; meet people face to face; have contact with distant family; or feel that they lack companionship or are left out.

However, many male connections are with more *distant* people where the *quality* of the connection is likely lower, and the potential for the connection to reduce loneliness is questionable. Other indicators suggest that men still retain an individualist, hegemonic masculine desire to remain emotionally aloof and instrumental in the conduct of friendships. Men are more likely to be kind to others from (rational) values than empathic emotion, be more transactional in cultivating 'use-value' friendships and strict repayment of favours and be less aware (that is, caring?) about unequal (that is, boorish) conversation dominance. Men are far less likely to plan or organize social and family activities. Men were less likely to help their children, friends or others manage difficult emotions. Ryan (2016) notes that developing 'horizontal' weak-tie networks may bring benefits and support beyond job and business prospects, but only if the network is not so weak that there is insufficient trust for resource sharing.

Critically, men seemed more likely to forgo building a wider network of strong, mutually supportive ties from a heteronormative (and hegemonic) masculine aspiration to be a 'good nuclear family man'; or, to paraphrase an old expression, many men seem to be guided by a rule of 'happy wives, happy social lives'. Indicators of this include men being more likely than women to: believe that having children increased their social standing; believe that family was more important than friends; rely on family over friends for support; avoid non-nuclear family members; have opposite sex (that is, female) friendships; see their (female) partner as their closest friend; and help manage their (female) partners' difficult emotions (who, in turn, help manage other's emotions). Men also strive to be independent leaders and providers for their families, in keeping with heteronormative/hegemonic desires to be demonstrably strong and capable. They were more likely to seek practical support and engagement from more distant sources, give and receive kindness from strangers, seek help with household jobs from more distant family or friends, and practical support (money, advice) from private and commercial sources (rather than friends or family).

Much of men's disconnection thus seems to be emotional in nature. It stems from the continued 'external' structural dominance of the institution of the nuclear family over the internal structures (that is, norms and networks) that shape social interaction processes and impact the experience and management of men's feelings of loneliness and isolation. Importantly, these findings point not only to individual men's behavioural preferences, but to continuing *hegemonic cultures* of male interaction that constrain social connection on a broad society-wide level. No matter how inclusive their values become, simply telling men to go out and 'make more friends' is problematic in a world where many other men are unpractised, unreceptive, instrumental and potentially intolerant towards forming emotional connections with anyone beyond their nuclear family – particularly with other men.

These findings prompt several policy recommendations, as well as issues relevant to future research. First, it is important to support initiatives that help boys and men build respectful interactive *attitudes and norms* not only towards women (Relationships Australia, 2018) but towards all those whom they would seek to form friendships with and encourage more emotional disclosure, assistance and reciprocity. Men might generally be okay with undertaking practical activities with more distant contacts and strangers. Still, many lack the normative, network, interactive or affective resources (that is, cultural, social or emotional capital [Cottingham, 2016]) to form more intimate bonds with anyone close to them other than their romantic partner, particularly when they are suspicious of other men's poor behaviour (Ratcliffe et al, 2021). Group-based training, education and role-play interventions to impart these interactive skills may be helpful.

Second, it is important to *re-examine the centrality of the nuclear family* and one's romantic partner in delivering support services as a key external structure shaping the internal structures of masculine social connectivity. Existing family-oriented supports may preserve men's social position (and privilege) at the apex of 'conventional' nuclear families. This may not only pressure women to compensate for men's 'social failings', but also pressure men to adjust to (likely) push-back from women to 'be more social' without the relevant supportive culture, capital and resources to do so (as evidenced here by men feeling pressured by their families about the way they organized their social life). Further research into the gendered inequalities and pressures associated with nuclear family social dynamics – and policy alternatives that might curb it – would be useful and timely.

Third, we should support initiatives encouraging men to *broaden their intimate networks* more generally. By focusing primarily on their domicile and immediate nuclear family ties, men are gambling that a house with a female partner can fulfil all their social and emotional intimacy needs. In doing so, men ignore the risks and fragility associated with a sense of 'home'. Cheshire et al (2021) note that the cosy notion of home as a haven, and a place of freedom and status away from the world, can be challenged by recognizing that it is embedded in wider and sometimes unstable social, political and economic relations (for example, housing markets, gentrification, neighbourly relations).

Combining these uncertainties with the relationship pressures of late modernity (Patulny and Olson, 2019), we can see the heightened risks that can result from men's excessive dependency on home and partner. Their limited social networks can encourage feelings of isolation even if their households remain intact (as shown by the evidence on support and feelings presented here), which become intensely magnified if their relationship breaks down. Men's looser and more instrumental 'horizontal' networks are unlikely to provide compensatory support if they lack the trust required for resource-sharing (Ryan, 2016).

It is important to support initiatives that teach men how to widen their emotional networks, and see possibilities for new connections and intimacies. In the context of late modern transformation and individualization and a rise in separated and single-person households (Patulny and Olson, 2019), wider emotional connectivity will not only help men who remain in nuclear families to buffer their networks, it will also help to provide a workable support system for a 'soft landing' should their relationship (and thus their core support base) break down and disappear.

Fourth, we should support initiatives that help men develop more *diverse* friendship groups and that have a conjoint focus on undoing hegemonic and toxic attitudes *and* building stronger social connections. Focusing on more inclusive masculine norms of interaction helps reduce wider social stigma. It will also help counteract the normative compulsion to uphold hegemonic, heteronormative nuclear family patterns, which risk marginalizing and stigmatizing those men who fall outside the norm, such as single men, single fathers and queer men. Younger people with more inclusive masculine attitudes are said to be leading the way in engaging here (Anderson and McCormack, 2018), but the findings here (many of which control for age) suggest there is still much work to be done across all age groups. Interventions focusing on men building broad networks, particularly through inclusive activities and mentorships, may be critical here. The finding that men are less likely than women to socialize digitally suggests digital interventions might be effective for improving men's diverse social interactions. However, digital interventions should be wary of online instrumental-hegemonic 'manosphere' communities that prey on loneliness to recruit vulnerable men. They should also be cognizant of literature suggesting that active (rather than passive) engagement with social media is oriented towards organizing physical get-togethers that reduce loneliness (Patulny and Bower, 2022).

There are limitations to this study, and it is recommended that future research seek to address them. Why has men's disconnection persisted over time? Is it primarily due to the continuance of hegemonic or toxic masculine norms of independence, isolation and delegation of social responsibility to female partners? Or due to men's continued commitment to long paid work hours and careers, keeping them away from forming better, more diversified and reciprocal relationships, networks and interactions with families, friends and the community? It is important to pull apart the normative, network and practice effects upon men's feelings of loneliness and isolation. This requires gathering the requisite questions on norms, networks, practices and feelings within the one dataset,[12] rather than piecing it together from multiple surveys across several waves. Such data will also be useful for establishing pathway and causal analysis between these components, and will eventually allow for the detailed empirical development and analysis of social interaction as a 'process'.

The data used here also has an insufficient sample of non-heterosexual, non-binary persons for analysis. This is an important area to redress for the future, most immediately with qualitative exploration, and in the longer run as part of a targeted survey of non-heterosexual persons households.

Notes

1. See Patulny and Petrolo (2024) for further elaboration on this.
2. $* = p < 0.1$, $** = p < 0.05$, $*** = p < 0.01$.
3. The identified differences remained significant even after controls were introduced, suggesting that this is not just a facet of generational replacement, and younger men (only) being more inclusive.
4. This gender difference was minorly significant ($p<0.1$) but strengthened to full significance ($p<0.05$) after controlling for older age.
5. This dynamic may pertain only to men in Western contexts; for example, *guanxi* relationships among Chinese men and women have been found to venerate longer-term relations and obligations (Feng and Patulny, 2020).
6. This is not to suggest that female partners are non-supportive (while a higher proportion of men than women rate their partner as their 'closest friend' this is still only 15 per cent of the male sample). Rather, it instead suggests particular kinds of men cannot get support even from their closest friend (who may indeed be male); multiple regressions revealed this was also concentrated among older retirees.
7. It is impossible to test this assertion without available data and analysis linking different types of social networks and support to different types of loneliness (for example, emotional, social, collective, and so on) for men and women. This is important work for future research.
8. Men were more likely to be kind to strangers in 2017, but the difference was non-significant.

9   It is worth noting that while the differences were non-significant, men were less likely to be socially engaged on all these indicators than women. Larger sample sizes might reveal more of these differences to be real and significant.
10 Although men may also be avoiding some of the pitfalls of digital connection; see Patulny (2020) for a discussion on whether social media makes us lonely.
11 It is unclear from the data whether they are referring to feelings of being loved, loving others, or both, but its absence on any interpretation conveys reduced feelings of intimate connection.
12 Preferably a longitudinal dataset, to allow analysis of changes over time.

References

Anderson, E. and McCormack, M. (2016) 'Inclusive masculinity theory: overview, reflection and refinement', *Journal of Gender Studies*, 27(5), 547–561.

Barretoa, M., Victor, C., Hammond, C., Eccles, A., Matt, T., Richins, M.T., et al (2021) 'Loneliness around the world: age, gender, and cultural differences in loneliness', *Personality and Individual Differences*, 169, Article 110066.

Bonsaksen, T., Ruffolo, M., Leung, J., Price, D., Thygesen, H., Schoultz, M., et al (2021) 'Loneliness and its association with social media use during the COVID-19 outbreak', *Social Media + Society*, 7(3).

Cheshire, L., Easthope, H. and ten Have, C. (2021) 'Unneighbourliness and the unmaking of home', *Housing, Theory and Society*, 38(2), 133–151.

Connell, R.W. and Messerschmidt, J.W. (2005) 'Hegemonic masculinity: rethinking the concept', *Gender & Society*, 19(6), 829–859.

Cottingham, M.D. (2016) 'Theorizing emotional capital', *Theory & Society*, 45(5), 451–470.

Feng, Z. and Patulny, R. (2020) 'Should I use my "weak" social capital or "strong" guanxi? Reviewing and critiquing two theories in the context of Western-Chinese migration', *Journal of Sociology*, 57(2), 464–482.

Flood, M. (2005) 'Mapping loneliness in Australia', Australia Institute Discussion Paper No. 76, The Australia Institute, Canberra.

Franklin, A. (2009) 'On loneliness', *Geografiska Annaler: Series B, Human Geography*, 91(4), 343–354.

Franklin, A., Barbosa Neves, B., Hookway, N., Patulny, R., Tranter, B. and Jaworski, K. (2019) 'Towards an understanding of loneliness among Australian men: gender cultures, embodied expression and the social bases of belonging', *Journal of Sociology*, 55(1), 124–143.

Goodman, A., Adams, A. and Swift, H.J. (2015) 'Hidden citizens: how can we identify the most lonely older adults? The Campaign to End Loneliness (CEL)', Report, Campaign to End Loneliness.

Heaney, J. (2023) '(Un)fixing habitus: affective transactions and the becoming body', *Distinktion Journal of Social Theory*, 1–20. https://doi.org/10.1080/1600910X

Holt-Lunstad, J., Smith, T.B., Baker, M., Harris, T. and Stephenson, D. (2015) 'Loneliness and social isolation as risk factors for mortality: a meta-analytic review', *Perspectives on Psychological Science*, 10(2), 227–237.

Hysinga, M., Petrieb, K.J., Bøea, T., Lønning, K.J. and Sivertsen, B. (2020) 'Only the lonely: a study of loneliness among university students in Norway', *Clinical Psychology in Europe*, 2(1), e2781.

Jeste, D.V., Lee, E.E. and Cacioppo, S. (2020) 'Battling the modern behavioral epidemic of loneliness: suggestions for research and interventions', *JAMA Psychiatry*, 77(6), 553–554.

Kidd, S.A. (2004) '"The walls are closing in, and we were trapped": a qualitative analysis of street youth suicide', *Youth and Society*, 36, 30–55.

Lim, M. (2018) 'Australian loneliness report: a survey exploring the loneliness levels of Australians and the impact on their health and wellbeing', *Australia Psychological Society Report*. https://doi.org/10.25916/sut.26279857

Patulny, R. (2009) 'The golden years? Social contact amongst retired men and women in Australia', *Family Matters*, 83, 39–47.

Patulny, R. (2020) 'Does social media make us more or less lonely? Depends on how you use it', *The Conversation*. Available at: https://theconversation.com/does-social-media-make-us-more-or-less-lonely-depends-on-how-you-use-it-128468 (Accessed 15 March 2025).

Patulny, R. (2021) '"The new economy and the privilege of feeling": towards a theory of emotional structuration', in J. Mckenzie and R. Patulny (eds) *Dystopian Emotions: Emotional Landscapes and Dark Futures*, Bristol University Press, pp 104–124.

Patulny, R. and Bower, M. (2022) 'Beware the "loneliness gap"? Examining emerging inequalities and long-term risks of loneliness and isolation from COVID-19', *Australian Journal of Social Issues*, 57(3), 562–583.

Patulny, R. and Olson, R. (2019) 'Emotions in late modernity', in R. Patulny, A. Bellocchi, R. Olson, S. Khorana, J. McKenzie and M. Peterie (eds) *Emotions in Late Modernity*, Routledge, pp 8–24.

Patulny, R. and Petrolo, B. (2024) 'Are we softly constructing more inclusive males? An examination of men's interpersonal emotion work for children and partners', *Emotions and Society*. https://doi.org/10.1332/26316897Y2024D000000047

Patulny, R. and Svendsen, G. (2007) 'The social capital grid: bonding, bridging, qualitative, quantitative', *International Journal of Sociology and Social Policy*, 27(1/2), 32–51.

Patulny, R., Smith, V. and Soh, K. (2017) 'Generalising men's affective experience', *International Journal for Masculinity Studies (NORMA)*, 12(3), 220–239.

Putnam, R.D. (2000) *Bowling Alone: The Collapse and Revival of American Community*, Touchstone Books/Simon & Schuster.

Ratcliffe, J., Kanaan, M. and Galdas, P. (2023) 'Reconceptualising men's loneliness: an interpretivist interview study of UK-based men', *Social Science & Medicine*, 332, Article 116129.

Ratcliffe, J., Galdas, P. and Kanaan, M. (2024) 'Older men and loneliness: a cross-sectional study of sex differences in the English Longitudinal Study of Ageing', *BMC Public Health*, 24, Article 354.

Relationships Australia (2018) 'Is Australia experiencing an epidemic of loneliness?', Working Paper 2018.

Ryan, L. (2016) 'Looking for weak ties: using a mixed methods approach to capture elusive connections', *The Sociological Review*, 64(4), 951–969. https://doi.org/10.1111/1467-954X.12395

Stones, R. (2005) *Structuration Theory*, Macmillan.

Totby, A. (2022) *They Call It Love: The Politics of Emotional Life*, Verso Books.

Willis, P. and Vickery, A. (2022) 'Loneliness, coping practices and masculinities in later life: findings from a study of older men living alone in England', *Health & Social Care in the Community*, 30, e2874–e2883.

Wong, Y.J., Granderson, R.M., Zounlome, N.O.O., McCullough, K.M., Hyman, J.E. and Schwabe, S.B. (2020) 'The assessment of subjective masculine norms in the United States', *Psychology of Men & Masculinities*, 21(4), 545–557.

3

Older Filipina Australians' Local and Transnational Connective Care Practices

Earvin Charles Cabalquinto

Introduction

The United Nations has recognized the world's increasingly ageing population. According to a report by the United Nations (2022), there were 771 million people aged 65 years or older globally in 2022. Notably, the Migration Data Portal (2023) reports that the United Nation's latest estimate for 2023 projects the number of older migrants (aged 65 and above) at 34.3 million, which constitutes 12.2 per cent of the 281 million migrants worldwide, based on data from mid-2020. In the digital age, older migrants utilize a variety of mobile devices, online channels and mobile applications to establish and navigate their personal, familial and social relationships (Baldassar and Wilding, 2019; Baldassar et al, 2020).

This chapter aims to investigate how older migrants enact social connections to perform, embody and negotiate personal and social care in both local and transnational settings. It also seeks to map the influences of social structures and technological infrastructures that facilitate and hinder everyday connective care practices. Older migrants are defined as individuals aged 65 years and older (United Nations, 2019). The chapter dives deep into the digital practices of 15 older Filipino Australians in Victoria, Australia. This cohort of women has been chosen as a case study for two reasons. First, there has been no prior research on the ways older Filipina Australians in Australia use digital technologies for social connection. Addressing this gap can enrich ongoing debates about the role of cultural backgrounds shape gendered ageing in a foreign land (Wilding et al, 2022). Second, it problematizes ageing in a foreign land through the perspective of social connection and intersectionality. An intersectional lens reveals how the intersecting domains of people's lives – such as age, class, ethnicity, gender and disability – reproduce marginality (Hill Collins and Bilge, 2016).

Drawing insights from data collected through in-depth interviews and photo elicitation in March 2023, I approach the participants' everyday digital care practices (Baldassar et al, 2007) as a form of social connectedness (Farmer et al, 2019). Additionally, I reflect on older migrants' social connectedness through the concept of bifocality (Vertovec, 2009), which refers to the ways migrants' experiences of being and belonging are shaped by local and transnational practices (Zontini, 2015). Importantly, this approach offers a critical stance on social connectedness by examining the influences of unequal social and digital resources (Helsper, 2021) in mediating connective care practices.

Older Filipina Australians: a brief overview

Australia has a growing population of Filipino-born migrants. According to a report from the Australian Bureau of Statistics (2021), 293,892 Filipino-born people are living in Australia, with 68,463 residing in Victoria. Among these, 8,625 individuals are between 55 and 64 years. This demographic information highlights the presence of an ageing Filipino community in Australia, which may have implications for social connections and care practices among older migrants.

The influx of Filipinos to Australia can be divided into three distinct waves (Espinosa, 2017). The first wave, occurring in the 1960s to 1970s, signalled the settlement of Filipinos as workers in the pearl and diving industry. From the 1970s onwards, the second wave was characterized by family reunification and marriages between Filipino Australians, facilitated through matchmaking services, exchanges of letters or online connections (Saroca, 2007; Espinosa, 2017). The third wave, beginning in the 1980s, saw an increase in the arrival of professional and skilled workers. Today, the Filipino community is considered the fifth-largest migrant community in Australia.

In Philippine culture, Filipina migrants are often expected to fulfil feminized and familial caring duties in their later years (Parreñas, 2020; Amrith, 2021; Cabalquinto, 2024). While living in the host country, they use modern communication technologies and online channels to forge and maintain ties within their distant networks by enacting these feminized and caring roles (Cabalquinto, 2024). However, caring at a distance among these networks has also become a site of tension.

Connective care practices in ageing migrants' digital lifeworlds

This section attempts to map key studies and concepts that examine the role of ubiquitous digital devices and online channels in shaping the everyday connective practices of ageing migrants. To begin, I approach the digital media practices of ageing migrants through the lens of social connectedness (Farmer et al, 2019). Farmer et al (2019) articulate this concept by moving away from a deficit-based perspective that focuses on 'the connections that people lack' (2019: 4). Instead, they advocate for a 'strengths-based approach to tackling issues of social isolation (2019: 2), which is mediated by an individual's resources, emotional attachments to family members and peers, human and non-human relations, and a variety of evolving connections. They emphasize the agency of individuals in using digital technologies, noting that positive outcomes are supported by access to a range of individual and social resources.

In the context of migrants, I interpret everyday social connectedness as a form of care practice often shaped by care obligations in a migrant household (Baldassar and Merla, 2014). For instance, in accordance with gendered care structures (Baldassar et al, 2007), grandmothers use digital technologies to perform various care practices for their children and grandchildren (Ho and Chiu, 2020; Baldassar et al, 2022). These grandmothers engage in care duties such as grocery shopping for the family, preparing meals and even picking up grandchildren from school (Ho and Chiu, 2020). In some instances, care is expressed through the sending of remittances and consumer goods that support the needs of distant family members and peers (Cabalquinto, 2024). These practices illuminate what Baldassar et al (2020) refer to as 'digital kinning', highlighting how digital media tools are utilized to fulfil and deliver local and transnational care.

The ways in which ageing migrants connect locally and transnationally to perform care is understood as bifocality (Vertovec, 2009). This concept refers to how migrants navigate the 'here' and 'there' which is 'discernible in social practices and conveyed in narratives' (Vertovec, 2009: 83). For instance, applying the notion of bifocality, Zontini (2015) examines how older Italian migrants in the UK connect locally with their co-ethnics in migrant spaces, such as churches or markets, and consume homeland products to imagine and embody a sense of belonging. They also do home visits to forge and sustain connections within distant networks. Zontini (2015) argues that bifocality enables positive experiences and enriches a migrant's quality of life.

In the digital era, mobile devices and online channels have mediated these diverse practices of connecting locally and transnationally. Numerous studies have shown that older migrants rely on digital communication technologies and online tools to forge and sustain ties among their dispersed networks across multiple locations (Baldassar and Wilding, 2019; Baldassar et al, 2020). Aging migrants use online media to consume homeland news (Ballantyne and Burke, 2017) and social media to stay connected with family members and peers (Khvorostianov et al, 2012).

However, I focus on how unequal social and technological factors often shape social connections in both local and transnational domains. Many studies on the intersections of digital media and migration have identified the deep interlinking of stringent family expectations and technological access and competencies as key influences that undermine the quality of connective practices (Parreñas, 2005; Madianou and Miller, 2012; Cabalquinto, 2022). In the case of ageing migrants, the obligation to care at a distance is constrained by digital access and capabilities among older migrants (Wilding, 2006; Baldassar et al, 2007; Brandhorst, 2017).

Additionally, digital exclusion manifests through language barriers (Georgeou et al, 2023), limited digital literacy (Millard et al, 2018) and other factors. Furthermore, connection by default does not necessarily compel distant networks to send financial support as a form of practical care. Given the economic disparities among members of a migrant family, it is often the ageing migrant who utilizes digital devices to send remittances (Amrith, 2021; Cabalquinto, 2024). Indeed, while the presence of mobile phones and online channels facilitates connective care practices, forced disconnection can also occur due to an individual's unequal access to resources and digital capacities.

Methodological considerations

This chapter reports on findings from in-depth interviews and photo elicitation conducted with 15 older Filipinas in Victoria, Australia. The interviews explored participants' migration histories to Australia, their ownership and use of digital devices and online channels, and the benefits and challenges associated with digital media use. Conducted in the participants' homes, the interviews lasted between 45 and 90 minutes.

Photo elicitation (Emmison and Smith, 2000) served as a supplementary aspect of the interview process. Participants were asked to share five images stored on their mobile devices that illustrate the way they connect with their local and transnational networks. They were also invited to discuss their feelings about the images they shared or received. This approach allowed participants to provide examples of content they produced, circulated and received in relation to their use of digital technologies and online channels in their connective practices.

Participants were recruited through various organizations for older Filipino Australians and other community networks. The 15 participants were based in Victoria, Australia. The majority migrated to Australia for marriage to their Australian partners (5) or through family sponsorship (5). Some participants migrants migrated for job opportunities (3), while one fled political chaos in the Philippines during Martial Law in the 1970s, and another followed a husband who received a job offer in Australia. Most participants moved to Australia in the 1980s (7), followed by the 1970s (4), 1990s (2) and 2000s (2).

The ages of the participants ranged from 66 to 78 years. Most were educated, with 12 having completed a bachelor's degree, one completed a pre-nursing degree through government funding, and the remainder having finished high school. One participant held several postgraduate degrees, one had a graduate diploma, and another one had two aged care certificates obtained in Australia. The majority were already retired; two were still working full-time, two were working in a part-time job, and one was volunteering in various institutions. In terms of living arrangements, most participants co-lived with their spouse (7) and family members (2), and the rest lived alone (5). One participant was renting a room in a shared house with four people.

The interviews were transcribed and coded using NVivo and analysed through thematic analysis (Saldaña, 2011). I coded the data based on the device and online channels used, the relationship with family members or peers that influenced use, the use of these technologies in local and transnational domains, and the benefits and challenges surrounding digital behaviours.

In terms of photo elicitation, a total of 155 photos were collected, which were manually coded using Excel. The thematic analysis of the photos (Rose, 2007) revealed that the most frequently shared content was about their positive leisurely experiences, such as cooking (20) and watching fun videos online (16) as well as their social relationships, including interactions with relatives overseas and their grandchildren in Australia (10). The least shared images depicted listening to Filipino music (2), watching a vlogger (1) and engaging with children (5).

This chapter includes selected quotes from the interview and discussions of the images with the participants. The project received ethics approval from Deakin University's Human Research Ethics Committee (DUHREC), with the approval number HAE-22-130.

Older migrants' everyday connection in a foreign land

The majority of the participants owned and accessed a range of mobile devices, online channels and mobile applications. They used these digital technologies and online channels to self-care and care for their family members and peers across, locally and transnationally. However, differing social structures and technological factors shape the connective care practices of older migrants.

Consuming culturally tailored contents as self-care

Participants accessed YouTube and Facebook for culturally tailored health-related, entertaining and religious content, which helped reaffirm their

Figure 3.1: The YouTube video on exercising (left) and the Apple watch (right)

identities (Zontini, 2015). For instance, Anna, a 67-year-old Filipina Australian, discussed how she manages her diabetes using digital devices in her home. She shared that she exercises indoors with her Apple watch and SMART TV (see Figure 3.1), both of which were given to her and set up by her son, who lives nearby. Reminded by her Apple watch, she engages in a daily 45-minute walk, following the routines demonstrated by Filipino trainers on YouTube. During the interview, she expressed a preference for walking indoors due to knee reconstruction and the risk of falling, as she feels dizzy when exercising outside.

For some participants, YouTube serves as a valuable source for health information often tied to their cultural roots. For example, Olga, a 78-year-old Filipina Australian with diabetes, shared that her doctor prescribed her medicines, but she sometimes feels uncertain about their side effects. To address this, she turns to Google and watches YouTube videos about herbal remedies, which reassures her by comparing the medication to the horse-radish tree (malunggay), commonly used in the Philippines to manage diabetes.

Similarly, Rita, a 75-year-old Filipina Australian mentioned that she watches videos by Doc Willie Ong (see Figure 3.2), a Filipino doctor with a substantial following on YouTube. As a diabetic, she finds his videos helpful, particularly in learning about the types of fruits she can safely consume.

Complementing the findings of Khvorostianov et al (2012), participants accessed online content for leisure. Several participants watched cooking videos to prepare their own Filipino dishes. For example, the 71-year-old Minda mentioned a Facebook page featuring Filipino recipes (see Figure 3.3).

Figure 3.2: The video of Doc Willie Ong

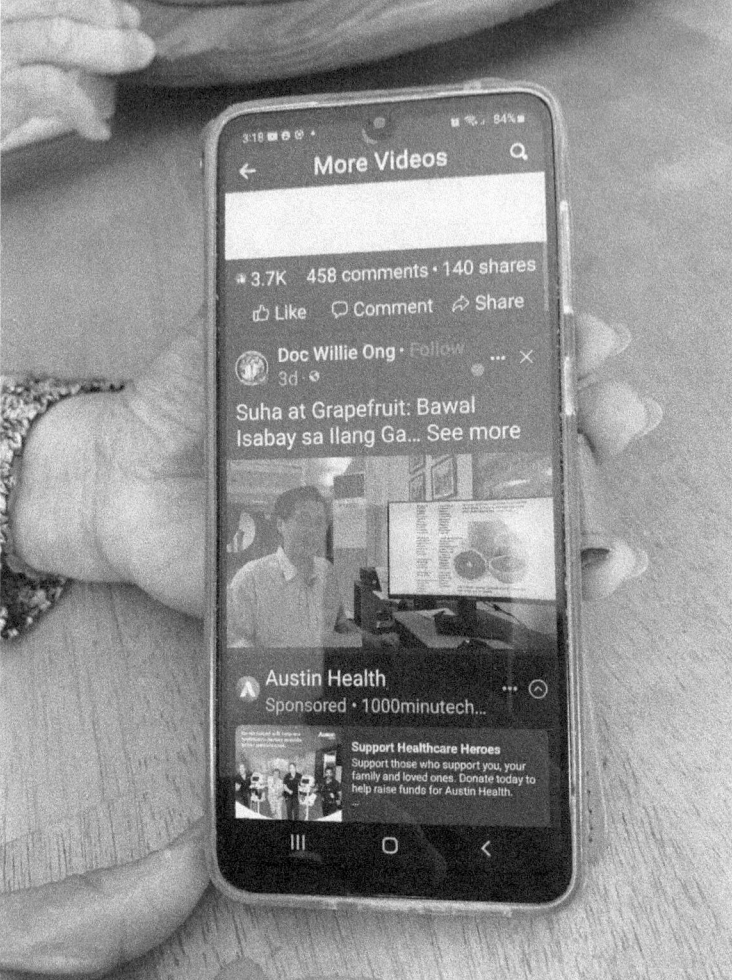

She shared that she watched some videos and tried cooking *adobo sa sprite* (chicken feet cooked with soy sauce) (see Figure 3.3). While she shared the dish with her friends, she did not offer it to her Australian husband, who dislikes it. When asked how she feels about cooking, she said, 'I am happy that I am able to taste different dishes.'

Caring locally and transnationally

Older migrants utilize various online channels to maintain connections with their local and transnational networks, enacting a sense of homeland – a form

Figure 3.3: The Facebook page (left) and the chicken feet recipe (right)

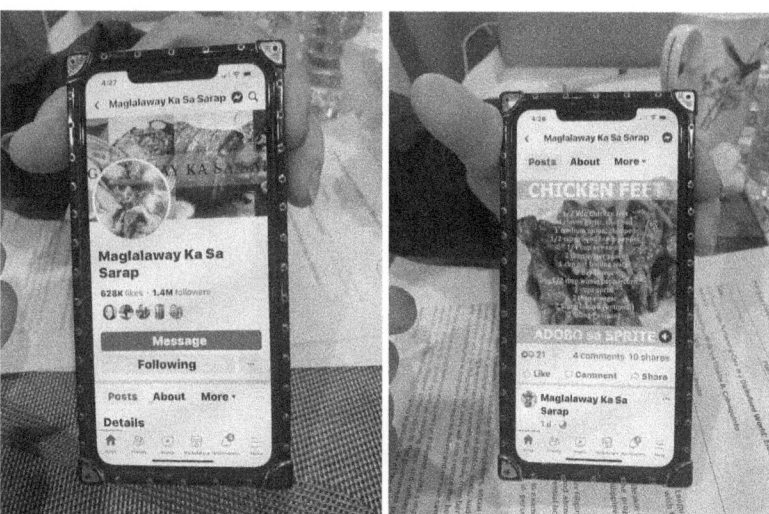

of bifocalism (Zontini, 2015). In the digital context, ageing migrants access digital devices and online channels to perform social connection and express care, often shaped by care and gendered structures (Baldassar et al, 2007).

During the fieldwork, I observed that some participants had a group chat dedicated to Australia-based family members. The group chat serves as an extended domestic space (Cabalquinto, 2022) where older participants and their children can exchange information, manage family matters and perform feminized care duties. For instance, Olivia, a 76-year-old Filipina Australian, mentioned that she is part of a WhatsApp group set up by her children. The group chat serves as a space for Olivia and her family to discuss random topics and coordinate family activities. Olivia shared: 'Sometimes we talk about the food. Sometimes, we discuss a trip. But sometimes, I tell them to bring the laundry into the house. ... I am used to doing their laundry, especially for my child, who has two children.'

Care practices also manifest in transnational connections. Carmen, a 79-year-old Filipina Australian, discussed the importance of a family group chat on Facebook. She explained that a group chat has enabled her and her family members to settle family matters, such as deciding to relocate their parents' tombs. They used the group chat to resolve the issue and pool financial resources.

Building on studies that explore how older migrants use digital technologies to care for their grandchildren (Ho and Chiu, 2020), I observed that participants with grandchildren used a messaging application to connect with them. For example, Rachel, a 71-year-old, shared her experiences

Figure 3.4: The photos of Rachel's grandchild learning to swim

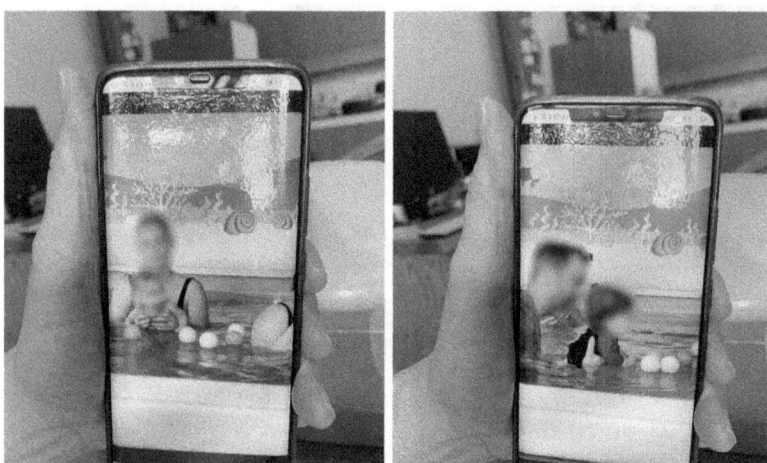

of receiving a photo of her three-month-old granddaughter via Facebook Messenger (Figure 3.4). The photo showed her granddaughter learning to swim, which brought Rachel immense joy; she expressed: 'I am very happy.'

In some cases, Facebook Messenger was also used to connect with grandchildren overseas. This was true for Sarah, a 73-year-old Filipina Australian, who frequently video calls her grandchildren in Singapore – one is nine months old, and the other is three years old. Sarah shared: 'They're all excited and they call me "Lola". Are you gonna come and see us?' When I asked Sarah how she responds, she said, 'I said, "When I have time, I'll come back" cause he [referring to the three-year-old grandchild] loves me picking him up and taking him to school. He's not supposed to have ice cream and I buy him ice cream.' These examples illustrate how online channels provide a crucial space for forging and reinforcing relationships between older migrants and their distant grandchildren, whether in Australia or overseas.

Social connectedness extends beyond relationships with children and grandchildren. The study shows that participants also used online channels to connect with distant peers and maintain communities internationally, echoing findings on older migrants' social capital building through digital means (Khvorostianov et al, 2012; Baldassar et al, 2022; Anschütz and Mazzucato, 2024). The experiences of Yasmin, a 67-year-old Filipina Australia, and Olivia, whom we met earlier, exemplify this connective practice.

Yasmin uses a group chat on Facebook Messenger to schedule and conduct prayer activities. She explained that the online group began after a high school reunion in the Philippines. In her words, 'I was the President of our class, so when I went home about ten years ago, I met some of them, and I haven't seen them for a long time.' From that meeting, the group formed, now consisting of 14 members who participate in online prayer sessions, with each member assigned a role.

Meanwhile, Olivia benefits from connecting with her former colleagues on Facebook Messenger, allowing her to ask questions about settling transactions back home. She expressed, 'I am satisfied that my questions are answered.' Notably, Facebook Messenger is also where she learned about the foot amputation of a former officemate, prompting her to extend support: 'I sometimes send ointment, and sometimes money. And when we were there, we gave a wheelchair.' In these instances, ageing migrants utilize online channels to sustain connections, receive assistance and provide support to friends facing hardships.

Troubled connections

Participants expressed the challenges they faced in using mobile devices and online channels as part of their everyday social connections. These findings contribute to a nuanced understanding of social connection by highlighting how unequal access to resources across different locations impacts connective care practices. Studies on older migrants' digital practices primarily emphasize connective challenges mediated by issues of access, use and digital capacities (Wilding, 2006; Baldassar et al, 2007; Brandhorst, 2017).

Most participants rely on digital technologies and online content for self-care practices, as consuming culturally tailored content fosters a sense of connection to their homeland. However, these connections can be disrupted by digital infrastructures, such as pop-up ads in online channels. For instance, when Carmen attempted to show the religious music she listened to, a pop-up appeared, prompting her to exclaim: 'Terrible, I dislike these ads.' Similarly, Olga showed her mobile device, which was inundated with non-stop notifications. She revealed that she did not know how to disable them, pointing to her digital illiteracy. During my fieldwork, I assisted her in disabling the notifications, and once everything was fixed, Olga said with a dose of relief: 'Thank you.'

Another technological factor that disrupts distant connections is an unstable internet connection. Numerous studies have shown how poor internet connectivity impedes communication among migrants (Wilding, 2006). For some participants in this study, a weak internet connection led to forced disconnection from distant family members. For example, Esther, 74, has siblings in the United States, the UK and Germany. She recounted that her youngest sister in Germany stopped contacting her, stating, 'When I was talking to my sister, she got angry, saying, "What's wrong with your phone?" Our connection kept dropping out every time we spoke.' As a result, her sister ceased calling her. When I asked Esther how she felt about this, she replied, 'I worry because I don't know what's happening to her.'

In such cases, forced disconnection signals a form of digital divide (Nguyen and Hargittai, 2023). The lack of digital literacy and stable internet connectivity among older migrants can lead to voluntary disconnection. The data reflects that this results in feelings of frustration and confusion, undermining the notion of healthy connections (Farmer et al, 2019).

Social structures and contexts can trigger 'emotional ambivalence' or conflicting emotions among older migrants. Burkitt (2017) emphasizes the relational dimension of emotions, noting how individuals respond to external situations based on circumstances, events and 'cultural meanings that give sense and feeling to them' (2017: 170). He also argues that people often experience mixed emotions, especially when they struggle to align their feelings with required cultural models or resist doing so (Burkitt, 2017: 171). As a form of emotional management (Hochschild, 1979), individuals navigate these tensions while maintaining connections with related others (Burkitt, 2017). The cases of Gigi and Carmen exemplify this emotional ambivalence.

For instance, Gigi, a 71-year-old Filipina Australian, revealed that she chooses not to participate in any group chats with her family in the Philippines. Instead, she only connects to them through one-on-one exchanges on Facebook Messenger. To manage family tensions, she expresses her feelings to her distant networks and opts to stay connected in a different way. She explained:

> I try to avoid [referring to being part of a group chat] because it stressed me out when I hear problems, and I take it seriously, and I can't sleep. I am not young anymore, so I told them, stop telling me all about whatever your complaint to one another or something because I get stressed here. I'm trying to get on with my life like you know. Because it worries me all the time, like you know, 'cause I'm the eldest. I'm the mother to them and a father to them already. ... So now I said, I'm a retired person now, it's time for me to enjoy, so stop giving me all these worries because I like to enjoy. (Gigi)

In the interview, I sought clarification on the complaints her siblings shared with her online. Gigi revealed that some of her siblings have misunderstandings, which often spill over into their conversations on Facebook Messenger. She also mentioned that she used to send money to some of her siblings to finance their education. However, now that she is retired, she has informed her family that she can only send money for special occasions and emergencies.

Another case is Carmen, whom we met earlier. The last time she was in the Philippines was 15 years ago. During the interview, she reflected on her connection with her family members back home: 'I have not established my relationship emotionally. But they haven't forgotten me. I'm sure, and I have not forgotten them. There is a relationship there but there is not much. And, before you can go, it takes a lot of effort. It takes a lot of expenses.'

Carmen also explained, 'I am really focused on my life here in Australia, and my family here in Australia. But of course, I do care about my cousins and all my families in the Philippines.' Despite this, she noted that her family members make an effort to greet her on her birthday via Facebook: 'It is a great revelation that they care about you, that they love you, that they respect you. They show it through communication and how much respect they demonstrate. ... Posts during birthdays and so on. I mean tagged greetings on Facebook, of course.' To reciprocate these messages, she also politely greets her distant family members on their birthdays and sends money in times of emergency.

Conclusion

This chapter has demonstrated how older Filipina Australians use mobile devices and social media to foster social connections and engage in self-care, as well as care for their networks both within and beyond Australia. Furthermore, it offers a nuanced perspective on the dynamics and outcomes of local and transnational connections by considering the influences of social and technological factors. Delving into the connective practices of older migrants serves as an entry point to extend the concept of bifocalism in a digital context.

What do the connective care practices of ageing Filipina Australians imply for policy? First, the chapter highlights the use of online channels and content for managing health and wellbeing in later years. The Australian government could rethink its approach to promoting positive healthy ageing by advocating for a repository of culturally tailored online resources that assist ageing migrants in maintaining their health and combating isolation. Collaborating with leaders of organizations for older migrants and investing in in-person cultural events could also foster a sense of community among older migrants.

Second, the chapter exposes the digital divide within the context of migration and aging. Barriers impact the digital practices of ageing migrants. A recent report from the Ethnic Communities Council of Victoria (2024) indicates that older migrants are at risk of online exploitation and digital exclusion. Echoing the work of Warschauer (2003), there is a need to rethink connections as influenced by multiple contact points linked to individuals' social and cultural backgrounds (Helsper, 2021). More work must be done to understand how transnational connections affect the health and wellbeing of older migrants. Insights generated from this understanding can be shared with relevant stakeholders to inform policies and interventions in both the host (Baldassar, 2016) and home countries of older migrants.

Ultimately, this chapter contributes to rethinking social connections enacted through care practices in both local and transnational settings among migrants. It presents a critical articulation of what it means to age in a foreign land while navigating the possibilities and challenges of connecting here, there and elsewhere.

Funding

The project received funding from the University of the Philippines Center for Women's and Gender Studies (UPCWGS) as part of the 2022 UPCWGS Research Grant (Grant number: 2022–3).

Acknowledgements

I would like to express my deepest gratitude to the older Filipina Australians who participated in the project, welcomed me into their homes and shared their stories. Thank you to Ms Norminda Forteza and Corina Dutlow of the Australian-Filipino Community Services and Ms Mila Cichello for promoting the call for participants and assisting in recruiting research participants.

References

Amrith, M. (2021) 'Ageing bodies, precarious futures: the (im)mobilities of "temporary" migrant domestic workers over time', *Mobilities*, 16, 1–13.

Anschütz, S. and Mazzucato, V. (2024) 'Pacing mobility trajectories: temporality and agency in "home" visits by migrant youth', *Population, Space and Place*, 30, e2762.

Australian Bureau of Statistics 2023 (2021) 'Census country of birth QuickStats: Philippines'. Available at: https://www.abs.gov.au/census/find-census-data/quickstats/2021/5204_AUS (Accessed 10 February 2025).

Baldassar, L. (2016) 'Mobilities and communication technologies: transforming care in family life', in M. Kilkey and E. Palenga-Möllenbeck (eds) *Family Life in an Age of Migration and Mobility: Global Perspectives through the Life Course*, Palgrave Macmillan, pp 19–42.

Baldassar, L. and Merla, L. (2014) 'Introduction: transnational family caregiving through the lens of circulation', in L. Baldassar and L. Merla (eds) *Transnational Families, Migration and the Circulation of Care: Understanding Mobility and Absence in Family Life*, New York: Routledge, pp 3–24.

Baldassar, L. and Wilding, R. (2019) 'Migration, aging, and digital kinning: the role of distant care support networks in experiences of aging well', *The Gerontological Society of America*, 60, 1–9.

Baldassar, L., Baldock, C. and Wilding, R. (2007) *Families Caring across Borders: Migration, Ageing and Transnational Caregiving*, Palgrave Macmillan.

Baldassar, L., Wilding, R. and Worrell, S. (2020) 'Elderly migrants, digital kinning and digital home making across time and distance', in B. Pasveer, O. Synnes and I. Moser (eds) *Ways of Home Making in Care for Later Life*, Palgrave Macmillan, pp 41–63.

Baldassar, L., Stevens, C. and Wilding, R. (2022) 'Digital anticipation: facilitating the pre-emptive futures of Chinese grandparent migrants in Australia', *American Behavioral Scientist*, 66, 1863–1879.

Ballantyne, G. and Burke, L. (2017) '"People live in their heads a lot": polymedia, life course, and meanings of home among Melbourne's older Irish community', *Transnational Social Review*, 7, 10–24.

Brandhorst, R.M. (2017) '"A lo lejos": aging in place and transnational care in the case of transnational migration between Cuba and Germany', *Transnational Social Review*, 7, 56–72.

Burkitt, I. (2017) 'Decentring emotion regulation: from emotion regulation to relational emotion', *Emotion Review*, 10, 167–173.

Cabalquinto, E.C. (2022) *(Im)mobile Homes: Family Life at a Distance in the Age of Mobile Media*, Oxford University Press.

Cabalquinto, E. (2024) 'The caregiving burden of ageing Filipino Australian women in the digital era', *Melbourne Asia Review*. Available at: https://www.melbourneasiareview.edu.au/the-caregiving-burden-of-ageing-filipino-australian-women-in-the-digital-era/ (Accessed 15 February 2025).

Emmison, M. and Smith, P. (2000) *Researching the Visual: Images, Objects, Contexts and Interactions in Social and Cultural Inquiry*, SAGE.

Espinosa, S.A. (2017) *Sexualised Citizenship: A Cultural History of Philippines-Australian Migration*, Palgrave Macmillan.

Ethnic Communities Council of Victoria (2024) 'The digital divide: impacts on older people from migrant communities'. Available at: https://eccv.org.au/wp-content/uploads/2024/09/Research-report-The-Digital-Divide.pdf (Accessed 15 February 2025).

Farmer, J.C., Jovanovski, N., De Cotta, T., Gaylor, E., Soltani Panah, A., Jones, H., et al (2019) *Healthy Social Connections: A Multidisciplinary Exploration*, Social Innovation Research Institute.

Georgeou, N., Schismenos, S., Wali, N., Mackay, K. and Moraitakis, E. (2023) 'A scoping review of aging experiences among culturally and linguistically diverse people in Australia: toward better aging policy and cultural well-being for migrant and refugee adults', *Gerontologist*, 63, 182–199.

Helsper, E. (2021) *The Digital Disconnect: The Social Causes and Consequences of Digital Inequalities*, SAGE.

Hill Collins, P. and Bilge, S. (2016) *Intersectionality*, Polity Press.

Ho, E.L.E. and Chiu, T.Y. (2020) 'Transnational ageing and "care technologies": Chinese grandparenting migrants in Singapore and Sydney', *Population, Space and Place*, 26, 1–11.

Hochschild, A.R. (1979) 'Emotion work, feeling rules, and social structure', *American Journal of Sociology*, 85, 551–575.

Khvorostianov, N., Elias, N. and Nimrod, G. (2012) '"Without it I am nothing": the internet in the lives of older immigrants', *New Media & Society*, 14, 583–599.

Madianou, M. and Miller, D. (2012) *Migration and New Media: Transnational Families and Polymedia*, Routledge.

Migration Data Portal (2023) 'Older persons and migration'. Available at: https://www.migrationdataportal.org/themes/older-persons-and-migration#key-trends (Accessed 13 February 2025).

Millard, A., Baldassar, L. and Wilding, R. (2018) 'The significance of digital citizenship in the well-being of older migrants', *Public Health*, 158, 144–148.

Nguyen, M.H. and Hargittai, E. (2023) 'Digital inequality in disconnection practices: voluntary nonuse during COVID-19', *Journal of Communication*, 73, 494–510.

Parreñas, R.S. (2005) 'Long distance intimacy: class, gender and intergenerational relations between mothers and children in Filipino transnational families', *Global Networks*, 5, 317–336.

Parreñas, R.S. (2020) *Servants of Globalization: Women, Migration and Domestic Work*, Stanford University Press.

Rose, G. (2007) *Visual Methodologies: An Introduction to the Interpretation of Visual Materials*, SAGE.

Saldaña, J. (2011) *Fundamentals of Qualitative Research*, Oxford University Press.

Saroca, C. (2007) 'Filipino women, migration and violence in Australia: lived reality and media image', *Kasarinlan: Philippine Journal of Third World Studies*, 21, 75–110.

United Nations (2019) 'World population ageing'. Available at: https://www.un.org/en/development/desa/population/publications/pdf/ageing/WorldPopulationAgeing2019-Highlights.pdf (Accessed 13 October 2024).

United Nations (2022) 'World population prospects'. Available at: https://www.un.org/development/desa/pd/sites/www.un.org.development.desa.pd/files/wpp2022_summary_of_results.pdf (Accessed 13 October 2024).

Vertovec, S. (2009) *Transnationalism*, Routledge.

Warschauer, M. (2003) *Technology and Social Inclusion: Rethinking the Digital Divide*, MIT Press.

Wilding, R. (2006) '"Virtual" intimacies? Families communicating across transnational contexts', *Global Networks*, 6, 125–142.

Wilding, R., Gamage, S., Worrell, S. and Baldassar, L. (2022) 'Practices of "digital homing" and gendered reproduction among older Sinhalese and Karen migrants in Australia', *Journal of Immigrant & Refugee Studies*, 20, 220–232.

Zontini, E. (2015) 'Growing old in a transnational social field: belonging, mobility and identity among Italian migrants', *Ethnic and Racial Studies*, 38, 326–341.

4

Social Connection by Design: Finnish Approaches to Long-Term Care

Jasmine Knox and Hannele Komu

Social isolation and loneliness are growing international public health issues that affect many older people (Boamah et al, 2021; Rodney et al, 2021; World Health Organization, 2021). Older adults residing in long-term care are particularly vulnerable to social isolation, loneliness, and related mental health issues such as depression and anxiety (Quan et al, 2020; World Health Organization, 2021). In Australia, for example, a recent government review found challenges with care facility design, insufficient staffing and poor training resulting in care that 'leaves too many older Australians isolated and disconnected' (Royal Commission into Aged Care Quality and Safety, 2021). These issues are reflected in care models for older people across other high-income countries (Theurer et al, 2015; Scales, 2021; Millett et al, 2024). Within facilities, poor social connection often stems from a 'one-size-fits-all' unimaginative approach to providing social activities such as bingo and crafts (Theurer et al, 2015; Neves et al, 2019), and a lack of integration of care facilities with the wider community. At the systems level, the organizational culture of the 'care industry' for older people has become distorted by funding, policy and related structural issues, meaning catering for immediate personal care needs and clinical healthcare are prioritized ahead of psychosocial wellbeing (Ludlow et al, 2020). It is increasingly acknowledged that social connection is an important issue for older people in long-term care that needs to be addressed (Gardiner et al, 2020; Quan et al, 2020; Millett et al, 2024) and ideas for how to do this are sought.

This chapter explores an alternative approach through the lens of Finnish long-term care homes, where social connection is considered and integrated into care delivery and care home operations. Drawing from observations and interviews across four regional facilities, we examine how Finland's Nordic welfare model shapes both policy and practice in supporting older people's social wellbeing. This chapter emerged from a partnership between an Australian PhD researcher and the service director of regional wellbeing services in Finland. Our collaboration brings together insights from both research and practice perspectives.

With a social equity and welfare model in place over the longer term, Finland has implemented changes to policy and practice to directly impact the social aspects of care for older people living in long-term care (Anttonen and Karsio, 2016), or elderly care homes, as residential care is commonly termed in Finland. Like many high-income countries, Finland has a rapidly ageing population (Valkama and Oulasvirta, 2021), so it is significant to understand how Finns aim to maintain social connection for the oldest age groups while providing services for a large proportion of the population. How Finland is proceeding should interest other high-income countries that also experience population ageing as studies suggest that rates of loneliness may have decreased (World Health Organization, 2021).

This chapter is structured in three parts. First, we explore current challenges to social connection in long-term care settings across high-income countries. We then present a detailed case study of regional care homes in Finland, examining how social connection is integrated into staff practices, care home design and management approaches. Finally, we present key learnings that can inform improvements in other contexts, offering practical insights for policy makers and practitioners seeking to enhance social connection in long-term care settings.

Social connection in long-term care

Before examining the Finnish approach in detail, it is important to establish our understanding of social connection, and the current challenges faced in long-term care settings. Social connection encompasses a range of satisfying and meaningful relationships with others that help to sustain overall health and wellbeing (Dunbar and Spoors, 1995; Seppala, 2014; Huxhold et al, 2020). This chapter adopts a strength-based approach to people's social interactions, focusing on how to build on people's intrinsic motivation to connect (Baumeister and Leary, 1995) rather than focusing on 'solving deficits' such as loneliness and isolation. This approach supports a sense of agency and minimizes the risk of stigmatizing individuals (Cacioppo and Cacioppo, 2014). Encouraging people to perceive any existing contacts or activities as valuable enables older people to identify where they are already connected and to consider if and how to build on this. Connections can be with social contacts and non-humans, including pets (see Chapter 5, this volume), connections to spiritual and cultural communities and sporting groups, and feelings of belonging to places or groups (Farmer et al, 2021; 2025).

Within care homes, social interaction takes multiple forms. Older people in long-term care may have social interaction with family and friends, other residents, community members, volunteers and staff members. Relationships with other residents and staff can play a crucial role in counteracting the loss of social networks that tends to occur when a person relocates into long-term care, helping to support residents' sense of security and identity (Sumaya-Smith, 1995; Grenade and Boldy, 2008; Thomas et al, 2013).

Challenges to social connection

Research across different countries consistently identifies several key challenges to fostering social connection in long-term care. These include:

- *Institutions, not homes*: The institutional scale and design of many long-term care facilities can detract from these places feeling homely and having a sense of community (Batchelor et al, 2020; Dyer et al, 2020; Royal Commission into Aged Care Quality and Safety, 2021). Evidence recommends that care homes should be arranged in smaller clustered units with a maximum of 15 people, with a home-like environment to foster social connection between residents (Batchelor et al, 2020; Dyer et al, 2020; Royal Commission into Aged Care Quality and Safety, 2021; Seemann et al, 2023).
- *Insufficient and under-appreciated workforce*: Understaffing, high staff turnover and lack of training are consistently reported internationally (Batchelor et al, 2020; Royal Commission into Aged Care Quality and Safety, 2021; Peters et al, 2021; Scales, 2021). These workforce issues directly impact residents' experiences of social connection as it becomes hard to create rapport and maintain ongoing relationships. Where staff are time-poor due to workforce shortages, they must prioritize personal care tasks, with little time left for social interaction and conversations with residents (Ludlow et al, 2020; Royal Commission into Aged Care Quality and Safety, 2021).
- *Standardized activities*: Rather than considering individual interests, staff and management may implement programmes they think most residents will be able to access rather than considering the differing interests of individuals. Such 'one-size-fits-all' programmes may deter residents who don't enjoy the activity and thus miss opportunities to connect with others (Neves et al, 2019). Many facilities lack appreciation of the benefits arising from social interaction, rather than just distracting or entertaining people *en masse* (Theurer et al, 2015; Neves et al, 2019).

- *Integration with local community*: Care facilities often operate as isolated environments, separate from their surrounding communities. Greater integration with the local community requires time and effort but would benefit both residents and the community. An Australian government report highlighted poor community integration and called for greater co-ordination between older people's care and other community services and activities provided by local government, community organizations and businesses (Royal Commission into Aged Care Quality and Safety, 2021).

Practice from regional Finland: a case study

Having identified these common challenges, this chapter examines how they are addressed within the Finnish context. The following case study presents findings from four care homes in regional Finland, offering insights into practical solutions for enhancing social connection in long-term care environments.

Methods

Four Finnish regional care homes were explored as part of one author's PhD studies to investigate social connection practices in different countries' models of long-term care of older people. Contact was made with the service director (Komu, co-author here). It was agreed that the Australian researcher would spend time immersed in the Finnish care home environment, observing and conducting interviews. The service director arranged for the researcher to meet with staff and residents at the four facilities. The study had ethics approval from the Swinburne University Ethics Committee (ref 20236970), and a research permit was approved by the county wellbeing services in Finland (ref 7§/2003).

The researcher spent one month embedded across four care homes, collecting data through participant observation and interviews with residents (8), staff members (5), managers (3) and visiting community artists (2). The researcher interviewed a policy expert and a Finnish elder care academic to understand the broader Finnish policy context. For interviews conducted in Finnish, the service director (Komu) or nursing staff helped translate the information during staff and resident interviews. While this isn't ideal due to possible bias or reticence to speak from interviewees, it was practical and less disruptive for residents than using an unknown translator. When feasible, interviews were conducted with staff in English. Observations were recorded after observation sessions, similarly, to avoid disruption to resident and staff routines. All interview data was collected with an audio-recording device, with the consent of participants. Reflections and questions from observations and interviews were discussed in regular conversations between the researcher and the service director (Komu). A manual thematic approach was used for data analysis (Braun and Clarke, 2006). The findings presented focus specifically on policy and practices that enhance social connection.

Context

Finland's population is one of the most rapidly ageing among Organization for Economic Co-operation and Development members (Valkama and Oulasvirta, 2021), with 28.9 per cent of people projected to be aged 65 years or over by 2060 (Pirhonen et al, 2020). North Karelia, the region where the facilities studied are located, is in Eastern Finland. It is home to 162,500 people, and 28.8 per cent of the population is over 65 years old (Statista, 2024).

The Finnish aged care system operates within a distinctive social framework. It is funded by tax revenue and provided by local government. The model of provision is predicated on equality, with no means-testing and universal access to services regardless of an individual's social and financial status (Anttonen and Karsio, 2016). Despite not being as wealthy as its Nordic neighbours, Denmark and Sweden, Finland demonstrates a pragmatic approach to service delivery. There is an accepted, general understanding of the importance of making evidence-informed decisions to provide quality public services, as captured in a popular Finnish expression that 'a poor man cannot afford bad quality'!

Over recent decades, Finland has significantly changed its aged care system. Following an ongoing trend of 'deinstitutionalization' (along with other parts of Europe), the country has closed large-scale facilities and replaced them with smaller, home-like environments (Komu et al, 2013; Anttonen and Karsio, 2016). Furthermore, the last 30 years have seen policy changes implemented that relate to improving the facility environment, staff education and training, mandatory staffing numbers and skill diversity to support older people's health and wellbeing (Supervision Law 741/2023, § 8; Komu et al, 2013; Quality recommendation, 2024). Notably, Finland is one of the few countries where there has been a decrease over the last 20 years in the use of antidepressant medication in long-term care (Roitto et al, 2019). This trend may be linked to a more socially-connected-oriented environment.

Current legislation shapes both the physical and social environment of Finnish care homes. According to legislation, environments in long-term care homes must be age-friendly and home-like (Komu et al, 2013; Quality recommendation, 2024). The law requires that the care home environment is safe, free of barriers and hazards, and that all necessary services are accessible (Quality recommendation, 2024). An 'age-friendly environment' supports residents' rights to self determination and promotes wellbeing and social interaction (Supervision Law 741/2023, § 8).

Several key policies specifically address social connection. The Finnish Elderly Care Law (980/2012) states that care must be implemented so that older people feel their lives are safe, meaningful and valuable, and that they can maintain social interaction and participate in various activities. Finnish legislation states that communal living in long-term care requires people to have an apartment within a care home that meets their needs and offers activities promoting social interaction (Social Care Law 1301/2014, § 21b). Long-term care environments must support older people's general wellbeing and social interaction (Supervision Law 741/2023, § 8). 'Community spirit' must be supported by places where residents can meet up with people who live in the community and participate in joint activities (Quality recommendation, 2024).

Staffing requirements are clearly defined in legislation. Care homes must have 0.6 staff employed in direct care work per resident. Staff qualifications and composition are also regulated. Staff training and task structure must correspond with the number and the needs of older people in their long-term care home.

The workforce combines both healthcare and social care expertise. Legislation mandating a care home requires a physiotherapist, social worker and mental health counsellors (Quality recommendation, 2024). Most staff are 'practical nurses' or nurses. A practical nurse has three years of training and education, including culturally appropriate social interaction and medical treatment skills. Practical nurses in eldercare work by legislated ethical principles and quality recommendations for services for older people. These include the fact that practical nurses must consider the residents' capabilities, resources and preferences, and support each older person's involvement in their care using a rehabilitative work approach (ePerusteet, 2024). For nurses, 3.5 years of tertiary education is required, with the option of completing specialist courses in memory care, palliative care or emergency care (Social and Healthcare Supervision 741, 2023).

In practice, these policies translate into a strong emphasis on creating home-like environments. Residents are empowered to participate in decision-making about the furnishing of communal areas and are able to have family or friends stay overnight. This approach reflects a broader philosophy of resident autonomy, captured in a common refrain from both staff and residents: 'they/I pay rent, so it's their/my choice'.

Homes, spaces and places

The following descriptions of two recently constructed care homes illustrate how Finnish design principles translate into practice.

Forest View

Forest View is a three-storey building with large windows across the front façade that provide views out onto the street and surrounding forest, as well to the garden and vegetable patch. It is home to 63 residents. Inside, residents' rooms are clustered into smaller units with 10–15 people. The interior features a classic Scandinavian design, with a muted colour scheme of greens and light wooden furniture. Each unit contains a lounge room, dining area, balcony and reading nook. The lounge has a sofa, chairs, a bookcase, a fireplace (faux) and a large television. There is also a sauna in the building that all residents share.

The building's design prioritizes sensory experiences. A kitchen is in the centre of the building on each of the three levels, so during mealtimes, the scent of whatever is cooking wafts through the living and dining spaces of each unit. During lunch observations, residents gathered around a long wooden table facing one another. Most residents collected their lunch from a kitchen hatch, and one staff member brought lunch trays over for those with mobility issues. Another staff member sat with residents, moving around the table, engaging residents in conversation and assisting those who needed it. Their tone was light, conversational, warm and familiar, and residents seemed engaged, occasionally laughing.

Residents' rooms function as studio apartments, with enough room for a single bed, a sofa or reading chair, a television, a small dining table or writing desk, and a bathroom. Residents and their families are encouraged by staff to furnish their rooms with art and furniture brought from home to support a home-like environment.

Autumn Leaves

Autumn Leaves is a large single-storey building that resembles the shape of the number eight. This innovative design creates a continuous walking loop inside the building. There are two garden areas in the middle, both with vegetable patches, outside dining areas and barbecues. These garden spaces are accessible 24/7, as they are fully enclosed and safe for residents with memory loss issues. Autumn Leaves is home to 60 residents, with approximately 30 residing in rooms around the two central gardens. The large lounge area in the middle features movable doors allowing the space to be reconfigured for various activities. Other communal spaces inside include a dining area and a sauna.

The design actively encourages staff–resident interaction. During a building tour, the physiotherapist explained that staff regularly take their portable laptop stations and sit outside to complete their paperwork during warmer weather. Offices and staff lunchrooms were designed to be small so that 'staff don't hide in the offices away from the residents'.

Residents' rooms are spacious and – similar to Forest View – resemble studio apartments designed to take in natural light from the street or the central gardens. Some rooms have their own direct access to the gardens, and double rooms are available for couples.

Job satisfaction: people and social connection

Each care home employs a multidisciplinary team to support residents' wellbeing. The team includes a social worker, a physiotherapist and a 'culture and wellbeing guide'. These staff members work five days a week alongside residents, planning and implementing daily social activities. In interviews, the team members emphasized how their collaborative approach enriches resident care. By combining their fitness, social support and art practice expertise, they create diverse and engaging programmes 'to come up with ideas for the residents' activities together'.

Direct care staff demonstrate a notably relaxed and positive approach to their work. During afternoons, they engage in personalized social activities with residents, such as reading a newspaper together in the lounge, watching a classic black-and-white movie, or sitting on the sofa with residents. When asked about these activities, staff consistently emphasized their integral role in care delivery, stating, 'This is part of my job' and 'We can sit, and we can talk with them. We can read [a] book to them'. They explained that they were encouraged by their managers to interact with residents and get to know them 'as you would entering someone's home'.

This approach reflects a broader cultural shift in Finnish aged care. The managers interviewed described interacting with residents and getting to know them as individuals as a shift that had taken place in Finland. They emphasized that connecting with residents personally signalled an intentional culture shift directed by national policy:

> That's our code, that every one of our staff can go and sit with elderly people and only discuss. It's also work. I think my staff work very hard, and they are very good in their work, but there are some old habits that we have to give away and take and act in a new way because we also have a law that requires that. (Regional manager)

The emphasis on meaningful social interaction appears to enhance job satisfaction. Staff were observed walking with residents in the neighbourhood or baking traditional sweets together. Several practical nurses and nurses expressed that they 'love their job'.

Social connection activities

The care homes offer diverse activities that encourage social connection to occur naturally. During nature trivia sessions, the 'culture and wellbeing guide' facilitates conversation and encourages residents to interact and answer questions. Art and craft sessions combine creativity with social engagement, as residents and staff learn about art practices to decorate the communal areas, working collaboratively to create arrangements made from nature, such as twigs and dried flowers or working collectively on a large mural. Other activities include bird variety memory card games around a table while chatting and making traditional cakes and sweets.

A new arts-based social programme demonstrates the care homes' commitment to innovation. The culture and wellbeing guide has collaborated with local artists to secure philanthropic funding to establish art, dance and movement workshops for residents and provide staff training. Group workshops unite residents and staff, singing, dancing or making music as a community. During these sessions, the artists encouraged residents to dance with each other and with staff, and at both facilities, residents and staff worked together to create a charcoal mural for the lounge area depicting a landscape. The programme extends beyond group activities; the artists also visited bed-bound residents and performed one-on-one music and art sessions in residents' rooms.

Staff development forms an integral part of the programme. Training includes how to engage residents in artistic practices and how to evaluate resident engagement in art-based activities. The culture and wellbeing guide emphasizes that this training was important so that care staff could build capacity and be supported to be 'more than just a nurse'.

Learnings for supporting social connection

The findings reveal several key themes about Finland's approach to creating socially connected care. These insights offer valuable considerations for policy makers and practitioners.

- *Policies to proactively support social connection*: Mandatory staffing numbers, skill diversity and legislation that informs the size and design of new facilities, for example, access to garden spaces and smaller density home-like living arrangements, ensure consistent standards that foster opportunities for residents to connect with staff and each other. Clear policy frameworks supporting the connection between residents, staff and the local community are essential to drive meaningful change and provide quality care that supports older people's wellbeing.
- *Approach to the 'work' of social connection*: In the Finnish settings, staff have time and encouragement to interact with residents outside of daily tasks like showering and assisting residents at mealtimes. Social engagement is considered an integral part of the job and is supported and encouraged by management. The diverse staff expertise – from social workers and physiotherapists to culture and wellbeing guides – enriches activity planning and delivery.
- *Creating care communities*: The Finnish care homes are relatively small, and within these, groups of 10–15 residents live in smaller clusters in

shared home-like environments. This design enables people to develop relationships and community with the number of people you would perhaps find in a neighbourhood. Smaller density living aligns with recommendations from studies on resident quality of life (Batchelor et al, 2020; Dyer et al, 2020; Seemann et al, 2023).

- *Spaces designed to support social connection*: The Finnish homes provide options for communal spaces in addition to lounge and dining areas. These include gardens with outside dining facilities, balconies and saunas. The design incorporates spaces for different types of social interaction; for example, a 'cat nook' in Forest View combines the bed of the resident cat, a comfortable chair positioned by a window, and garden views and a radio (see Figure 4.1). This space exemplifies how design can support various forms of connection – allowing residents to be present in shared

Figure 4.1: The 'cat nook' in a long-term care facility in Finland

areas while engaging with animals, nature or music rather than direct human interaction.
- Medical equipment remains hidden from view, and communal spaces such as the lounge and dining areas feature warm and inviting decor, with furniture positioned to encourage interaction (Seemann et al, 2023). Nature is a consistent design element throughout the buildings. Natural elements appear in artwork, and large windows provide views of the garden spaces outside, creating an interplay between the interior and the nature surrounding the building. Residents enjoy 'barrier-free' access to multiple garden spaces.
- *Social connection activities in care settings*: The Finnish approach emphasizes purposeful interaction through shared activities. These include creating murals, participating in group quizzes, gardening or baking traditional cakes. Activities that encourage individuals to work together and problem-solve enable social connection to occur naturally as a by-product (Farmer et al, 2021; 2025). Similarly, synchronous activities, where people do the same activity together in groups (singing, dancing and movement activities), form a regular part of daily life in Finnish care homes.
- *Integration with local community*: Care homes in Finland maintain active partnerships with local artists, museums, activity workers and community groups. These partnerships help bridge the gap between facilities and the broader community by bringing community members *into the facility* to interact with residents, creating opportunities for residents to develop new and different types of social connection.

Conclusion

Creating environments that nurture social connection in long-term care requires systematic changes across multiple dimensions. The Finnish example demonstrates how this can be achieved through three key elements: clear policy frameworks; practical operational approaches; and purposeful design. While these elements operate within Finland's distinct funding model and cultural context, they offer valuable, adaptable insights for other countries.

The Finnish facilities show how social connection can become central to care delivery when:

- Policy actively supports social connection through staffing requirements and design standards.
- Management encourages staff to prioritize social interaction as core work.
- Facility design intentionally creates spaces for various forms of connection.
- Activities emerge from resident interests rather than institutional convenience.

These practical approaches can be adapted to different contexts, regardless of funding models or cultural frameworks. As aged care systems globally seek solutions to social isolation and loneliness, the Finnish model offers evidence that systematic, non-pharmacological approaches can successfully support older people's social and emotional wellbeing. Most importantly, it demonstrates that creating socially connected care environments is both achievable and essential for quality aged care delivery.

References

Anttonen, A. and Karsio, O. (2016) 'Eldercare service redesign in Finland: deinstitutionalization of long-term care', *Journal of Social Service Research*, 42(2), 151–166.

Batchelor, F., Savvas, S., Dang, C., Goh, A.M.Y., Levinger, P., Peck, A., et al (2020) *Inside the System: Aged Care Residents' Perspectives*, National Ageing Research Institute.

Baumeister, R.F. and Leary, M.R. (1995) 'The need to belong: desire for interpersonal attachments as a fundamental human motivation', *Psychological Bulletin*, 117(3), 497–529.

Boamah, S.A., Weldrick, R., Lee, T.S.J. and Taylor, N. (2021) 'Social isolation among older adults in long-term care: a scoping review', *Journal of Aging and Health*, 33(7–8), 618–632.

Braun, V. and Clarke, V. (2006) 'Using thematic analysis in psychology', *Qualitative Research in Psychology*, 3(2), 77–101.

Cacioppo, J.T. and Cacioppo, S. (2014) 'Social relationships and health: the toxic effects of perceived social isolation', *Social and Personality Psychology Compass*, 8(2), 58–72.

Dunbar, R. and Spoors, M. (1995) 'Social networks, support cliques and kinship', *Human Nature*, 6(3), 273–290.

Dyer, S.M., Valeri, M., Arora, N., Tilden, D. and Crotty, M. (2020) 'Is Australia over-reliant on residential aged care to support our older population?' *The Medical Journal of Australia*, 213(4), 156–157.

ePerusteet (2024) 'For practical nurse education'. Available at: https://eperusteet.opintopolku.fi/#/fi/kooste/ammatillinen/8531450 (Accessed 11 November 2024).

Farmer, J., De Cotta, T., Savic, M., Rowe, C., Verhagen, J., Sivasubramaniam, D., et al (2025) *Social Connection 101*, revised edition, Swinburne University of Technology. https://doi.org/10.25916/sut.28415261

Gardiner, C., Laud, P., Heaton, T. and Gott, M. (2020) 'What is the prevalence of loneliness amongst older people living in residential and nursing care homes? A systematic review and meta-analysis', *Age and Ageing*, 49(5), 748–757.

Grenade, L. and Boldy, D. (2008) 'Social isolation and loneliness among older people: issues and future challenges in community and residential settings', *Australian Health Review*, 32(3), 468–478.

Huxhold, O., Fiori, K.L., Webster, N.J. and Antonucci, T.C. (2020) 'The strength of weaker ties: an underexplored resource for maintaining emotional well-being in later life', *The Journals of Gerontology: Series B*, 75(7), 1433–1442.

Komu, H., Rissanen, S. and Kälviäinen, M. (2013) 'Physical environment of care homes: some Finnish case examples', in A. Hujala, S. Rissanen and Vihma (eds) *Designing Wellbeing in Elderly Care Homes*, Aalto University, pp 192–204.

Ludlow, K., Churruca, K., Mumford, V., Ellis, L.A. and Braithwaite, J. (2020) 'Staff members' prioritisation of care in residential aged care facilities: a Q methodology study', *BMC Health Services Research*, 20, 1–14. https://doi.org/10.1186/s12913-020-05127-3

Millett, G., Franco, G. and Fiocco, A.J. (2024) 'Understanding the social and leisure needs of lonely and socially isolated older adults living in residential care: a qualitative study', *Aging & Mental Health*, 28(2), 344–352.

Neves, B.B., Sanders, A. and Kokanović, R. (2019) '"It's the worst bloody feeling in the world": experiences of loneliness and social isolation among older people living in care homes', *Journal of Aging Studies*, 49, 74–84.

Peters, M.D., Marnie, C. and Butler, A. (2021) 'Royal Commission into Aged Care recommendations on minimum staff time standard for nursing homes', *Australian Health Review*, 46(4), 388–390. https://doi.org/10.1071/AH21283

Pirhonen, J., Lolich, L., Tuominen, K., Jolanki, O. and Timonen, V. (2020) '"These devices have not been made for older people's needs": older adults' perceptions of digital technologies in Finland and Ireland', *Technology in Society*, 62, Article 101287.

Quality recommendation for the organization of active and functional aging and sustainable services 2024–2027 (2024) Available at: https://julkaisut.valtioneuvosto.fi/bitstream/handle/10024/165460/STM_2024_4_J.pdf?sequence=1&isAllowed=y (Accessed 11 November 2024).

Quan, N.G., Lohman, M.C., Resciniti, N.V. and Friedman, D.B. (2020) 'A systematic review of interventions for loneliness among older adults living in long-term care facilities', *Aging & Mental Health*, 24(12), 1945–1955.

Rodney, T., Josiah, N. and Baptiste, D.L. (2021) 'Loneliness in the time of COVID-19: impact on older adults', *Journal of Advanced Nursing*, 77(9), e24.

Roitto, H.M., Kautiainen, H., Aalto, U.L., Öhman, H., Laurila, J. and Pitkälä, K.H. (2019) 'Fourteen-year trends in the use of psychotropic medications, opioids, and other sedatives among institutionalized older people in Helsinki, Finland', *Journal of the American Medical Directors Association*, 20(3), 305–311.

Royal Commission into Aged Care Quality and Safety (2021) *Final Report: Care, Dignity and Respect*, Commonwealth of Australia. Available at: https://agedcare.royalcommission.gov.au/publications/final-report (Accessed 11 November 2024).

Scales, K. (2021) 'It is time to resolve the direct care workforce crisis in long-term care', *The Gerontologist*, 61(4), 497–504.

Seemann, N., Fuggle, L., Week, D., Westera, A., Morris, D., Loggie, C., et al (2023) *Final Report on the Development of the Draft National Aged Care Design Principles and Guidelines*. Australian Health Services Research Institute, University of Wollongong.

Seppala, E. (2014) 'Connectedness & health: the science of social connection'. Available at: https://ccare.stanford.edu/uncategorized/connectedness-health-the-science-of-social-connection-infographic/ (Accessed 6 August 2024).

Statista (2024) 'Share of population aged 65 years and older in Finland 2023, by region'. Available at: https://www.statista.com/statistics/529453/share-of-individuals-aged-65-years-and-older-in-finland-by-region/ (Accessed 17 November 2024).

Sumaya-Smith, I. (1995) 'Caregiver/resident relationships: surrogate family bonds and surrogate grieving in a skilled nursing facility', *Journal of Advanced Nursing*, 21(3), 447–451.

Theurer, K., Mortenson, W.B., Stone, R., Suto, M., Timonen, V. and Rozanova, J. (2015) 'The need for a social revolution in residential care', *Journal of Aging Studies*, 35, 201–210.

Thomas, J.E., O'Connell, B. and Gaskin, C.J. (2013) 'Residents' perceptions and experiences of social interaction and participation in leisure activities in residential aged care', *Contemporary Nurse*, 45(2), 244–254.

Valkama, P. and Oulasvirta, L. (2021) 'How Finland copes with an ageing population: adjusting structures and equalising the financial capabilities of local governments', *Local Government Studies*, 47(3), 429–452.

World Health Organization (2021) 'Social isolation and loneliness among older people: advocacy brief'. Available at: https://www.who.int/publications/i/item/9789240030749 (Accessed 22 November 2024).

5

Companionship in Times of Uncertainty: The Role of Pets for Families with Children during COVID-19

Shannon K. Bennetts, Sharinne B. Crawford, Tiffani J. Howell, Fiona C. Giles and Kylie Burke

As inherently social creatures, humans have an intrinsic need for regular, ongoing and meaningful social connections and support (Cacioppo and Patrick, 2008). The absence of such connections can exacerbate feelings of loneliness, boredom, anxiety and depression, especially for children and adolescents (Loades et al, 2020). The COVID-19 pandemic was declared a public health emergency of international concern in January 2020 and a global pandemic in March 2020, prompting widespread and significant changes to the ways that we work, live and study. Efforts to mitigate the spread of the SARS-CoV-2 virus included mandatory isolation and social distancing, disrupting opportunities to engage in the social interactions that keep us well (Okabe-Miyamoto et al, 2021). Australian efforts to curb transmission included strict 'stay at home' orders, remote school learning and working, curfews, business closures, and restrictions on daily movements. With families spending more time at home than ever before, demand for pet adoptions surged, primarily for dogs and cats. This generated considerable dialogue and media attention about the role that pets play during times of change and uncertainty (Selinger-Morris, 2020).

In a book exploring how social connections manifest in diverse contexts, we would be remiss not to consider our non-human companions. Australia has one of the highest rates of pet ownership worldwide, with over two-thirds of households (69 per cent) now owning a pet, including around 6.3 million dogs and 5.3 million cats (Animal Medicines Australia, 2022).

By comparison, pet ownership rates are estimated to be around 66 per cent in the United States (Brown, 2023) and 57 per cent in the United Kingdom (Statista, 2024).

We saw the pandemic as a unique opportunity to better understand how pets shape our social worlds during a time when our usual human-to-human interactions were restricted and fragmented. Drawing on our large online survey of Australian parents during the pandemic, this chapter reflects on the role of pets for social connection and wellbeing. We consider the role of the pet in two ways: first, the bond between human and pet as a relationship that offers (direct) companionship and non-judgemental support; and second, the (indirect) role of the pet in facilitating human-to-human connection. We view these human–pet connections through an attachment lens. Attachment refers to the deep and enduring emotional connections we form, typically between two people, in which each seeks closeness and feels more secure when the attachment figure is present. Although originally applied to infant–parent relationships (Bretherton, 1992), Attachment Theory has more recently been considered in the context of human–pet relationships (Zilcha-Mano et al, 2011), such that pets are viewed as offering a 'safe haven' or 'secure base'.

The study of human–animal interactions

The multidisciplinary study of interactions between human and non-human animals – 'anthrozoology' – is a relatively recent field. It emerged in the early 1980s following reports that human–pet interactions could have mental and physical health benefits (Fine, 2020). Since then, both psychological and physical benefits have been well-documented, such as enhanced self-esteem, increased physical activity, improved hormonal levels and reduced heart rate (Handlin et al, 2011; McConnell et al, 2011; Janssens et al, 2020). For children, interacting with pets is linked to better physical health, more physical activity, less parental concern about the child's mood, behaviour and learning ability, and better emotion regulation and social skills (Hawkins et al, 2019; Christian et al, 2020; Dueñas et al, 2021). Pets can offer unconditional and non-judgemental companionship, which can be particularly beneficial for those with pre-existing mental health conditions or those who have experienced trauma (Brooks et al, 2018).

However, a recent systematic review reported mixed findings on the links between pets and quality of life, with 54 studies concluding positive (n=17), mixed (n=19) and no impact (n=13) (Scoresby et al, 2021). This speaks to the challenges and responsibilities of caring for pets such as behavioural issues like aggression (Arhant et al, 2017), trouble adapting to new routines (Applebaum et al, 2020) and associated disrupted sleep (Hoffman et al, 2018).

Interestingly, strong human–pet bonds have been linked to *greater* psychological distress, including depression and anxiety (Peacock et al, 2012). This association has also been reported in elderly populations (Miltiades and Shearer, 2011) and workers in high-risk occupations such as emergency services (Lass-Hennemann et al, 2020). Without robust longitudinal data, it is not possible to fully explain these links. Do pets *cause* distress (for example, worry about the pet's care and wellbeing)? Or do distressed people adopt pets partly to support their wellbeing? There is evidence that this negative relationship between pet attachment and mental health is mediated by owners' attachment style towards humans (that is, an insecure attachment to humans is associated with poorer mental health, not the relationship with the dog, per se [Lass-Hennemann et al, 2022]), but it is necessary to replicate this study to determine if the pattern is generalizable to other pet owners.

The COVID-19 context

In addition to the health impacts of contracting SARS-CoV-2, pandemic restrictions caused significant global economic and social upheaval (Churchill, 2021), disrupting social connections and increasing loneliness (Vasan et al, 2022). A representative survey in March 2020 found that Australian adults were experiencing substantially elevated anxiety and depression symptoms compared to population norms (Dawel et al, 2020). Parents experienced particularly high stress levels and poorer mental health (Brown et al, 2020), often juggling work and homeschooling, social isolation, loss of income, and less access to support (Griffiths et al, 2021). Mental health impacts were strongest for Australian parents with pre-existing mental health risks, socioeconomic disadvantage or pandemic-related work impacts (Westrupp et al, 2021).

Open-ended responses from a 2020 survey revealed that US dog owners felt their dogs had contributed to reduced feelings of loneliness and isolation and protected their mental and physical health (Bussolari et al, 2021). Conversely, quantitative data from US pet owners suggested that the impact of pet attachment differed by pre-pandemic mental health status; pet attachment was found to be protective for those with moderate or high distress, but those with strong pet attachment and severe distress were likely to continue to experience severe distress (McDonald et al, 2021). Evidence from UK lockdowns has shown that stronger pet attachment was associated with more psychological distress (Ratschen et al, 2020).

Method

In response to the emerging pandemic in March 2020, we rapidly designed and implemented a national online survey to capture a 'snapshot' of how

Australian families with children and a cat or dog viewed and engaged with their pets. Given mixed previous evidence, our broad aim was to investigate the role of pets for families with children during the pandemic. For the purpose of this chapter, we focus on: (1) how human–pet bonds were associated with parent/child wellbeing; and (2) how parents described the benefits and challenges of having a pet during the pandemic. Detailed findings have been reported elsewhere (Bennetts et al, 2022a; 2022b; 2023).

Data for the *Parents, Pets & Pandemic Survey* were collected over 12 weeks, from July 2020 to October 2020. Participants were required to be: over 18 years old; living in Australia; living with at least one child under 18 years at least some of the time; and living with at least one cat or dog. Our team of experts in psychology, public health and anthrozoology designed a brief 15-minute survey. The survey included validated measures of human–pet bonds, including the brief Human–Animal Attachment Scale (Bures et al, 2019) and the Cat/Dog Owner Relationship Scale (Howell et al, 2017), as well as validated measures of parent/child wellbeing, including the K6 for adults (Kessler et al, 2002) and the brief Spence Child Anxiety scale (Reardon et al, 2018). We also asked how often families engaged in a list of pet-related activities and open-ended questions about the benefits and challenges of having a pet. For simplicity, parents with more than one child were asked to respond regarding the child with the next birthday. The rollout of the survey coincided with the 'second wave' of COVID-19 in Australia.

Participants were recruited using both paid and unpaid Facebook advertising. Unpaid advertising involved posting about the survey on Facebook pages or groups (for example, pet groups, parent groups), while paid advertising involved Facebook campaigns conducted via the Facebook Ads Manager. Although this was a rapidly collected convenience sample, we proactively monitored for 'gaps' in participant sub-groups (for example, fathers) and adjusted recruitment strategies accordingly. This approach is effective and necessary for social media-based research recruitment (Bennetts et al, 2019).

Who participated?

As summarized in Table 5.1, over 1,000 parents took part across all Australian states and territories, with a mean age of 43 years (±6.9, range 20–65). Most participants were female. Overall, participants were living in slightly less disadvantaged neighbourhoods compared to the Australian mean, based on the Australian Bureau of Statistics Index of Relative Socio-Economic Disadvantage. One-fifth had introduced a new cat or dog during the COVID-19 pandemic (since March 2020).

Table 5.1: Characteristics of survey respondents (N=1,034)

Parent	N (%)
Parent gender	
Female	803 (77.7)
Male	225 (21.8)
Non-binary	1 (0.1)
Prefer not to say	5 (0.5)
Tertiary qualification	620 (61.6)
Single parent	164 (15.9)
Indigenous	14 (1.4)
Language other than English	74 (7.2)
Focus child	**n (%)**
Child age, years	
0–4	144 (13.9)
5–9	277 (26.8)
10–14	395 (38.2)
15–17	218 (21.1)
Child gender	
Female	489 (47.3)
Male	537 (51.9)
Non-binary	5 (0.5)
Prefer not to say	3 (0.3)
Only child	355 (34.5)
Pet	**n (%)**
Focus pet type	
Cat	364 (35.2)
Dog	670 (64.8)
During COVID-19 (since March 2020)	
Got a new pet	206 (20.0)
Pet died	82 (8.0)
Pet surrendered	6 (0.6)
Family	**n (%)**
Location	
Victoria	636 (61.5)
New South Wales	315 (30.5)
Queensland	136 (13.2)
Western Australia	68 (6.6)
South Australia	52 (5.0)
Australian Capital Territory	35 (3.4)
Tasmania	28 (2.7)
Northern Territory	2 (0.2)
Socioeconomic status	
Quintile 1 (most disadvantaged)	103 (10.2)
Quintile 2	138 (13.7)
Quintile 3	205 (20.4)
Quintile 4	214 (21.3)
Quintile 5 (least disadvantaged)	347 (34.5)

Note: * Not all rows add to 1,034 due to small amount of missing data. Socioeconomic status based on family's residential postcode; Index for Relative Socio-economic Disadvantage from Australian Bureau of Statistics.

Findings

Pet attachment, pet-related activities and family wellbeing

Participants reported on how frequently they engaged in various pet-related activities (Table 5.2). As expected, parents and children with stronger attachment to their pet engaged in more of these activities more frequently. Most parents reported their pet was helpful for their own (78 per cent) and their child's mental health (80 per cent).

Survey responses showed that 14 per cent of parents were experiencing clinical levels of psychological distress and 20 per cent of children were experiencing clinical levels of anxiety (based on parent report). After adjusting for key demographics, we found that parents with clinical psychological distress were 2.5 times more likely to be worried about their pet's care, wellbeing and behaviour (OR=2.56, p<0.001). Clinically anxious children were almost twice as likely to live in a family who engaged frequently in pet-related activities (for example, cooked treats and taught tricks, OR= 1.82, p<0.01).

Children with stronger pet bonds were more likely to be anxious (parent-reported, p<0.001). Parent–pet attachment was not associated with self-reported psychological distress (p=0.42), however, parents with a strong emotional closeness with their pet reported greater psychological distress (p=0.002).

Table 5.2: Pet-related activities ordered by frequency

Pet-related activities	Often or every day, N (%)
Talked to them as if they understand you	848 (82.2)
Referred to yourself as their 'parent'	751 (72.9)
Given them premium/expensive pet food or human food	641 (62.1)
Allowed them to sleep in/on the same bed as you or your child	632 (61.2)
Given them treats or new toys	579 (56.1)
Participated in cat/dog groups or pages on social media	417 (40.6)
Left on the heating/cooling, lights or TV/radio for them	405 (39.2)
Taught them tricks or trained them to do something	359 (34.9)
Cooked or made treats for them	301 (29.3)
Rearranged personal commitments around them	296 (28.7)
Created or posted content to a social media account for them	246 (23.9)
Dressed them in outfits/costumes	50 (4.9)
Worn matching outfits/accessories with them	5 (0.5)

In parents' own words

As part of the survey, 611 parents provided free-text responses about the benefits and challenges of having a cat or dog for their family during the pandemic. We used inductive template thematic analysis (Brooks et al, 2015) to identify codes, then we mapped codes onto a Biopsychosocial Model (Gee et al, 2021). This biopsychosocial perspective describes how biological, psychological and social factors influence one another, and contribute to human health and wellbeing (presented here in Figure 5.1 as three separate but overlapping spheres).

As illustrated in Figure 5.1, many of these codes – both positive (normal text) and negative (italic) – mapped onto the *social* sphere. This underscores the significant social impacts of the pandemic on families (for example, physical distancing, isolation, limited social interaction) and suggests that family pets played a critical role in addressing this 'gap'. Findings highlight the powerful role of pets in providing non-judgemental companionship, comfort and support for families with children (for example, family time, fun and entertainment) – but also brings attention to the difficulties of juggling children and pets during restrictions and without usual social supports (for example, disruption, access to training and socialization). Pets offered companionship and helped to build social connections between humans within and outside of the household (for example, an opportunity to connect with others).

One of the most common experiences shared by parents in our survey was the sense of companionship provided by the cat or dog during the pandemic. For children without siblings, this was seen as particularly important: 'My daughter is an only child, and the dog is her best friend' (mother of one child, one dog, Victoria). At a time when human social supports were limited, these roles were often filled by pets: 'I love being able to talk to my cats and dog, sit and watch a movie together' (father of one child, two cats, one dog, Victoria). Pets often helped to ease tension or anxiety within the family unit, providing opportunities for physical affection and unconditional love: '[Our dog is] always ready for a cuddle or pat, which can be soothing in times of uncertainty' (mother of one child, one dog, Northern Territory).

Pets often indirectly facilitated connection between humans, such as by encouraging parents and children to spend time together. Interactions were often filled with 'fun', 'silliness' and 'laughs'. The humour and entertainment of pets' antics was sometimes shared with others, as a way to connect and as a topic of conversation: 'They join remote school classes and liven up the classes, not just ours but all the classmates' pets as well' (mother of one child, two cats, Victoria). Pets were often viewed as a talking point or an 'ice breaker', when families were unable to engage in their normal activities.

Figure 5.1: Social benefits (normal text) and challenges (italic) raised by parents regarding the role of pets for family wellbeing during the COVID-19 pandemic

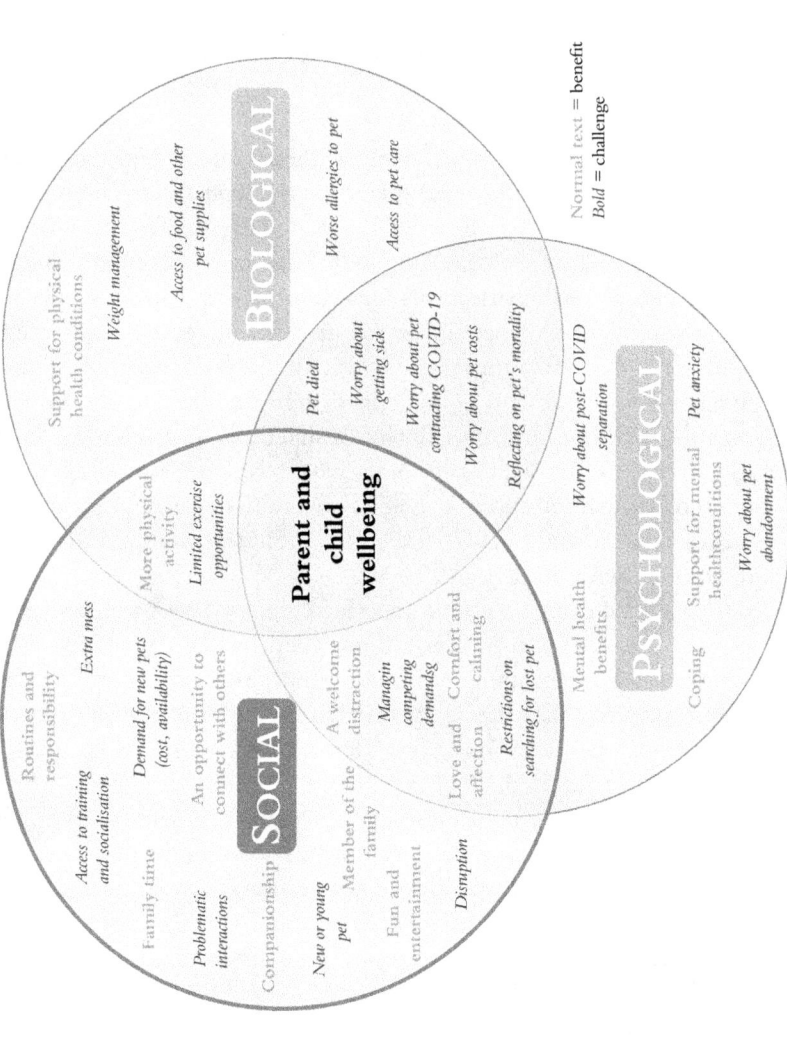

Especially when families were struggling with feeling overwhelmed, anxious or isolated, pets provided much-needed structure and routine which helped families to regain a sense of normality: for example, 'No matter what kind of mood we are in, we still have to get up and look after her needs' (mother of two children, one cat, Queensland). Having a 'reason to get up' was seen as beneficial for both parents and children, at a time 'when everything else feels so uncertain'.

While community spaces such as dog parks often facilitate human–human, human–dog and dog–dog connections, these opportunities were restricted during the pandemic. For example, one participant described 'wanting to socialize whilst exercising the dog, and breaking the habit of approaching other dog owners for a chat when out at the park' (mother of three children, one dog, Victoria). However, a few participants described how pets facilitated some positive community interactions:

> Staff and other customers at pet supply shops, as well as people at dog parks, have a common interest in pets, so interactions with them while other businesses and social venues are closed is an opportunity for face to face communication with people with similar outlook and experience of the current situation. (Father of two children, two cats, two dogs, South Australia)

Although pets clearly offered families critical social support, there were numerous challenges associated with spending more time together. Especially for those with newly adopted pets, a lack of access to training or opportunities for socialization was problematic, and there were concerns that this would lead to long-term issues. For example: 'The restrictions are concerning regarding socializing him as planned, as puppy school has been cancelled and being unable to socialize him with friends ... [it's] been impossible. I just hope this doesn't create any long-time behavioural issues' (mother of two children, one dog, Victoria).

Many parents described wanting to introduce a new cat or dog, but they encountered issues with availability or soaring costs: 'Shame we can't afford a new dog as the price has become inflated' (mother of five children, one dog, Western Australia). Other social concerns included dogs disrupting parents during work meetings or while children completed remote learning activities. There were also challenges with juggling competing demands when everyone was spending more time at home: 'Although it was assumed there was more time to support a new pet, to adjust because I was home, there were new tasks that made it difficult to give adequate time and energy to the task, i.e., home schooling, working from home, childcare, having a new baby' (father of three children, two dogs, New South Wales). Some parents also described difficulties in managing interactions between children and pets: 'It's a challenge when the arousal level of the dogs and children peak' (mother of two children, two dogs, New South Wales).

Conclusion

There is now strengthening evidence – including from our own work described earlier – that people experiencing social adversity, isolation, loneliness or inadequate (human) social support tend to have particularly strong bonds with their pets (Lass-Hennemann et al, 2022; Ellis et al, 2024). Children and adolescents who demonstrate compassionate responses to self and others have also been found to have stronger connections to their pet (Bosacki et al, 2022). Findings from our national survey highlight the important role that pets play in providing and facilitating the social connections that are integral to wellbeing, especially during times of change and uncertainty. It was apparent that families were turning to their pets as a source of comfort when human-to-human social supports were less accessible. As echoed elsewhere, pets can provide a sense of purpose, meaning and a reason to keep going in tough times (Hawkins et al, 2021). Pets became a 'talking point' among parents' work colleagues or children's school friends; an opportunity to build positive connections during remote work and learning.

Although the link between stronger human–pet bonds and poorer mental health might seem counter-intuitive, this finding has been reported in other studies both prior to and during the pandemic (for example, Peacock et al, 2012; Lass-Hennemann et al, 2020). We cannot infer causality here, but there are two possibilities. First, parents and children who were feeling unsettled during the pandemic were gravitating towards pets to seek additional comfort; this is supported by the results of Lass-Hennemann et al (2022), who found that insecure attachments to other humans fully mediate the relationship between pet attachment and poor mental health outcomes. Second, stronger pet attachment contributes to greater distress (for example, through the burden of responsibility, as highlighted in our qualitative findings). The reality may reflect a combination of the two. The pandemic created a highly stressful environment for some families negotiating the challenges of working and learning from home with pets, operating without their usual social supports and outlets. These circumstances were particularly challenging for those with pre-existing physical or mental health difficulties. Longitudinal evidence is required to delineate the mechanisms underpinning pet attachment, social connection and wellbeing.

While the pandemic brought newfound attention to the role of the family pet, the importance of pets for both companionship and as a 'conduit for social capital' (Wood et al, 2005) is not new. Our national survey offers further insight with multidisciplinary relevance across education, psychology, social work and public health. We have aimed to move beyond simply considering pet 'ownership' or 'guardianship' to consider – both quantitatively and qualitatively – the nature of the connections we build with our pets and how these connections link to wellbeing. There remain opportunities to explore the long-term impacts of human–pet connections for both human and pet wellbeing and as a facilitator of human-to-human social connection. People experiencing isolation or social adversity, including children, the elderly and people with physical or mental health difficulties, may benefit from the companionship, sense of purpose and meaningful connection that pets may offer. Professionals must be cognizant of the important role pets can play in people's lives, acknowledging the potential for pets to both enhance wellbeing and social support while also understanding that this is not universally the case for all pet owners.

References

Animal Medicines Australia (2022) *Pets in Australia: A National Survey of Pets and People.* Available at: https://animalmedicinesaustralia.org.au/wp-content/uploads/2022/11/AMAU008-Pet-Ownership22-Report_v1.6_WEB.pdf (Accessed 15 November 2024).

Applebaum, J.W., Tomlinson, C.A., Matijczak, A., McDonald, S.E. and Zsembik, B.A. (2020) 'The concerns, difficulties, and stressors of caring for pets during COVID-19: results from a large survey of U.S. pet owners', *Animals*, 10(10), Article 1882. https://doi.org/10.3390/ani10101882

Arhant, C., Beetz, A.M. and Troxler, J. (2017) 'Caregiver reports of interactions between children up to 6 years and their family dog: implications for dog bite prevention', *Frontiers in Veterinary Science*, 4(130). https://doi.org/10.3389/fvets.2017.00130

Bennetts, S.K., Hokke, S., Crawford, S., Hackworth, N.J., Leach, L.S., Nguyen, C., et al (2019) 'Using paid and free Facebook methods to recruit Australian parents to an online survey: an evaluation', *Journal of Medical Internet Research*, 21(3), e11206. https://doi.org/10.2196/11206

Bennetts, S.K., Crawford, S., Howell, T., Burgemeister, F., Chamberlain, C., Burke, K., et al (2022a) 'Parent and child mental health during COVID-19 in Australia: the role of pet attachment', *PLOS ONE*. https://doi.org/10.1371/journal.pone.0271687

Bennetts, S.K., Crawford, S.B., Howell, T., Ignacio, B., Burgemeister, F., Burke, K., et al (2022b) 'Companionship and worries in uncertain times: Australian parents' experiences of children and pets during COVID-19', *Anthrozoös*, 35(6). https://doi.org/10.1080/08927936.2022.2051931

Bennetts, S.K., Howell, T., Crawford, S., Burgemeister, F., Burke, K. and Nicholson, J.M. (2023) 'Family bonds with pets and mental health during COVID-19 in Australia: a complex picture', *International Journal of Environmental Research and Public Health*, 20(7), Article 5245. https://doi.org/10.3390/ijerph20075245

Bosacki, S., Tardif-Williams, C.Y. and Roma, R.P.S. (2022) 'Children's and adolescents' pet attachment, empathy, and compassionate responding to self and others', *Adolescents*, 2(4), 493–507. https://doi.org/10.3390/adolescents2040039

Bretherton, I. (1992) 'The origins of attachment theory: John Bowlby and Mary Ainsworth', *Developmental Psychology*, 28(5), 759–775. https://doi.org/10.1037/0012-1649.28.5.759

Brooks, H.L., Rushton, K., Lovell, K., Bee, P., Walker, L., Grant, L., et al (2018) 'The power of support from companion animals for people living with mental health problems: a systematic review and narrative synthesis of the evidence', *BMC Psychiatry*, 18(1), Article 31. https://doi.org/10.1186/s12888-018-1613-2

Brooks, J., McCluskey, S., Turley, E. and King, N. (2015) 'The utility of template analysis in qualitative psychology research', *Qualitative Research in Psychology*, 12(2), 202–222. https://doi.org/10.1080/14780887.2014.955224

Brown, A. (2023) 'About half of U.S. pet owners say their pets are as much a part of their family as a human member', Pew Research Center. Available at: https://www.pewresearch.org/short-reads/2023/07/07/about-half-us-of-pet-owners-say-their-pets-are-as-much-a-part-of-their-family-as-a-human-member/ (Accessed 15 September 2024).

Brown, S.M., Doom, J.R., Lechuga-Peña, S., Watamura, S.E. and Koppels, T. (2020) 'Stress and parenting during the global COVID-19 pandemic', *Child Abuse & Neglect*, Article 104699. https://doi.org/10.1016/j.chiabu.2020.104699

Bures, R.M., Mueller, M.K. and Gee, N.R. (2019) 'Measuring human-animal attachment in a large US survey: two brief measures for children and their primary caregivers', *Frontiers in Public Health*, 7, Article 107. https://doi.org/10.3389/fpubh.2019.00107

Bussolari, C., Currin-McCulloch, J., Packman, W., Kogan, L. and Erdman, P. (2021) '"I couldn't have asked for a better quarantine partner!": experiences with companion dogs during COVID-19', *Animals*, 11(330), 1–14. https://doi.org/10.3390/ani11020330

Cacioppo, J. and Patrick, W. (2008) *Loneliness: Human Nature and the Need for Social Connection*, W.W. Norton & Co.

Christian, H., Mitrou, F., Cunneen, R. and Zubrick, S.R. (2020) 'Pets are associated with fewer peer problems and emotional symptoms, and better prosocial behavior: findings from the Longitudinal Study of Australian Children', *Journal of Pediatrics*, 220, 200–206. https://doi.org/10.1016/j.jpeds.2020.01.012

Churchill, B. (2021) 'COVID-19 and the immediate impact on young people and employment in Australia: a gendered analysis', *Gender, Work & Organization*, 28(2), 783–794. https://doi.org/10.1111/gwao.12563

Dawel, A., Shou, Y., Smithson, M., Cherbuin, N., Banfield, M., Calear, A.L., et al (2020) 'The effect of COVID-19 on mental health and wellbeing in a representative sample of Australian adults', *Frontiers in Psychiatry*, 11, 1026. https://doi.org/10.3389/fpsyt.2020.579985

Dueñas, J.-M., Gonzàlez, L., Forcada, R., Duran-Bonavila, S. and Ferre-Rey, G. (2021) 'The relationship between living with dogs and social and emotional development in childhood', *Anthrozoös*, 34(1), 33–46. https://doi.org/10.1080/08927936.2021.1878680

Ellis, A., Stanton, S.C.E., Hawkins, R.D. and Loughnan, S. (2024) 'The link between the nature of the human–companion animal relationship and well-being outcomes in companion animal owners', *Animals*, 14(3), Article 441. https://doi.org/10.3390/ani14030441

Fine, A.H. (2020) 'The psycho-social impact of human-animal interactions', *International Journal of Environmental Research and Public Health*, 17(11). https://doi.org/10.3390/ijerph17113964

Gee, N.R., Rodriguez, K.E., Fine, A.H. and Trammell, J.P. (2021) 'Dogs supporting human health and well-being: a biopsychosocial approach', *Frontiers in Veterinary Science*, 8. https://doi.org/10.3389/fvets.2021.630465

Griffiths, D., Sheehan, L., van Vreden, C., Petrie, D., Grant, G., Whiteford, P., et al (2021) 'The impact of work loss on mental and physical health during the COVID-19 pandemic: baseline findings from a prospective cohort study', *Journal of Occupational Rehabilitation*, 31(3), 455–462. https://doi.org/10.1007/s10926-021-09958-7

Handlin, L., Hydbring-Sandberg, E., Nilsson, A., Ejdebäck, M., Jansson, A. and Uvnäs-Moberg, K. (2011) 'Short-term interaction between dogs and their owners: effects on oxytocin, cortisol, insulin and heart rate – an exploratory study', *Anthrozoös*, 24(3), 301–315. https://doi.org/10.2752/175303711X13045914865385

Hawkins, R.D., McDonald, S.E., O'Connor, K., Matijczak, A., Ascione, F.R. and Williams, J.H. (2019) 'Exposure to intimate partner violence and internalizing symptoms: the moderating effects of positive relationships with pets and animal cruelty exposure', *Child Abuse & Neglect*, 98, Article 104166. https://doi.org/10.1016/j.chiabu.2019.104166

Hawkins, R.D., Hawkins, E.L. and Tip, L. (2021) '"I can't give up when I have them to care for": people's experiences of pets and their mental health', *Anthrozoös*, 34(4), 543–562. https://doi.org/10.1080/08927936.2021.1914434

Hoffman, C.L., Stutz, K. and Vasilopoulos, T. (2018) 'An examination of adult women's sleep quality and sleep routines in relation to pet ownership and bedsharing', *Anthrozoös*, 31(6), 711–725. https://doi.org/10.1080/08927936.2018.1529354

Howell, T.J., Bowen, J., Fatjó, J., Calvo, P., Holloway, A. and Bennett, P.C. (2017) 'Development of the cat-owner relationship scale (CORS)', *Behavioural Processes*, 141, 305–315. https://doi.org/10.1016/j.beproc.2017.02.024

Janssens, M., Eshuis, J., Peeters, S., Lataster, J., Reijnders, J., Enders-Slegers, M.-J., et al (2020) 'The pet-effect in daily life: an experience sampling study on emotional wellbeing in pet owners', *Anthrozoös*, 33(4), 579–588. https://doi.org/10.1080/08927936.2020.1771061

Kessler, R.C., Andrews, G., Colpe, L.J., Hiripi, E., Mroczek, D.K., Normand, S.L., et al (2002) 'Short screening scales to monitor population prevalences and trends in non-specific psychological distress', *Psychological Medicine*, 32(6), 959–976. https://doi.org/10.1017/S0033291702006074

Lass-Hennemann, J., Schäfer, S.K., Sopp, M.R. and Michael, T. (2020) 'The relationship between dog ownership, psychopathological symptoms and health-benefitting factors in occupations at risk for traumatization', *International Journal of Environmental Research and Public Health*, 17(7), Article 2562. https://doi.org/10.3390/ijerph17072562

Lass-Hennemann, J., Schäfer, S.K., Sopp, M.R. and Michael, T. (2022) 'The relationship between attachment to pets and mental health: the shared link via attachment to humans', *BMC Psychiatry*, 22(1), Article 586. https://doi.org/10.1186/s12888-022-04199-1

Loades, M.E., Chatburn, E., Higson-Sweeney, N., Reynolds, S., Shafran, R., Brigden, A., et al (2020) 'Rapid systematic review: the impact of social isolation and loneliness on the mental health of children and adolescents in the context of COVID-19', *Journal of the American Academy of Child and Adolescent Psychiatry*, 59(11), 1218–1239.

McConnell, A.R., Brown, C.M., Shoda, T.M., Stayton, L.E. and Martin, C.E. (2011) 'Friends with benefits: on the positive consequences of pet ownership', *Journal of Personality and Social Psychology*, 101(6), 1239–1252. https://doi.org/10.1037/a0024506

McDonald, S.E., O'Connor, K.E., Matijczak, A., Tomlinson, C.A., Applebaum, J.W., Murphy, J.L., et al (2021) 'Attachment to pets moderates transitions in latent patterns of mental health following the onset of the COVID-19 pandemic: results of a survey of US adults', *Animals*, 11(3), Article 895. https://doi.org/10.3390/ani11030895

Miltiades, H. and Shearer, J. (2011) 'Attachment to pet dogs and depression in rural older adults', *Anthrozoös*, 24(2), 147–154. https://doi.org/10.2752/175303711X12998632257585

Okabe-Miyamoto, K., Folk, D., Lyubomirsky, S. and Dunn, E.W. (2021) 'Changes in social connection during COVID-19 social distancing: it's not (household) size that matters, it's who you're with', *PLOS ONE*, 16(1), e0245009. https://doi.org/10.1371/journal.pone.0245009

Peacock, J., Chur-Hansen, A. and Winefield, H. (2012) 'Mental health implications of human attachment to companion animals', *Journal of Clinical Psychology*, 68(3), 292–303. https://doi.org/10.1002/jclp.20866

Ratschen, E., Shoesmith, E., Shahab, L., Silva, K., Kale, D., Toner, P., et al (2020) 'Human-animal relationships and interactions during the COVID-19 lockdown phase in the UK: investigating links with mental health and loneliness', *PLOS ONE*, 15(9), e0239397. https://doi.org/10.1371/journal.pone.0239397

Reardon, T., Spence, S.H., Hesse, J., Shakir, A. and Creswell, C. (2018) 'Identifying children with anxiety disorders using brief versions of the Spence Children's Anxiety Scale for children, parents, and teachers', *Psychological Assessment*, 30(10), 1342–1355. https://doi.org/10.1037/pas0000570

Scoresby, K.J., Strand, E.B., Ng, Z., Brown, K.C., Stilz, C.R., Strobel, K., et al (2021) 'Pet ownership and quality of life: a systematic review of the literature', *Veterinary Sciences*, 8(12), Article 332. https://doi.org/10.3390/vetsci8120332

Selinger-Morris, S. (2020) 'Silver linings: Australia's dogs and cats are living their best lives', Sydney Morning Herald. Available at: https://www.smh.com.au/lifestyle/life-and-relationships/silver-linings-australia-s-dogs-and-cats-are-living-their-best-lives-20200319-p54bnq.html (Accessed 15 October 2024).

Statista (2024) 'Share of households owning a pet in the United Kingdom (UK) from 2012 to 2023'. Available at: https://www.statista.com/statistics/308235/estimated-pet-ownership-in-the-united-kingdom-uk/ (Accessed 24 June 2024).

Vasan, S., Lambert, E., Eikelis, N. and Lim, M.H. (2022) 'Impact of loneliness on health-related factors in Australia during the COVID-19 pandemic: a retrospective study', *Health & Social Care in the Community*, 30(6), e5293–e5304.

Westrupp, E.M., Stokes, M.A., Fuller-Tyszkiewicz, M., Berkowitz, T.S., Capic, T., Khor, S., et al (2021) 'Subjective wellbeing in parents during the COVID-19 pandemic in Australia', *Journal of Psychosomatic Research*, 145, Article 110482. https://doi.org/10.1016/j.jpsychores.2021.110482

Wood, L., Giles-Corti, B. and Bulsara, M. (2005) 'The pet connection: pets as a conduit for social capital?', *Social Science & Medicine*, 61(6), 1159–1173. https://doi.org/10.1016/j.socscimed.2005.01.017

Zilcha-Mano, S., Mikulincer, M. and Shaver, P.R. (2011) 'An attachment perspective on human–pet relationships: conceptualization and assessment of pet attachment orientations', *Journal of Research in Personality*, 45(4), 345–357. https://doi.org/10.1016/j.jrp.2011.04.001

PART II

Physical Spaces

6

Can Our Housing Environments Impact Loneliness? A Tale of Two Studies

Marlee Bower, Caitlin Buckle, Jennifer Kent, Lily Teesson, Roger Patulny, Laura McGrath and Emily Rugel

Introduction

Loneliness is a pressing public health issue. Estimates indicate that just over one in six Australians, approximately 4.3 million individuals, experienced loneliness in 2022 (AIHW, 2024). This is concerning because loneliness is linked with mental health conditions such as depression, anxiety and suicide (Hawkley, 2020). Loneliness is characterized by an aversive emotional response associated with a feeling that one's social needs are unmet (Badcock et al, 2022). Some of the literature details the multidimensionality of loneliness, with two main sub-types. Social loneliness is a feeling associated with a lack of high-quality relationships, often associated with a perceived lack of close friendships. Emotional loneliness is a lack of meaningful, intimate relationships, often associated with the lack of an intimate partner or family members (Weiss, 1973). However, most empirical studies fail to examine loneliness as multidimensional, and the links between different types of loneliness and social connections in different social contexts remain undeveloped.

Before progressing further, it is important to understand the definition of loneliness as distinct from other similar concepts like 'social connection', which is an umbrella term for the relationships, interactions and bonds individuals have with others, encompassing a sense of belonging, support and meaningful engagement within their social networks (Holt-Lunstad, 2022). It includes various dimensions, such as the quantity and quality of relationships, the frequency of interactions and the depth of emotional connections. Social connection is related to, but not the opposite of, loneliness. The absence of loneliness does not necessarily imply the presence of strong social connections, and vice versa (Holt-Lunstad, 2022). A person may not feel lonely yet still lack meaningful connections, or they may feel lonely even in the presence of others if those connections are superficial or unfulfilling. Therefore, fostering social connection involves more than just reducing loneliness; it requires building and sustaining meaningful and supportive relationships.

Academic literature on loneliness has tended to focus on individual-based solutions, such as one-to-one psychological therapies like cognitive behavioural therapy (Hickin et al, 2021). Another more 'upstream' approach is social prescribing, an initiative with increasing prominence in both the United Kingdom and Australia, and globally, based on a social model of mental health (Sonke et al, 2023). Social prescribing involves healthcare professionals recognizing the therapeutic benefits of activities, such as non-clinical social services or activities, and referring individuals to external providers of these services (Reinhardt et al, 2021). However, given the scale of loneliness in Australia and globally, it is clear that approaches are needed, which, on a broader scale, is a public health issue (Amaro, 2014). Individualistic prescribing models of treatment focused on individualized rather than collective responses are insufficient, and it is necessary to implement more meso- and macro-level interventions that address the causes and treatment of loneliness on a broader scale. Outside academia, there has been a burgeoning interest in how built environments – defined as the 'human-made space(s) in which people live, work and recreate on a day-to-day basis' (Roof and Oleru, 2008: 24) – influence loneliness. These environments include housing, neighbourhoods, workplaces, urban design, green spaces (for example, parkland) and blue spaces (for example, oceans, lakes), among others. It has been proposed that such environments can improve public health by directly or indirectly reducing loneliness.

The Foundation for Social Connection (United States) recently published a White Paper exploring this issue, highlighting the fact that these environments can both facilitate and impede social connections, depending on their design (Krombach et al, 2024). Government policies are also being implemented to identify facilitative elements in community spaces to reduce loneliness. For instance, the United Kingdom's 2018 Loneliness Strategy highlights the importance of community-centric housing design, using underutilized community spaces, and creating transport networks that support social connections.

Non-government organizations have also released reports linking built environments to loneliness, particularly in the context of housing for older people (Wood and Salter, 2016), and the corporate development sector is starting to address how their products might impact loneliness. For example,

Lendlease UK published a blog post in 2021 discussing how localized infrastructure improvements, such as public benches and pedestrianized spaces, may reduce loneliness (Power, 2021). In 2020, global engineering firm WSP launched a 'thought leadership series' that integrated insights from architecture, transport planning and urban design experts to advance designs that foster connections (WSP, 2020). The Australian property development company Frasers has financially invested in loneliness initiatives, identifying increasing belonging and reducing loneliness as their core drivers (Calautti, 2023). Taken together, it is clear the prevention of loneliness is gaining legitimacy as a focus across multiple sectors and even as a market for new initiatives and products in and of itself. This agenda is progressing even though the evidence that built environments can reduce or prevent loneliness retains elements of ambiguity.

Due to the rising interest in the relationship between place and loneliness, a clear and critical understanding of the strengths and limitations of the current evidence base is essential. For instance, it is unclear if designing places that facilitate social connection among people who might otherwise be strangers is sufficient for reducing loneliness. It is difficult to assess the effectiveness of these endeavours in the absence of a clear conceptualization of the nature of loneliness and social connection. For example, conceptions of social connection focusing on the structure, function and quality of individual connections (Holt-Lunstad, 2022) may unduly shift emphasis away from the meso- and macro-level factors that impact social connection, such as the built or lived environment.

Furthermore, delineating such an understanding inherently requires an interdisciplinary framework. Fields such as environmental psychology and environmental epidemiology have increasingly described, categorized and measured associations between built environments and human health, albeit often in siloes. Contemporaneously, urban planners have begun studying designs thought to facilitate interactions. Unfortunately, although many individual studies include researchers from distinct fields, we lack the common understanding and communication tools needed to fully integrate research across disciplines and within practice.

This chapter builds on two pieces of published research that sought to bridge this gap by exploring how housing and local neighbourhood settings influence loneliness, using a multidisciplinary lens aimed at developing implications for policy and practice.

Study 1

Our first study aimed to understand the relationship between housing, local neighbourhoods and loneliness on a much broader scale. We used a systematic review methodology to explore all academic literature exploring the relationship between the built environment and loneliness published since 2000 (Bower et al, 2023b). We took an intentionally interdisciplinary approach, with co-authors representing psychology, urban planning, public health and sociology. We felt this diverse viewpoint would be vital. We worked hard as a team to form a common language across the different disciplines, consistently questioning various core assumptions underpinning the work. These robust debates and discussions produced a more meaningful paper with directly applicable findings to multiple fields.

Our rigorous systematic review methodology drew from seven broad interdisciplinary databases and started with a pool of over 7,000 unique studies, ending with 57 included studies. Although there was a significant amount of good-quality research exploring this research area, studies could have been of better quality. In addition, most studies were conducted in the Global North, with large geographic gaps; for example, no studies were from South Asian nations.

Our results revealed that specific housing characteristics *can* reduce loneliness, but this relationship is complex, contextual and multidirectional. The research fits into two streams: the 'structured environment', referring to material aspects like housing size and proximity to parks, and the 'lived environment', encompassing personal, experiential and relational interactions within the structured environment. Impacts on loneliness were found to occur through interactions between these constructs, influenced by contextual factors such as socioeconomic status and personal experiences.

Structured environment

Studies on apartment size (for example, Volk, 2009) showed that a key impact of a small apartment was a reduced ability to host and socialize, preventing a sense of belonging at home, or the capacity to conduct hobbies and other personally meaningful activities (Volk, 2009; En Wee et al, 2019; Kalina, 2021). Housing disrepair had a similar impact, where issues like plumbing, mould and general dissatisfaction with housing conditions were associated with higher loneliness (Finlay et al, 2020; Bower et al, 2023a).

Housing type had mixed impacts on loneliness. While some studies suggested that living in apartments was less lonely than living in detached dwellings or standalone houses, others suggested no effect. In either case, this impact was inseparable from a person's broader context. In initial analyses, two studies found that apartment dwellers were lonelier than residents of other dwelling types. Still, these effects turned out to be driven by a higher concentration of younger, less wealthy residents living in apartments and became insignificant after adjusting for sociodemographics and age (Kearns et al, 2015; van den Berg et al, 2016). Living in apartments (versus semi-detached homes) was more associated with loneliness in those under 65 (van den Berg et al, 2016). However, this finding was complicated because detached dwellings were more often located in higher-income areas, which tended to have more established communities and were less affordable for younger people. And another study found that living in standalone housing could also be associated with isolation and loneliness among low-income people, especially in areas that lacked nearby safe, public and free spaces to gather and socialize (Finlay and Kobayashi, 2018).

The quality of living spaces at home was also important as they allowed individuals to feel safe, have a sense of control over their spaces and live out their social identity. For example, housing that allowed for some personalization in interiors (Kalina, 2021), had adequate natural light (Kalina, 2021), was not too cold (Cotter et al, 2012) and was constructed of quality building materials which made people more likely to invite others over to socialize (Nzabona et al, 2016) were all independently found to reduce loneliness, as was having adequate common spaces (Rusinovic et al, 2019; Grenier et al, 2021; Kalina, 2021). Co-housing reduces loneliness, but only when people have the ability to have some independence and choice in their day-to-day living (Rusinovic et al, 2019).

Socioeconomic status had a substantial impact on each of these factors: people with low socioeconomic status were more likely to live in the kinds of housing and neighbourhood conditions that produce loneliness. For instance, they were more likely to reside in apartments rather than detached dwellings (van den Berg et al, 2016), further away from public infrastructure like parks (Finlay and Kobayashi, 2018) or in cold housing (Cotter et al, 2012).

The lived environment

Our findings indicate that living in unaffordable housing significantly contributes to feelings of loneliness. When housing is affordable, individuals are more likely to choose their living arrangements based on feelings of safety, comfort and connection rather than financial constraints (Morgan et al, 2019; Morris and Verdasco, 2020). Conversely, unaffordable housing leaves people with less disposable income after paying rent or mortgages, limiting their ability to engage in social activities, such as dining out or participating in shared experiences (Morris and Verdasco, 2020). Additionally, those facing structural housing issues – such as mould, cracks in walls or poor ventilation – often report lower personal satisfaction with their living conditions. This dissatisfaction can heighten their need for belonging within their neighbourhood, as their homes may fail to fulfil their social identity needs, leading them to rely more heavily on the broader community to meet these requirements (Bower et al, 2023a).

Findings regarding the impact of housing tenure – whether social or private rentals versus home ownership – on loneliness were mixed and closely tied to socioeconomic context. Individuals renting publicly or privately generally had less financial capital than homeowners, which limited their ability to invest in housing improvements, often resulting in poorer living conditions and neighbourhoods. This lack of resources further exacerbated feelings of loneliness. One study indicated that differences in loneliness between social renters and public renters could be attributed to the regulated cap on rental costs in public housing, which allowed public renters more disposable income for social activities (Morris and Verdasco, 2020). However, other research suggests that this increased financial flexibility does not necessarily translate into greater social support, as public housing renters often lack the resources to assist one another compared to private renters and homeowners (Patulny and Morris, 2012). In fact, our Alone Together study found that the differences in housing tenure and loneliness diminished when accounting for participants' income and employment status (Bower et al, 2023a).

Study 2

During the COVID-19 pandemic, governments around the world, including Australia (Parliament of Australia, 2020), implemented stay-at-home orders as a critical measure to reduce the risk of infection. These restrictions created a unique and unprecedented situation that fundamentally altered the ways in which individuals interacted with and perceived their built environments.

This context provided a valuable opportunity to observe and analyse how people's perceptions and usage of their residential spaces and local neighbourhoods evolved when confined to these areas for extended periods. As individuals spent significantly more time in their homes, insights emerged regarding which aspects of their living environments were most valued and perceived as detrimental or insufficient to meet their social and emotional needs, ultimately contributing to feelings of loneliness and isolation.

Moreover, the restrictions illuminated the role of individual built environments in fulfilling social needs, particularly when access to external or communal spaces was severely limited. This situation underscored the importance of adaptable living spaces and thoughtful community planning, emphasizing the need for environments that can support social interaction and foster a sense of belonging, even in times of crisis. Understanding these dynamics is crucial for informing future urban design and public health strategies to enhance social connectivity and wellbeing.

The Alone Together study took advantage of this natural experiment by adopting social determinants of mental health approach, using a survey methodology to explore the role that impacts factors like housing, income, equality, education and resources had on changes in mental health across the two-year follow-up period during the COVID-19 pandemic among over 2,000 Australians (Bower et al, 2023a). Initiated in July 2020, shortly after the onset of the pandemic, this longitudinal study aimed to capture the evolving mental health landscape during this unprecedented time (Bower et al, 2023a).

The sample was not nationally representative. Instead, purposive sampling was undertaken to include people who may be less likely to participate in research and may also be more likely to suffer during the pandemic. This included people experiencing disability, living in places badged as infection 'hot spots', with low incomes, in precarious housing situations, experiencing homelessness and older people.

The examination of housing conditions was particularly important in the context of understanding the impact of the built environment on social connectivity and loneliness. To facilitate this, we actively recruited from services catering to people with more acute housing needs, including offices of community housing providers, tenants' unions, homelessness drop-in services and welfare support services. We also utilized housing type and quality questions adapted from the Australian Housing Conditions Dataset (Baker et al, 2019). The findings reported here are derived from the study's baseline data, which was collected in the second half of 2020, and focus on just one of many mental health and wellbeing outcomes assessed across the course of the complete Alone Together study – loneliness. We used a mixed methods approach to examine this specific outcome, integrating quantitative housing data with data from the De Jong Gierveld Loneliness Scale (De Jong Gierveld and Van Tilburg, 2010) and qualitative and quantitative data about participant housing adequacy.

The quantitative analysis indicated that various aspects of the 'lived environment' related to housing were significantly linked to feelings of loneliness among participants. Notably, a lower sense of community belonging correlated with increased loneliness. Additionally, several non-social factors emerged as significant contributors to loneliness, including dissatisfaction with natural light within the home, major structural issues, disturbances from noise and the burden of unaffordable housing. While these factors are not inherently social, their effects were often realized – or exacerbated – within diminished social interactions. This reveals the complex interplay between physical living conditions and social wellbeing, highlighting how inadequate housing can contribute to isolation and disconnection from the community.

Using the findings from Study 1, qualitative responses revealed a deeper understanding of how people experienced their homes as their primary, and often sole, 'structured environment' for daily activities during the COVID-19 pandemic. Rather than introducing new stressors, the pandemic intensified and highlighted existing negative aspects of their 'lived environment' related to housing. Participants described how a small house felt even smaller, while unsafe neighbourhoods and substandard housing situations appeared increasingly perilous. With the inability to leave their residencies, issues associated with their living conditions became more pronounced, urgent and impossible to overlook.

The ability to manage and access natural light emerged as a crucial factor in their overall wellbeing. Financial security and housing affordability played significant roles, as those with greater resources could adapt their living spaces to better meet their needs – whether by establishing a home office or addressing issues like mould. Additionally, housing tenure significantly influenced these negative outcomes; renters often lacked the agency to make the necessary repairs or personalize their living spaces, both of which are factors that Study 1 identified as essential for reducing feelings of loneliness.

Without the chance to escape their homes and have access to the spaces they enjoyed while not under COVID-19 restrictions, people focused their attention on the boundaries (or lack thereof) between their homes and their immediate surroundings (for example, neighbours and local streets). For example, environmental noise within and surrounding the home was described as making it difficult to engage in work, leisure activities and routine effectively, and placed significant strains on relationships with neighbours. One participant said their neighbour relationships 'deteriorated', while another expressed 'hate' towards their neighbours due to disruptive noise levels.

This struggle was particularly problematic among those individuals working from home. As mentioned earlier, for many participants, homes moved from being one of many spaces in their everyday lives to being the primary, or only, space for activities. For some participants, this restriction was associated with a reduced capacity to manage emotions, resulting in feelings of claustrophobia and entrapment driven by the loss of other everyday spaces and the lack of agency to leave home and then return to it for specific purposes (for example, sleep, leisure). Similarly, for some participants whose homes were not places of safety, the pandemic led to decreased access to spaces of refuge. For example, one participant noted: 'I would typically work over 30 hours a week on top of a full-time study in order to avoid being home, and with the pandemic, I no longer have the option to distance myself from my abusive living situation.'

Participants also described how the changing use of their homes and neighbourhoods during COVID-19 influenced their social identity and, subsequently, appeared to feel more susceptible to loneliness. Some participants who reported not 'fitting in' with their local neighbourhood described how being unable to visit other neighbourhoods in which they did 'fit in' left them feeling isolated. For example, one individual living in a social rental reflected that lockdown left them feeling that 'no matter how hard I work in my job, I will always be a "houso" [social housing resident]'. For this person, lockdown meant their reality was grounded in their local social context and the symbolic value this held for their identity.

Restriction to one's local neighbourhood highlighted that not everyone had access to high-quality green spaces or public amenities within their allowed travel radius. For example, one participant noted: 'Only being able to walk in the local area since COVID-19 it has made me dislike the suburbs more so. I'd rather be in the country or by the ocean.'

This study uncovered the intricate relationship between the built environment, housing conditions, access to amenities and neighbourhood characteristics in relation to loneliness. Although COVID-19 lockdowns are no longer in effect, the significance of having access to welcoming neighbourhoods, quality housing and well-maintained natural environments remains critical for enhancing social connections and promoting mental health.

Conclusion

This research illustrates that housing significantly influences an individual's likelihood of experiencing loneliness. While the relationship between specific housing characteristics and loneliness or social connection is not strictly deterministic, several factors generally serve to mitigate feelings of loneliness and isolation. High-quality, well-maintained housing that offers adequate space and flexibility for essential activities – such as work, rest, leisure and socializing – plays a crucial role in fostering social connections. Additionally, the ability to personalize one's living space to reflect individual identity is equally important.

Other urban environmental factors, such as welcoming and inclusive neighbourhoods, as well as affordable housing located near essential amenities, further contribute to this dynamic. These findings indicate that social connection encompasses more than just the microstructural, functional and qualitative aspects of individual networks (Holt-Lunstad, 2022); it also necessitates consideration of meso- and macro-level relational components to fully understand its complexity.

Our findings carry significant implications for housing design and policy addressing the loneliness epidemic. Policy makers have the opportunity to directly influence loneliness by ensuring that housing and urban spaces are designed, maintained or retrofitted to align with the conditions identified in our research. Based on the results of our two studies, we recommend the following:

- *Designing housing to mitigate loneliness*: Housing should be constructed to be safe, secure and appropriately sized to foster social connections and

reduce feelings of loneliness. To enhance mental health among vulnerable populations, housing policies must prioritize affordability without compromising quality, adequate space or access to nearby public amenities.
- *Ensuring high-quality housing*: High-quality housing – characterized by safety, sufficient space and the ability to adapt environments to meet personal and social needs – is essential for promoting social health among residents, regardless of socioeconomic status. This is particularly crucial for individuals with limited capacity to modify their living conditions due to lower socioeconomic status, insecure tenure or restrictive regulations associated with social housing. Therefore, both private and public rental agreements should include clauses that allow for the personalization of living spaces, fostering a sense of control and belonging.
- *Prioritizing maintenance and improvements*: Ongoing maintenance and periodic improvements to housing are vital for social wellbeing, irrespective of whether individuals rent or own their properties. Australian states could benefit from enforcing minimum housing standards similar to those in New Zealand (Tenancy Services New Zealand Government, 2021) and initiatives currently being implemented in Victoria, Australia (Moore et al, 2024).
- *Investing in social infrastructure*: Governments should commit to equitable access to social infrastructure and neighbourhood amenities, particularly for isolated and marginalized populations. This includes ensuring that neighbourhoods are welcoming and inclusive, providing ample opportunities for social connection and fostering a sense of belonging among residents.

References

AIHW (2024) *Social Isolation and Loneliness*. Available at: https://www.aihw.gov.au/mental-health/topic-areas/social-isolation-and-loneliness#key_points (Accessed 13 September 2024).

Amaro, H. (2014) 'The action is upstream: place-based approaches for achieving population health and health equity', *American Journal of Public Health*, 104(6), Article 964.

Badcock, J.C., Holt-Lunstad, J., Garcia, E., Bombaci, P. and Lim, M.H. (2022) 'Position statement: addressing social isolation and loneliness and the power of human connection', Global Initiative on Loneliness and Connection.

Baker, E., Beer, A., Zillante, G., London, K., Bentley, R., Hulse, K., et al (2019) *The Australian Housing Conditions Dataset*. ADA Dataverse. Available at: https://doi.org/10.26193/RDMRD3 (Accessed 15 September 2024).

Bower, M., Buckle, C., Rugel, E., Donohoe-Bales, A., Mcgrath, L., Gournay, K., et al (2023a) '"Trapped", "anxious" and "traumatised": COVID-19 intensified the impact of housing inequality on Australians' mental health', *International Journal of Housing Policy*, 23, 260–291.

Bower, M., Kent, J., Patulny, R., Green, O., Mcgrath, L., Teesson, L., et al (2023b) 'The impact of the built environment on loneliness: a systematic review and narrative synthesis', *Health Place*, 79, Article 102962.

Calautti, L. (2023) 'How a mission to create belonging led to focus on health plight', *AREAs*. Available at: https://www.realestate.com.au/news/areas-2023-how-a-mission-to-create-belonging-led-to-focus-on-health-plight/ (Accessed 15 August 2024).

Cotter, N., Monahan, E., Mcavoy, H. and Goodman, P. (2012) 'Coping with the cold: exploring relationships between cold housing, health and social wellbeing in a sample of older people in Ireland', *Quality in Ageing and Older Adults*, 13, 38–47.

De Jong Gierveld, J. and Van Tilburg, T. (2010) 'The De Jong Gierveld short scales for emotional and social loneliness: tested on data from 7 countries in the UN generations and gender surveys', *European Journal of Ageing*, 7, 121–130.

En Wee, L., Tsang, T.Y.Y., Yi, H., Toh, S.A., Lee, G.L., Yee, J., et al (2019) 'Loneliness amongst low-socioeconomic status elderly Singaporeans and its association with perceptions of the neighbourhood environment', *International Journal of Environmental Research and Public Health*, 16, Article 967.

Finlay, J.M. and Kobayashi, L.C. (2018) 'Social isolation and loneliness in later life: a parallel convergent mixed-methods case study of older adults and their residential contexts in the Minneapolis metropolitan area, USA', *Social Science & Medicine*, 208, 25–33.

Finlay, J.M., Gaugler, J.E. and Kane, R.L. (2020) 'Ageing in the margins: expectations of and struggles for "a good place to grow old" among low-income older Minnesotans', *Ageing & Society*, 40, 759–783.

Grenier, A., Burke, E., Currie, G., Watson, S. and Ward, J. (2021) 'Social isolation in later life: the importance of place, disadvantage and diversity', *Journal of Aging and Social Policy*, 1–26.

Hawkley, L. (2020) 'Social isolation, loneliness, and health', in J. Lobel and P.S. Smith (eds) *Solitary Confinement: Effects, Practices, and Pathways toward reform*, Oxford University Press, pp 185–198.

Hickin, N., Käll, A., Shafran, R., Sutcliffe, S., Manzotti, G. and Langan, D. (2021) 'The effectiveness of psychological interventions for loneliness: a systematic review and meta-analysis', *Clinical Psychology Review*, 88, Article 102066.

Holt-Lunstad, J. (2022) 'Social connection as a public health issue: the evidence and a systemic framework for prioritizing the "social" in social determinants of health', *Annual Review of Public Health*, 43, 193–213.

Kalina, M. (2021) '"A neighbourhood of necessity": creating home and neighbourhood within subsidised aged housing in Durban, South Africa', *Journal of Housing and the Built Environment*, 36, 1671–1697.

Kearns, A., Whitley, E., Tannahill, C. and Ellaway, A. (2015) '"Lonesome town"? Is loneliness associated with the residential environment, including housing and neighborhood factors?', *Journal of Community Psychology*, 43, 849–867.

Krombach, A., Peavey, E., Wilkerson, R. and Barth, A. (2024) *Systems of Cross-Sector Integration and Action across the Lifespan (SOCIAL) Framework Report*, Foundation for Social Connection.

Moore, T., Baker, E., Daniel, L. and Willand, N. (2024) 'Victoria is raising minimum rental standards – it's good news for tenants and the environment', *The Conversation*, 7 June. Available at: https://theconversation.com/victoria-is-raising-minimum-rental-standards-its-good-news-for-tenants-and-the-environment-231679 (Accessed 15 June 2024).

Morgan, T., Wiles, J.L., Park, H.-J., Moeke-Maxwell, T., Dewes, O., Black, S., et al (2019) 'Social connectedness: what matters to older people?', *Ageing and Society*, 41, 1126–1144.

Morris, A. and Verdasco, A. (2020) 'Loneliness and housing tenure: older private renters and social housing tenants in Australia', *Journal of Sociology*, 57, 763–779.

Nzabona, A., Ntozi, J. and Rutaremwa, G. (2016) 'Loneliness among older persons in Uganda: examining social, economic and demographic risk factors', *Ageing & Society*, 36, 860–888.

Parliament of Australia (2020) 'COVID-19: a chronology of state and territory government announcements (up until 30 June 2020)'. Available at: https://www.aph.gov.au/About_Parliament/Parliamentary_departments/Parliamentary_Library/pubs/rp/rp2021/Chronologies/COVID-19StateTerritoryGovernmentAnnouncements#_Toc52275800 (Accessed 15 September 2024).

Patulny, R.V. and Morris, A. (2012) 'Questioning the need for social mix: the implications of friendship diversity amongst Australian social housing tenants', *Urban Studies*, 49, 3365–3384.

Power, G. (2021) 'Designing out loneliness from the built environment', *MIPIM World Blog* [blog], 14 October. Available at: https://blog.mipimworld.com/rising-star/designing-out-loneliness-from-the-built-environment/ (Accessed 16 May 2024).

Reinhardt, G., Vidovic, D. and Hammerton, C. (2021) 'Understanding loneliness: a systematic review of the impact of social prescribing initiatives on loneliness', *Perspectives in Public Health*, 141, 204–213.

Roof, K. and Oleru, N. (2008) 'Public health: Seattle and King County's push for the built environment', *Journal of Environmental Health*, 71, 24–27.

Rusinovic, K., Bochove, M.V. and Sande, J.V.D. (2019) 'Senior co-housing in the Netherlands: benefits and drawbacks for its residents', *International Journal of Environmental Research and Public Health*, 16(19), 3776.

Sonke, J., Manhas, N., Belden, C., Morgan-Daniel, J., Akram, S., Marjani, S., et al (2023) 'Social prescribing outcomes: a mapping review of the evidence from 13 countries to identify key common outcomes', *Frontiers in Medicine*, 10, 1266429.

Tenancy Services New Zealand Government (2021) *Healthy Homes*. Available at: https://www.tenancy.govt.nz/healthy-homes?gclid=CjwKCAjwzruGBhBAEiwAUqMR8D_8i2aT9qhWxQYueQZBdx8robQzWCzENNY93zsCHFDYucMJIGrl7BoCwcsQAvD_BwE (Accessed 15 April 2024).

van den Berg, P., Kemperman, A., De Kleijn, B. and Borgers, A. (2016) 'Ageing and loneliness: the role of mobility and the built environment', *Travel Behaviour and Society*, 5, 48–55.

Volk, L. (2009) '"Kull wahad la haalu": feelings of isolation and distress among Yemeni immigrant women in San Francisco's Tenderloin', *Medical Anthropology Quarterly*, 23, 397–416.

Weiss, R.S. (1973) *Loneliness: The Experience of Emotional and Social Isolation*, MIT Press.

Wood, C. and Salter, J. (2016) *Building Companionship: How Better Design Can Combat Loneliness in Later Life*, DEMOS.

WSP (2020) 'WSP and Helen Clark Foundation tackle loneliness in the built environment', 13 October. Available at: https://www.wsp.com/en-nz/news/2020/wsp-helen-clark-foundation-tackle-loneliness-built-environment (Accessed 25 October 2024).

7

Urban–Rural Disparities in Social Network Profiles Among Older Koreans at the Early Stage of the Pandemic

Pildoo Sung

Introduction

Social networks play a crucial role in the health and wellbeing of older adults (Cornwell et al, 2008). They provide emotional, instrumental and informational support and foster a sense of belonging and attachment (Kawachi and Berkman, 2001). However, the COVID-19 pandemic disrupted older adults' social networks. Social distancing measures and shelter-in-place orders reduced face-to-face interactions and social activities (Van Orden et al, 2021; Fuller et al, 2022). The pandemic, however, did not uniformly affect all aspects of older adults' social networks, highlighting the need for a multidimensional approach (see also Chapter 2, this volume). For instance, while face-to-face contact with friends and neighbours declined during the pandemic (Lachance, 2021), communication with close family – particularly via electronic devices – may have remained stable or even increased (Freedman et al, 2022; Litwin and Levinsky, 2022; Peng and Roth, 2022).

Researchers have employed a clustering approach to capture the multidimensionality of social networks. This method classifies older adults into distinct social network profiles based on several dimensions, such as marital status, contact with family and friends, and social engagement (Litwin, 1995; Wenger, 1997). Identifying prevalent and unique social network profiles helps elucidate the interplay among these dimensions (Kim et al, 2016; Park et al, 2018).

Relevant studies have identified four common social network profiles among older adults: diverse, family-focused, friend-oriented and restricted (Wenger, 1997; Fiori et al, 2006). A diverse profile reflects active social interactions with family, friends and acquaintances. In contrast, a friend-oriented profile is characterized by social ties predominantly with friends. A family-focused profile represents older adults whose social networks primarily comprise immediate and extended family members. Lastly, a restricted profile denotes limited social relationships. Further research indicates that older adults with a diverse profile tend to experience better mental health outcomes than those with the restricted profile (Fiori et al, 2006; Park et al, 2018).

In addition, older adults' social networks are often geographically bounded, particularly by mobility limitations (see also Chapters 6 and 12, this volume), with notable urban–rural differences previously identified (Levasseur et al, 2015; Liu et al, 2020; Shang, 2020). Urban residents typically have more diverse but sparser social networks. In contrast, rural residents tend to have smaller, more tightly knit networks, although the extent of these differences varies by the type and size of communities (Hofferth and Iceland, 1998; Zheng and Chen, 2020). However, it remains uncertain whether these urban–rural differences in social networks persisted during the pandemic. Were urban or rural older adults more likely to maintain diverse or restricted social network profiles during the pandemic? Did the mental health implications of social networks vary by place of residence?

This chapter aims to identify and compare prevalent social network profiles among older adults and their association with mental health in urban and rural areas of South Korea during the COVID-19 pandemic. South Korea's effective pandemic response has garnered global recognition. Early in the pandemic, the country successfully curbed the initial peak of infections through extensive testing, contact tracing and information sharing, all while avoiding drastic lockdowns or immigration controls (Kang et al, 2020). The sociopolitical context, characterized by democracy, equity and solidarity, also played a vital role in the successful implementation of these measures (Kim, 2020). Nevertheless, little research has examined how the pandemic may have affected older adults' social relationships and whether urban–rural disparities emerged during this period.

South Korea is rapidly ageing, with individuals aged 65 or older making up 19 per cent of the population in 2023, a figure expected to reach nearly 40 per cent by 2050 (United Nations, 2023). The country's strong collectivistic culture and Confucian legacy have emphasized filial piety and in-group bonding based on blood, region and education (Horak and Klein, 2016). These traditions have fostered family-based social networks among older adults (Kim et al, 2016). Yet, with over 80 per cent of the population living in cities, rapid ageing and urbanization may have led to different social network profiles among older adults in urban and rural settings.

Social networks and social cohesion are vital during crises when other institutional support is limited (see also Chapters 11 and 13, this volume). Specifically, the pivotal role of social capital, broadly defined as the resources and benefits derived from social connectedness, cohesion and solidarity, has been documented in responding to disasters and crises (Aldrich and Meyer, 2015). Recent studies also report the benefits of social capital in weathering adversities during the COVID-19 pandemic (Bartscher et al, 2021; Makridis and Wu, 2021; Wu, 2021). Given the rampant poverty and mental health problems among older Koreans (Kang et al, 2022), identifying social network profiles among urban and rural residents and their mental health implications during the pandemic could raise public awareness of vulnerable, socially isolated older adults and inform policy and practice for designing tailored interventions.

Methods

The Korean Longitudinal Study of Aging is a nationally representative survey that collects data on family and social relationships, health and wellbeing, and financial status of older adults in Korea. This study utilized data from the eighth wave, conducted between August and December 2020, following the onset of the COVID-19 pandemic (The KLoSA Task Force, 2023). The analytic sample consisted of 6,488 respondents aged 57 or older in 2020. Of those, 5,001 respondents were classified as urban residents, including those living in metropolitan areas and small and medium-sized cities. In contrast, 1,487 respondents were categorized as rural residents, residing in -eup, -myeon, -ri rural administrative districts, where the majority of inhabitants are engaged in farming or fishing.

Measures

Social network indicators

Five social network indicators were used to identify social network profiles:

1. marital status (married versus unmarried/divorced/separated);
2. weekly contact with one or more children by phone or email;
3. weekly meeting with one or more child in person;
4. weekly meeting with friends or relatives; and
5. weekly engaging in social activities, such as religious groups, social clubs, leisure/culture/sports groups and alumni/hometown/family associations.

Items 2 and 3 were only asked of respondents who did not live with their children. Therefore, those living with their children were treated separately, resulting in three categories: 'Weekly or more frequent contact/meeting with children', 'Less frequent than weekly contact/meeting with children' and 'Coresidence'. For items 4 and 5, the variables were dichotomized into 'Weekly' versus 'Less frequently than weekly'.

Mental health

Mental health was assessed using the ten-item Center for Epidemiologic Studies Depression Scale (Kohout et al, 1993). Items such as 'I felt depressed' or 'My sleep was restless' were included, with four response categories ranging from 'rarely or none=0' to 'most of the time=3'. The summative scale ranged from 0 to 30, with higher scores indicating more severe depression.

Covariates

Sociodemographic characteristics and health status, which are associated with older adults' mental health, were accounted for. Sociodemographic characteristics included *age* (57–102 years), *gender* (woman=1), *living alone* (living alone=1), *household income* (logged), *education* (less than primary school=1; middle school=2; high school=3; university or higher=4), *working status* (currently working=1; not working=0), *chronic medical conditions* (the sum of 11 chronic conditions diagnosed by a health professional, such as cancer, diabetes and hypertension) and *functional limitations* (the sum of ten difficulties with instrumental activities of daily living, including preparing meals, cleaning or shopping).

Analytic strategies

To compare distinct social network profiles between urban and rural residents, latent class analysis (LCA) was employed separately for urban and rural respondents (Collins and Lanza, 2010). In this study, LCA grouped older adults with similar social network characteristics into different profiles based on their responses to five social network indicators. To determine the optimal number of profiles, model fit indices from various models – each with a different number of sub-groups – were compared (Nylund-Gibson and Choi, 2018).

Once the model was selected, each respondent was assigned to the most likely profile based on the highest posterior probabilities. Multivariable linear regression was then used to examine the association between social network profiles and depressive symptoms, adjusting for other covariates. Missing data were addressed using the LCA's full information maximum likelihood method and multiple imputation by predictive mean matching in the regression model (Morris et al, 2014).

Results

Sample characteristics

Table 7.1 presents the descriptive statistics for the study variables, comparing urban (n=5,001) and rural (n=1,487) respondents. Statistically significant differences were found across most social network indicators, except for weekly engagement in social activities. Urban respondents were slightly more likely to be married, meet their children in person weekly, and have weekly meetings with close friends or relatives than rural respondents. Conversely, rural respondents were more likely to have weekly contact with their children by phone or email, possibly due to greater physical distance between parents and children and pandemic-related travel restrictions.

Rural respondents were significantly older, and a higher percentage of them lived alone. Urban respondents, on average, had slightly higher household incomes and higher levels of education. A greater proportion of rural respondents were employed, and they reported slightly more functional limitations. However, no significant differences were found in the number of chronic conditions or levels of depressive symptoms between urban and rural respondents.

Characteristics of the social network profiles

Model fit comparisons indicated that a six-profile solution was optimal for urban respondents and a four-profile solution was best for rural respondents (results available upon request). Figures 7.1 and 7.2 illustrate the characteristics of the social network profiles for urban and rural respondents, respectively, based on each group's probability of responding 'yes' to the five social network indicators.

Among urban respondents, six social network profiles were identified and labelled as diverse-social, friend-social, child-focused, restricted, coresident-friend and coresident-restricted. The first four profiles included urban respondents who did not live with their children. The diverse social profile (21.3 per cent of urban respondents) consisted of older adults who frequently maintained contact with their children, met with close friends or relatives, and engaged in social activities. The friend-social profile (6.5 per cent) represented older adults actively involved in social activities and maintained ties with friends or relatives, with less emphasis on contact with their children. The child-focused profile (31.5 per cent) encompassed older adults whose social relationships primarily involved meeting and contacting their children. The restricted profile (18.1 per cent) comprised older adults with limited social networks.

The remaining two profiles included urban respondents who lived with their children. The coresident-friend profile (10.2 per cent) was characterized

Table 7.1: Study variables

Variables (range)	Urban (n=5,001)	Rural (n=1,487)	Test of difference
	Mean (SD)/%		
Social network indicators			
Married			$\chi= 4.39$*
No	25.1%	27.8%	
Yes	74.9%	72.2%	
Weekly contact with children by phone or email			$\chi= 144.12$***
No	29.1%	37.1%	
Yes	48.3%	54.1%	
Coresidence	22.6%	8.8%	
Weekly meeting with children in person			$\chi= 186.60$***
No	42.7%	59.7%	
Yes	34.7%	31.5%	
Coresidence	22.6%	8.8%	
Weekly meeting with friends/relatives			$\chi= 105.39$***
No	20.1%	38.7%	
Yes	79.9%	61.3%	
Weekly engage in social activities			$\chi= 0.43$
No	75.4%	76.3%	
Yes	24.6%	23.7%	
Mental health			
Depressive symptoms (0–30)	5.78 (5.15)	5.61 (4.70)	$t= -1.11$
Sociodemographic characteristics			
Age (57–102)	70.23 (9.56)	73.44 (9.54)	$t= 11.38$***
Woman	57.7%	58.8%	$\chi= 0.54$
Living alone	12.1%	17.7%	$\chi= 30.40$***
Household income (0.69–11.72)	7.77 (0.90)	7.48 (0.86)	$t= -11.13$***
Education (1–4)	2.35 (1.08)	1.77 (0.99)	$t= -18.58$***
Working	33.8%	40.0%	$\chi= 19.70$***
Health status			
Chronic conditions (0–8)	1.43 (1.25)	1.45 (1.24)	$t= 0.47$
Functional limitations (0–10)	0.57 (1.97)	0.75 (2.24)	$t= 2.88$**

Note: * $p<0.05$, ** $p<0.01$, *** $p<0.001$.

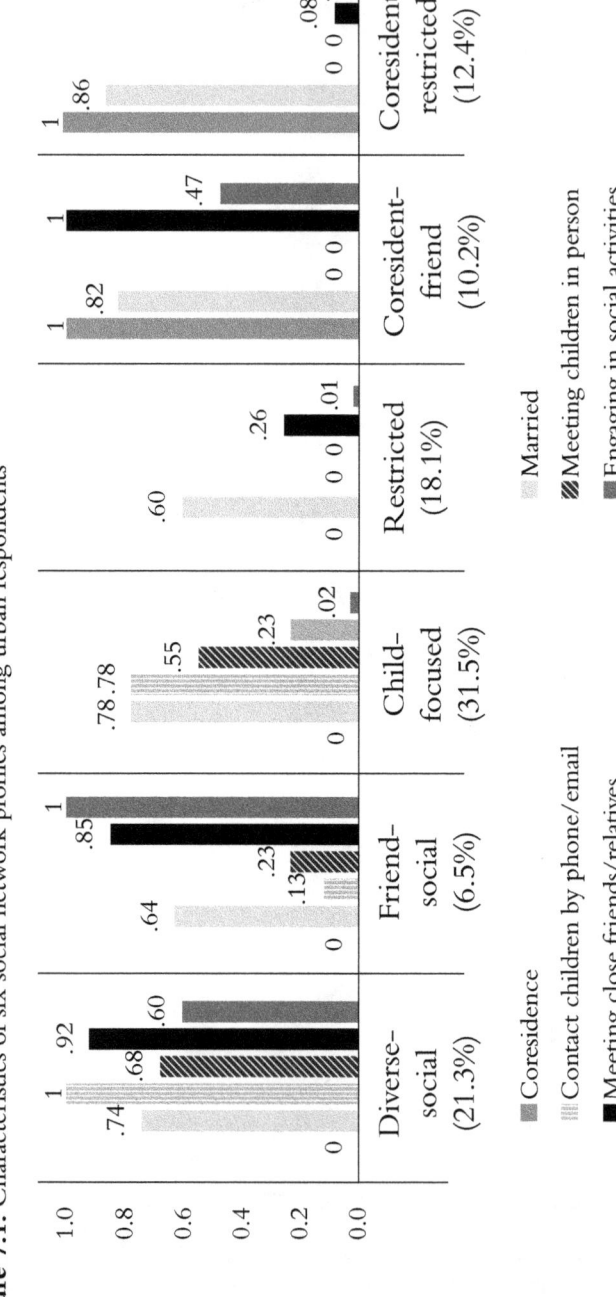

Figure 7.1: Characteristics of six social network profiles among urban respondents

by older adults who lived with their children while maintaining frequent contact with friends. In contrast, the coresident-restricted profile (12.4 per cent) indicated older adults living with their children but experiencing limited social connectedness.

As shown in Figure 7.2, four distinct social network profiles emerged among rural respondents: *diverse-social* (22.5 per cent of the rural respondents), *child-focused* (43.0 per cent), *restricted* (25.7 per cent) and *coresident-friend* (8.8 per cent). These profiles shared characteristics similar to those identified among urban respondents, except for the *coresident-friend* profile, defined by coresidency combined with moderate levels of friend contact and social engagement. Compared to their urban counterparts, a larger proportion of rural respondents fell into the *child-focused* and *restricted* profiles, leading to less variation in their overall social network profiles.

Mental health implications of social network profiles

Table 7.2 presents the linear regression results examining the association between social network profiles and depressive symptoms separately for urban and rural respondents. The *child-focused* profile, the largest group in both urban and rural samples, was used as the reference category. The models adjusted for sociodemographic and health covariates.

Among urban respondents, older adults in the *diverse-social* and *coresident-friend* profiles reported lower levels of depressive symptoms compared to those in the *child-focused* profile. In contrast, those in the *restricted* and *coresident-restricted* profiles reported higher levels of depressive symptoms. Among rural respondents, the *diverse-social* profile was associated with lower depressive symptoms, while the *coresident* profile was linked to higher depressive symptoms relative to the *child-focused* profile.

Discussion

This chapter contributes to the literature by employing a clustering approach to examine social network profiles of older adults in urban and rural areas, using national data collected during the early stages of the COVID-19 pandemic in South Korea.

The analysis revealed that urban respondents exhibited a greater variety of social network profiles compared to their rural counterparts. Specifically, a higher proportion of urban respondents lived with their children, leading to the identification of two distinct profiles: *coresident-friend* and *coresident-restricted*. In contrast, rapid urbanization in South Korea may have limited the opportunity for coresidence among older adults in rural areas, resulting in the identification of only a single *coresident* profile.

Figure 7.2: Characteristics of four social network profiles among rural respondents

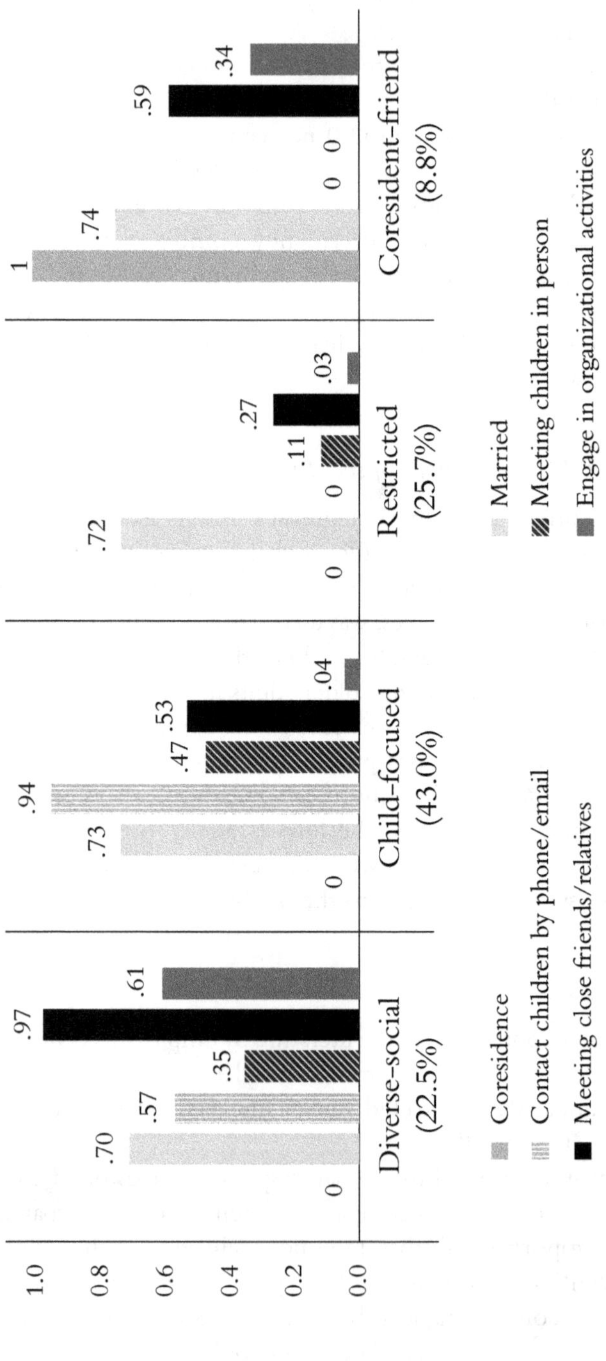

Profile	Coresidence	Contact children by phone/email	Meeting close friends/relatives	Married	Meeting children in person	Engage in organizational activities
Diverse-social (22.5%)	0	.57	.97	.70	.35	.61
Child-focused (43.0%)	0	.94	.53	.73	.47	.04
Restricted (25.7%)	0	0	.27	.72	.11	.03
Coresident-friend (8.8%)	1	0	.59	.74	0	.34

Table 7.2: Linear regression of social network profiles on depressive symptoms

Outcome: depressive symptoms	Urban respondents		Rural respondents	
	β	95% CI	β	95% CI
Urban social network profiles				
Diverse-social	−1.33***	[−1.71, −0.95]		
Friend-social	−0.02	[−0.60, 0.56]		
Child-focused	Reference			
Restricted	0.68***	[0.28, 1.07]		
Coresident-friend	−0.85***	[−1.36, −0.35]		
Coresident-restricted	1.27***	[0.80, 1.74]		
Rural social network profiles				
Diverse-social			−1.26***	[−1.85, −0.68]
Child-focused			Reference	
Restricted			0.43	[−0.12, 0.99]
Coresident			1.39**	[0.56, 2.23]
N	5001		1,487	

Note: CI: Confidence Interval. Results are based on 20 imputed datasets for urban respondents and 10 imputed datasets for rural respondents. Covariates (age, women, living alone, household income, education, working, chronic conditions, functional limitations) were adjusted for.
* $p<0.05$, ** $p<0.01$, *** $p<0.001$.

Additionally, a small but notable percentage of urban respondents (6.5 per cent) were classified under the *friend-social* profile – characterized by weekly meetings with friends/relatives and active social engagement – a profile absent among rural respondents. This aligns with the literature on urban–rural differences in social networks, where more diverse and weaker social networks can be established in urban settings (Hofferth and Iceland, 1998; Zheng and Chen, 2020).

Despite these differences, the *child-focused* profile emerged as the most common among both urban and rural respondents, reflecting South Korea's collectivistic culture, filial piety, and the importance of intergenerational contact and support exchange (Lee et al, 2014). Moreover, even during the pandemic, about 30 per cent of urban respondents in the *diverse-social* and *coresident-friend* profiles, as well as a similar proportion of rural respondents in the *diverse-social* profile, likely maintained weekly contact with children, weekly meetings with friends/relatives and active social engagement. This may be attributed to South Korea's effective pandemic countermeasures, which avoided a nationwide lockdown in 2020.

Who, then, was more likely to have diverse active or *restricted* profiles? Supplementary analyses explored the association of sociodemographic characteristics and health status with social network profiles (tables available on request). The results showed that older adults with functional limitations were less likely to belong to the *diverse-active* profile in both urban and rural areas. Additionally, urban respondents with functional limitations were more likely to fall into the *coresident-restricted* profile. These support the health selection perspective, proposing that good health is essential for initiating, expanding and maintaining social networks in later life (Schafer, 2013).

Among urban respondents, gender and education disparities were pronounced: older women and those with higher levels of education were more likely to belong to the *diverse-active* profile (Van Groenou and Van Tilburg, 2003; Ajrouch et al, 2005). In contrast, these factors did not significantly differentiate social network profiles among rural respondents. Instead, working status and health were influential, with working respondents and those in poor health less likely to have a diverse social profile. While employment can enrich social network diversity (Haynes et al, 2014), older adults in rural Korea predominantly engage in low-status jobs, such as farming or fishing, leaving them with fewer resources and less time to build and maintain diverse and active social networks.

Irrespective of urban or rural residence, older adults with a diverse social profile tended to report lower levels of depressive symptoms than those with a *child-focused* profile. These findings reaffirm the importance of social relationships in promoting or protecting mental health (Kawachi and Berkman, 2001; Fiori et al, 2006). Interestingly, older adults in the *coresident-restricted* profile in urban areas and those in the *coresident* profile in rural areas reported higher levels of depressive symptoms compared to those in the *child-focused* profile. This contrasts with existing literature, which often highlights the mental health benefits of parent–child coresidence, primarily due to the intergenerational support exchanges (Do and Malhotra, 2012; Grundy and Murphy, 2018). This discrepancy requires careful interpretation, as the reasons for coresidence may vary: older adults may live with their children out of necessity due to health conditions, and this dependency could negatively impact their mental health (Xu et al, 2019). Also, depending on the context, intergenerational coresidence may lead to emotional stress and relationship conflict, potentially deteriorating mental health (Seo and Kim, 2022).

From a practical standpoint, policy makers should prioritize older adults in both urban and rural areas whose social networks are restricted to their immediate family (spouse or children). The findings indicate that approximately 60 per cent of older adults in both settings had limited connections with friends and minimal social engagement and reported higher levels of depressive symptoms. Additionally, older adults living with their children but experiencing limited social interactions outside the household were also prone to depressive symptoms, highlighting the need for increased public awareness.

Various interventions have been developed to combat social isolation among older adults (Gardiner et al, 2018; Fakoya et al, 2020). In particular, long-term group-based participatory activities that offer social support and/or counselling/therapy have proven to be more effective than non-participatory, one-to-one interventions (Dickens et al, 2011). In addition, promoting online modes of social connection (see Chapters 14 and 15, this volume) or outreach services (for example, home visits or befriending schemes) could be beneficial for older adults in rural areas or for those living with their children.

This study has several limitations. First, the cross-sectional design precludes causal inference regarding the association between social network profiles and mental health. In terms of directionality, both social causation (where social networks influence mental health) and health selection (where mental health shapes social networks) may apply, suggesting a reciprocal relationship (Son and Sung, 2023). Second, the social network indicators used to derive social network profiles were less comprehensive. Specifically, the absence of more refined measures, such as phone or email contact with friends and relatives, limited the ability to make more nuanced distinctions between social network profiles. Third, the observed urban–rural differences may not be generalizable due to the specific timing and context of this study.

Despite these limitations, this chapter has revealed differences in the social network profiles of older Koreans in urban and rural settings during the pandemic and their implications for mental health. The findings call for future studies to explore the intersection of social networks, place of residence and mental health among older adults. Further research is warranted to investigate whether and to what extent older adults' social network profiles vary by place of residence, as well as their antecedents and consequences in other sociocultural contexts.

References

Ajrouch, K.J., Blandon, A.Y. and Antonucci, T.C. (2005) 'Social networks among men and women: the effects of age and socioeconomic status', *The Journals of Gerontology: Series B*, 60, S311–S317. https://doi.org/10.1093/geronb/60.6.S311

Aldrich, D.P. and Meyer, M.A. (2015) 'Social capital and community resilience', *American Behavioral Scientist*, 59, 254–269. https://doi.org/10.1177/0002764214550299

Bartscher, A.K., Seitz, S., Siegloch, S., Slotwinski, M. and Wehrhöfer, N. (2021) 'Social capital and the spread of COVID-19: insights from European countries', *Journal of Health Economics*, 80, Article 102531. https://doi.org/10.1016/j.jhealeco.2021.102531

Collins, L.M. and Lanza, S.T. (2010) *Latent Class and Latent Transition Analysis: With Applications in the Social, Behavioral, and Health Sciences*, John Wiley & Sons.

Cornwell, B., Laumann, E.O. and Schumm, L.P. (2008) 'The social connectedness of older adults: a national profile', *American Sociological Review*, 73, 185–203. https://doi.org/10.1177/000312240807300201

Dickens, A.P., Richards, S.H., Greaves, C.J. and Campbell, J.L. (2011) 'Interventions targeting social isolation in older people: a systematic review', *BMC Public Health*, 11, Article 647. https://doi.org/10.1186/1471-2458-11-647

Do, Y.K. and Malhotra, C. (2012) 'The effect of coresidence with an adult child on depressive symptoms among older widowed women in South Korea: an instrumental variables estimation', *The Journals of Gerontology: Series B*, 67B, 384–391. https://doi.org/10.1093/geronb/gbs033

Fakoya, O.A., McCorry, N.K. and Donnelly, M. (2020) 'Loneliness and social isolation interventions for older adults: a scoping review of reviews', *BMC Public Health*, 20, Article 129. https://doi.org/10.1186/s12889-020-8251-6

Fiori, K.L., Antonucci, T.C. and Cortina, K.S. (2006) 'Social network typologies and mental health among older adults', *The Journals of Gerontology: Series B*, 61, P25–P32. https://doi.org/10.1093/geronb/61.1.P25

Freedman, V.A., Hu, M. and Kasper, J.D. (2022) 'Changes in older adults' social contact during the COVID-19 pandemic', *The Journals of Gerontology: Series B*, 77, e160–e166. https://doi.org/10.1093/geronb/gbab166

Fuller, H.R., Huseth-Zosel, A., Hofmann, B., Van Vleet, B., Kinkade, E., Carlson, S.L., et al (2022) 'Shifts in older adults' social connections throughout the initial year of the COVID-19 pandemic', *The Gerontologist*, 62, 1160–1172. https://doi.org/10.1093/geront/gnac030

Gardiner, C., Geldenhuys, G. and Gott, M. (2018) 'Interventions to reduce social isolation and loneliness among older people: an integrative review', *Health & Social Care in the Community*, 26, 147–157. https://doi.org/10.1111/hsc.12367

Grundy, E. and Murphy, M. (2018) 'Coresidence with a child and happiness among older widows in Europe: does gender of the child matter?', *Population, Space and Place*, 24, e2102. https://doi.org/10.1002/psp.2102

Haynes, P., Banks, L. and Hill, M. (2014) 'The relationship between employment and social networks in the older population', *International Journal of Social Economics*, 41, 321–335. https://doi.org/10.1108/IJSE-10-2012-0201

Hofferth, S.L. and Iceland, J. (1998) 'Social capital in rural and urban communities', *Rural Sociology*, 63, 574–598. https://doi.org/10.1111/j.1549-0831.1998.tb00693.x

Horak, S. and Klein, A. (2016) 'Persistence of informal social networks in East Asia: evidence from South Korea', *Asia Pacific Journal of Management*, 33, 673–694. https://doi.org/10.1007/s10490-015-9416-1

Kang, J., Jang, Y.Y., Kim, J., Han, S.-H., Lee, K.R., Kim, M., et al (2020) 'South Korea's responses to stop the COVID-19 pandemic', *American Journal of Infection Control*, 48, 1080–1086. https://doi.org/10.1016/j.ajic.2020.06.003

Kang, J., Park, J. and Cho, J. (2022) 'Inclusive aging in Korea: eradicating senior poverty', *International Journal of Environmental Research and Public Health*, 19, Article 2121. https://doi.org/10.3390/ijerph19042121

Kawachi, I. and Berkman, L.F. (2001) 'Social ties and mental health', *Journal of Urban Health*, 78, 458–467. https://doi.org/10.1093/jurban/78.3.458

Kim, B., Park, S. and Antonucci, T.C. (2016) 'Longitudinal changes in social networks, health and wellbeing among older Koreans', *Ageing & Society*, 36, 1915–1936. https://doi.org/10.1017/S0144686X15000811

Kim, H. (2020) 'The sociopolitical context of the COVID-19 response in South Korea', *BMJ Global Health*, 5, e002714. https://doi.org/10.1136/bmjgh-2020-002714

The KLoSA Task Force (2023) *User's Guide for the 2020 Korean Longitudinal Study of Ageing (KLoSA), Wave 8*, Korea Employment Information Service.

Kohout, F.J., Berkman, L.F., Evans, D.A. and Cornoni-Huntley, J. (1993) 'Two shorter forms of the CES-D Depression Symptoms Index', *Journal of Aging and Health*, 5, 179–193. https://doi.org/10.1177/089826439300500202

Lachance, E.L. (2021) 'COVID-19 and its impact on volunteering: moving towards virtual volunteering', *Leisure Sciences*, 43, 104–110. https://doi.org/10.1080/01490400.2020.1773990

Lee, H.J., Lyu, J., Lee, C.M. and Burr, J.A. (2014) 'Intergenerational financial exchange and the psychological well-being of older adults in the Republic of Korea', *Aging & Mental Health*, 18, 30–39. https://doi.org/10.1080/13607863.2013.784955

Levasseur, M., Cohen, A.A., Dubois, M.-F., Généreux, M., Richard, L., Therrien, F.-H., et al (2015) 'Environmental factors associated with social participation of older adults living in metropolitan, urban, and rural areas: the NuAge study', *American Journal of Public Health*, 105, 1718–1725. https://doi.org/10.2105/AJPH.2014.302415

Litwin, H. (1995) 'The social networks of elderly immigrants: an analytic typology', *Journal of Aging Studies*, 9, 155–174. https://doi.org/10.1016/0890-4065(95)90009-8

Litwin, H. and Levinsky, M. (2022) 'Social networks and mental health change in older adults after the COVID-19 outbreak', *Aging & Mental Health*, 26, 925–931. https://doi.org/10.1080/13607863.2021.1902468

Liu, D., Xi, J., Hall, B.J., Fu, M., Zhang, B., Guo, J., et al (2020) 'Attitudes toward aging, social support and depression among older adults: difference by urban and rural areas in China', *Journal of Affective Disorders*, 274, 85–92. https://doi.org/10.1016/j.jad.2020.05.052

Makridis, C.A. and Wu, C. (2021) 'How social capital helps communities weather the COVID-19 pandemic', *PLOS ONE*, 16, e0245135. https://doi.org/10.1371/journal.pone.0245135

Morris, T.P., White, I.R. and Royston, P. (2014) 'Tuning multiple imputation by predictive mean matching and local residual draws', *BMC Medical Research Methodology*, 14, 1–13. https://doi.org/10.1186/1471-2288-14-75

Nylund-Gibson, K. and Choi, A.Y. (2018) 'Ten frequently asked questions about latent class analysis', *Translational Issues in Psychological Science*, 4, 440–461. https://doi.org/10.1037/tps0000176

Park, N.S., Jang, Y., Lee, B.S., Chiriboga, D.A., Chang, S. and Kim, S.Y. (2018) 'Associations of a social network typology with physical and mental health risks among older adults in South Korea', *Aging & Mental Health*, 22, 631–638. https://doi.org/10.1080/13607863.2017.1286456

Peng, S. and Roth, A.R. (2022) 'Social isolation and loneliness before and during the COVID-19 pandemic: a longitudinal study of U.S. adults older than 50', *The Journals of Gerontology: Series B*, 77, e185–e190. https://doi.org/10.1093/geronb/gbab068

Schafer, M.H. (2013) 'Structural advantages of good health in old age: investigating the health-begets-position hypothesis with a full social network', *Research on Aging*, 35, 348–370. https://doi.org/10.1177/0164027512441612

Seo, B.K. and Kim, J.H. (2022) 'Intergenerational coresidence and life satisfaction in old age: the moderating role of homeownership', *Applied Research Quality Life*, 17, 3199–3216. https://doi.org/10.1007/s11482-022-10062-y

Shang, Q. (2020) 'Social support, rural/urban residence, and depressive symptoms among Chinese adults', *Journal of Community Psychology*, 48, 849–861. https://doi.org/10.1002/jcop.22302

Son, J. and Sung, P. (2023) 'Does a reciprocal relationship exist between social engagement and depression in later life?', *Aging & Mental Health*, 27, 70–80. https://doi.org/10.1080/13607863.2021.2024794

United Nations (2023) *Leaving No One Behind in an Ageing World, World Social Report 2023*, Department of Economic and Social Affairs.

Van Groenou, M.I.B. and Van Tilburg, T. (2003) 'Network size and support in old age: differentials by socio-economic status in childhood and adulthood', *Ageing & Society*, 23, 625–645. https://doi.org/10.1017/S0144686X0300134X

Van Orden, K.A., Bower, E., Lutz, J., Silva, C., Gallegos, A.M., Podgorski, C.A., et al (2021) 'Strategies to promote social connections among older adults during "social distancing" restrictions', *The American Journal of Geriatric Psychiatry*, 29, 816–827. https://doi.org/10.1016/j.jagp.2020.05.004

Wenger, G.C. (1997) 'Social networks and the prediction of elderly people at risk', *Aging & Mental Health*, 1, 311–320. https://doi.org/10.1080/13607869757001

Wu, C. (2021) 'Social capital and COVID-19: a multidimensional and multilevel approach', *Chinese Sociological Review*, 53, 27–54. https://doi.org/10.1080/21620555.2020.1814139

Xu, Q., Wang, J. and Qi, J. (2019) 'Intergenerational coresidence and the subjective well-being of older adults in China: the moderating effect of living arrangement preference and intergenerational contact', *Demographic Research*, 41, 1347–1372.

Zheng, Z. and Chen, H. (2020) 'Age sequences of the elderly social network and its efficacies on well-being: an urban-rural comparison in China', *BMC Geriatrics*, 20, Article 372. https://doi.org/10.1186/s12877-020-01773-8

8

The Rise of Parkrun: Collective Positivity, Rituals and Episodic Togetherness in an Age of Loneliness

Nicholas Hookway and Zack Dwyer

Introduction

Traditional club-based sport is often regarded as the 'lifeblood' of communities heralded for enhancing physical health but also social connection and social cohesion (Davies et al, 2021). There is compelling evidence, however, that club-based sports participation in Australia and internationally is declining (Seippel et al, 2020; Jeanes et al, 2024). One significant but emerging community-orientated sporting activity that bucks these trends is the rise of parkrun (written with a lowercase 'p' throughout to reflect the organization's branding). Parkrun is a not-for-profit organization that provides free-to-attend, timed, five-kilometre events in public spaces, such as community parks and green environments, every Saturday around the world. Parkrun began in 2004 with 13 runners and five volunteers in Bushy Park (London) in the UK and is now an international phenomenon with over nine million parkrunners (parkrun, 2024). Parkrun spans large city centres such as London, where flagship events such as Bushy Park attract over 1,000 weekly participants, to smaller regional and remote events.

The parkrun community is based on the simple principle that it is 'weekly, free, for everyone and forever' (parkrun, 2024). While primarily a physical activity, where people walk, jog or run, parkrun (outside of a small group of paid staff who oversee global and national operations) is also entirely volunteer-led, with every event organized and delivered by the participants themselves. Parkrun is best conceptualized as a fusion between 'informal' and 'formal' sports. On the one hand, parkrun's open, free and casual participation and collective use of public space are reminiscent of informal sports (Neal et al, 2023). Informal sport promotes open and casual access where individuals can join in on what might be a routine schedule but do so on a 'turn up and play' basis (Neal et al, 2023: 3). This flexible model allows individuals to create shared meanings and connections via more informal or casual participation. Examples of informal sports include street football, community basketball and urban cycling groups (Jeanes et al, 2024). On the other hand, parkrun's overarching organizational structure means it shares qualities with formal community and club-based sporting organizations (Wiltshire et al, 2018). While existing parkrun research has mostly focused on the health and physical benefits of parkrun, less is known about the nature and quality of social connection generated at parkrun and how this is experienced. This chapter analyses parkrun as a specific site to investigate everyday ways of making and experiencing social connection in the context of declining membership of traditional sporting clubs and associations.

Real community? Theorizing social connection at parkrun

Despite the physical and social benefits of informal sports (for example, street football, community basketball, urban cycling groups), there is a strong critique that they do not afford the same social quality and depth as traditional sports clubs. Putnam, for example, is critical that informal physical activities are not as 'social' (2000: 109) as organized group or team sports. While people can attend the gym with others and jog or walk with friends, sociability compared to traditional group-based sports is limited (Hajkowicz et al, 2013). The recent shift towards individual-focused sporting activities is argued to threaten the social capital outcomes typically fostered by civil society organizations, such as norms of reciprocity, a sense of community connectedness and collective identities (Putnam, 2000; Tonts, 2005). Where then does the rise of parkrun fit within this picture of declining, or at least changing, sporting community membership and how can parkrun social connection be theorized?

Drawing upon Bauman (2001), parkrun can be framed as an example of contemporary 'aesthetic communities'. Aesthetic communities are collectives that generate short-term bonds that lack long-term commitments, obligations and ethical responsibilities (Bauman, 2001). For Bauman, aesthetic communities are fragile and transitory gatherings that reflect the loneliness and disconnection of 'liquid' times (Bauman, 2005). Parkrun, then, in Bauman's (2001: 69) terms, 'conjures up the experience of community without real community, the joy of belonging without the discomfort of being bound'. Following Bauman, we can speculate that parkrun's more 'no strings attached' type community means it cannot produce the same strength of social bonds, especially without the common goal or objective of club-based sports and the in-group bonding that occurs through competition.

Maffesoli's (1996) concept of 'neo-tribalism' offers an alternative and more positive lens to theorize parkrun social connection. 'Neo-tribes' are characterized by an intensive emotional bonding aroused through shared leisure activities and lifestyles (Bennett, 1999). Whereas Bauman (2001) positions 'aesthetic communities' as reflective of fragile social bonds and loneliness in 'liquid modernity', Maffesoli's 'neo-tribalism' underscores the return of new forms of being together moulded in the shape of Durkheimian 'collective effervescence'. Neo-tribes are localized 'micro-groups' (Maffesoli, 1996: 6) where individuals build powerful affective energy through meaningful and ritualized interactions. While recent scholarly work on parkrun has led scholars to proclaim that parkrunners are a distinct group of leisure enthusiasts who cultivate a powerful 'family' or 'community' spirit (Wiltshire and Stevinson, 2018: 47; Bowness et al, 2021: 44; Hindley, 2022: 101), further research is needed to examine how rituals produce community. I draw here upon Collins' (2004: 7) work, which defines interaction rituals as 'a mechanism of mutually focused emotion and attention, producing a momentarily shared reality, which thereby generates solidarity and symbols of group membership'. Collins' (2004) theory on rituals and emotions is useful for analysing how social connections are generated at parkrun.

Methods

The study involved a qualitative analysis of 33 semi-structured interviews with participants in parkrun events across Tasmania (Australia). On average, a total of 1,725 people complete a Tasmanian parkrun event as a participant (that is, walk or run) each week, while 197 attend a Tasmanian parkrun event each week as a volunteer (parkrun, 2024). The largest parkruns in Tasmania (Launceston in the North, Bellerive in the South) regularly attract over 300 participants each Saturday morning (parkrun, 2024). Interviews formed the second stage of a larger multi-method survey-interview project investigating the personal, health and social impacts of parkrun participation in 2019. Upon completing the survey, participants were invited to participate in a follow-up one-hour interview to deepen the knowledge of their experiences. Interviewees were asked about the process of becoming and being a parkunner, including its impacts on health, identity and social connection. This chapter focuses on reporting the findings on social connection.

Most interviews (n=27) were conducted in person with the remaining undertaken via Skype or telephone. The age range was 22–74 with a mean age of 48. Sixteen interviewees were male and 17 were female. Eighteen interviewees held a bachelor's degree while four possessed a postgraduate qualification. At the time of data collection, the majority (n= 22) of participants were employed full-time while six were retired. The average period of doing parkrun was 3.5 years and most participated (n= 24) in parkrun – as either a volunteer or participant – 'regularly' (weekly or fortnightly). Five participated 'semi-regularly' (once a month to once every three months) and four participated on an 'irregular' basis (once every six months or less). Interviews ranged from 22 to 87 minutes in length, with most around 55 minutes. Data were thematically analysed guided by Braun and Clarke's (2019) reflexive thematic analysis (RTA) approach. Themes were generated using both inductive and deductive coding and involved familiarization by reading and re-reading transcripts, developing initial codes, merging codes into themes, refining themes and reporting using extracts and quotations (Byrne, 2022). Guided by RTA, data analysis focused on interpreting and telling stories rather than 'uncovering' an objective truth (Braun and Clarke, 2019: 591).

The 'church of humanity': social connection and the collective ethos of positivity

Social connection was one of parkrun's big drawcards. Mirroring existing research (Bowness et al, 2021; Hindley, 2022), feelings of belonging and community were paramount to why participants started and continue to do parkrun. While many participants discussed how they initially joined parkrun to improve their health or fitness, the social elements of parkrun were central for everyone from 'casual' to 'serious' parkrunners. Participants said: 'It's the social side that's important' (Harry, 53); 'It became a real social thing' (Suellen, 44); 'There's something about the community-feel of parkrun that other events don't have' (Josh 46); 'I really like the social stuff ... and parkrun offers that more than other events do' (Tyler, 50). Many expressed the social elation of 'meeting more and more people', 'making new friends' and 'meeting different sorts of people'. Richard and Melissa, two older participants, captured the emotional 'excitement' of making social connections at parkrun that cemented their commitment and devotion:

> As I met more and more people it became very exciting. Suddenly parkrun became a big part of my weekend and my life because of that. (Richard, 64)

> I met all sorts of different people – and that was exciting. After I got to know them, I started to really enjoy it and it became a weekly thing. (Melissa, 56)

Indeed, several participants noted that parkrun was less about running and more about social connection. Adam (22) said: 'For me it's about the social connections that it brings and the conversations I have. The actual running itself? Sometimes I can take it or leave it.' Similarly, Jeremy (52) explained how 'It's not just running. It allows people to become ... social. It really is a social thing', while Margaret (72) stated 'I don't even think about running really. When I'm there I'm looking for people to talk to or to catch-up with.' The emphasis on parkrun as an almost 'non-running' community renders it unique from other running-based leisure communities where there is a stricter focus on running as a bodily, disciplinary and emotional practice (Shipway et al, 2013). In this sense, parkrun is less about running and more about coming together to celebrate 'the social'.

Feelings of belonging at parkrun were linked to the generation of a 'clan morality' (Maffesoli, 1996) marked by shared beliefs and emotions. This resonates with Hindley's (2022) research, which claims that parkrunners belong to an identifiable group with shared meanings, norms and values. Emily (52), Harry (53) and Eliza (27), for example, explained how at parkrun 'everyone is pretty like-minded', 'feels the same way about things', 'have a similar purpose' and that it is 'a connection point for people who have similar goals and interests'.

To be a *parkrunner* – as opposed to someone who just *does* parkrun – was to possess a shared commitment to prosocial emotions such as positivity, kindness and happiness. For example, Dianne (65) remarked that 'It's all about positivity' and Linda (55) added that parkrun was 'about sharing and kindness'. Emotions of positivity were particularly revered. There was almost a quasi-religious sense of the importance attached to positivity as a collective emotion. Harry (53) explained: 'I liken parkrun to church. It's a church of humanity that doesn't involve God. It's a church of positivity where people go and support and connect with others around that spirit of positivity.'

Positivity is a central emotion in facilitating social connection at parkrun. Positivity had an emotional 'contagion' effect, with participants often noting that they 'always come away from parkrun happy' (Kate 47). Kate said that it's a 'positivity that's surreal in a lot of ways because you adopt it almost subconsciously'. The shared emphasis on collective positivity makes parkrun a highly appealing event. Parkrun's own branding states: 'join the feel-good movement'. As Kišjuhas (2023: 369) argues in relation to leisure rituals, humans are drawn towards 'social forms that generate positive feelings'. The focus on expressing positive emotions meant that participants performed 'emotional work' (Hochschild, 1979) to police 'deviant' emotions in themselves and others (Thoits, 1990). Failure to display positive emotions – to be a parkrun 'killjoy' (Ahmed, 2010) – meant risking not being accepted at parkrun. Jeremy (53), for example, described how 'If you come without that positivity, you stand out like a sore thumb.' Oscar (59) shared a story about the community response to someone who was 'hitting tree branches out of frustration' because they did not run well: 'We ignore them if they're like that, or they're told not to come back.' More serious or elite runners were identified as most commonly violating the 'feeling rules' (Hochschild, 1979) of parkrun by being 'too competitive', 'not volunteering' or just 'missing what parkrun is about' (Diane, 65; Tyler, 50). This finding echoes Bowness et al's (2021) finding that the 'community feel' of parkrun can exclude some individuals. The following section highlights the importance of rituals in generating social connection (and disconnection) at parkrun events.

Rituals and social connection: generating belonging at parkrun

The ritualized practices of parkrun were key to creating experiences of social connection. Rituals have been identified as central to leisure practices (Kišjuhas, 2023) but little research has applied theories of ritual to analyse the production of parkrun social connection. Four 'interaction rituals' (Collins, 2004) were developed from the interview data that were important for producing social connection. First, the 'pre-run briefing' ritualistically begins the community interaction. Performed by the Run Director, all participants are expected to attend (and actively listen) as course specifics are outlined, visitors and first-timers are acknowledged and volunteer and milestone achievements are recognized (parkrun, 2024). As Tyler said: 'It's where the community starts.' Participants highlighted in particular how the celebration of achievement milestones at the pre-run briefing strengthened feelings of belonging by 'letting you know you're part of the group' (Josh, 47) and 'solidified the accomplishment and your position in the community' (Ruth, 35). Attending and actively listening to the parkrun briefing – and 'congratulating the milestones' – was also discussed as part of conforming to the 'feeling rules' (Hochschild, 1979) of being 'respectful and kind' (Linda, 55) at parkrun.

Second, solidarity at parkrun is established through the ritualistic 'collective bodywork' (Wiltshire et al, 2018) of walking, running or volunteering together weekly at the same time and in the same place. As Hindley (2022) argues, the collective act of exercising together at parkrun creates a 'shared communal experience'. These collective rituals see ordinary community parks transformed every Saturday morning for two or three hours creating a shared focus charged with emotions based on 'chains' of previous encounters (Collins, 2004). Parkrun is also known for its course positivity, with participants regularly high-fiving and encouraging each other, thanking volunteers mid-run and early finishers, and helping and applauding others across the finish line.

Third, parkrunners use clothing ritualistically to symbolize their belonging by wearing, for example, purchased milestone t-shirts (for example, 50 runs, 100, 250, and so on). In Justin's words, 'You wear the shirts to let others know you're one of them.' This aligns with Hindley's (2018) research, which showed how milestone t-shirts express parkrunners' shared identity and value within the community. Participants also used clothing to establish belonging during themed days such as 'everyone wearing red' to celebrate a parkrun's birthday while others dressed up for 'Star Wars Day' and relished the 'camaraderie' and the 'strange looks from passers-by' (George, 50). While 'individual careers' are enabled – and celebrated through symbols such as milestone t-shirts – they also function to demonstrate commitment to the group. While there can be tension between individual achievement and community belonging, the parkrun ethos emphasizes the latter. This emphasis on participation over performance played out in a recent decision by parkrun to remove the publication of individual speed-based records (for example, course records; sub-20-minute times for women; sub-17-minute times for men) from its website to ensure the data 'doesn't imply that parkrun is a race'.

Finally, participants identified the post-run coffee as a significant ritual that crystallized post-event social connection. If the pre-run briefing signalled the 'start' of the parkrun community, the post-run coffee enabled the community to extend beyond the run. Lisa (54) said: 'Rather than parkrun ending and everyone getting in their car and going home, those who go to the café carry on and process the results or chat about the run.' The post-run coffee ritual was so central that for some its loss had a negative impact on the parkrun social experience. Tanya (72), for example, shared how her experience of parkrun belonging 'splintered' when a café decided to stop opening early while Tyler (50) discussed how after losing the 'connection point' of the café that 'parkrun is worse off for it'. Existing research by Hindley (2018) identifies how parkrun fulfils certain 'third space' (Oldenburg, 1999) elements – a public place outside of work and home where people can gather voluntarily, informally and habitually to foster belonging. While the formality, size and high-profile nature of parkrun means it is quite different from traditional third spaces, here parkrun works in tandem with the café as a more traditional third space to foster community interaction. The final section analyses how parkrun tends to produce what we call 'episodic togetherness' but also more enduring relationships that may assuage isolation and loneliness.

Episodic togetherness and beyond: friendship, loneliness and emotional talk

Most participants emphasized how parkrun had a strong 'community feel' (Richard, 64) but 'dissipated' (Tanya, 72) or 'faded into the background' (Fred) post-event. Josh, for example, described parkrun as a type of community that 'pops up and then disperses' while parkrun for Kate was about an 'essence of togetherness and a very loose sense of being part of a group'. Most interviewees described parkrun social connections as 'acquaintances' rather than 'friends' and the sense of belonging using words such as 'loose', 'fleeting', 'casual' and 'surface level'. This dominant experience of social connection at parkrun can be described as 'episodic togetherness'. Episodic togetherness captures the power of parkrun as a short-term, loose and light-touch form of community that is experienced as a joyful 'essence of togetherness' that goes beyond a shared passion or interest in parkrun. Episodic togetherness is distinct from Bauman's (2001) 'aesthetic communities' in that it does not misplace short-term togetherness for loneliness or dismiss it as not 'real' community, nor does it reduce social connection to something expressed purely around a shared interest as Maffesoli's 'neo-tribalism'.

Episodic togetherness can be distinguished from the types of social connection experienced in more traditional sporting clubs. Participants differentiated the deeper, enduring and tightly bound community formed in traditional sporting clubs with the more fleeting and less committed social connection developed at parkrun. While participants noted the benefits of not being 'locked into any commitment' (Adam), parkrun did not produce the same social capital benefits of club-based sports. Lyn (31), for instance, explained that 'I can't depend on people at parkrun in the same way I can from netball – or even tennis' while Josh (46) added, 'Football is where I can rely more on others ... they're the people I trust and am closer to.' Parkrun's episodic togetherness meant that for many participants it did not generate bonding social capital in the way that group-based community sports can (Tonts, 2005; Spaaij, 2009).

On the other hand, there was a core group of participants where parkrun social connection went beyond weaker and temporary social bonds. A small group of men, for example, underlined how parkrun had helped them cope with and reduce loneliness and isolation, particularly when they first moved to the state. George (50), for example, stated: 'I got all my first friends in Tasmania through parkrun ... all my current friends do parkrun. parkrun is certainly the social hub of my life' while Jeremy said: 'I moved from Sydney and ended up with severe depression ... what had happened was that I'd isolated myself. So, the social aspect of parkrun was good to me.' Similarly, Rhys identified he 'faced some lonely times' moving to Tasmania from another country and parkrun was helpful as he 'didn't have anything in terms of social connections'. Other men, like Adam (22) discussed the benefits of parkrun easing the burden of arranging social life and admitted he 'required that external organization'. The gendered aspects of parkrun social connection align with evidence that suggests men can experience entrenched loneliness across the life course and strengthen calls for loneliness to be tackled through initiatives that 'reactivate' the public realm (Franklin et al, 2019; Chapter 2, this volume).

Other participants said that they developed ongoing, emotionally deep and trusting friendships through parkrun. For example, Dianne said: 'I've made new friends and trust them a lot. We talk quite deeply about our family and mental health issues', while Suellen (44) expressed how her parkrun friends 'are people who have shared their life history with me, and I've shared with them ... we trust each other enough to confide about our lives'. There appears to be a gendered dimension to this emotional talk, with fewer men discussing how parkrun was a space where they would have vulnerable, deep and expressive conversations (see Chapter 2, this volume). Men and women did both favourably compare opportunities for social connection at parkrun with work. Rhys, for example, said he'd 'only made one friend through work' while Emily (52) compared her 'like-minded' friends at parkrun to her work colleagues who she is 'not that close to ... because we don't really share interests'.

Finally, several participants discussed how parkrun can help reverse the negative effects of 'hurried' lives on maintaining social connections with friends and family. As Lyn said: 'It can be hard with everyone working or starting families to find that time these days.' Comparing parkrun to coffee catch-ups that 'usually fall through', the strength of parkrun was that it created a 'pre-arranged' (Lyn, 55) space for social connection. Participants similarly commented about parkrun as a routinized space for connecting and 'becoming closer with family' (Eliza, 28). Multiple parents discussed how running with their children was a highlight that strengthened family connections. This strengthening of connections between parents and children is an example of how parkrun can generate bonding social capital (Putnam, 2000). For participants like Harry (50) bonding capital was not limited to face-to-face interactions with the international nature of parkrun helping him keep connected with his son living overseas: 'We do ours in the morning here, and then 13 hours later he does his. Every Sunday I wake up to a message from him about his run – and that's great. We're on opposite sides of the world but parkrun is everywhere.'

Conclusion

This chapter analysed parkrun as an everyday space to spotlight the new and creative ways people are making and doing social connection. The international rise and success of parkrun was positioned as a possible antidote to wider anxieties about 'broken communities' and declining membership in traditional community sports organizations. Parkrun was positioned as a fusion activity that shares the open and casual access elements of 'informal' sport and the more formal organizational structures of community sports organizations. Bauman's (2001) 'aesthetic communities' and Maffesoli's (1996) 'neo-tribalism' – extended through

Collins' (2004) interaction rituals – were introduced as theoretical devices to interpret the characteristics of social connection and ritual at parkrun. The chapter introduces 'episodic togetherness' as an alternative to Bauman and Maffesoli's theories, capturing a powerful but short-term feeling of community that neither reduces new forms of social connection to the loneliness of late-modernity nor focuses exclusively on emotional affinities that develop around shared interests.

Three key themes were developed in the empirical analysis. The first highlighted the overwhelming pull of social connection for participants starting and continuing parkrun. All participants identified that they were drawn to parkrun – and remained in parkrun – due to its social connection benefits. Social connection, for many, was more important than running itself. The social connection was linked to 'feeling rules' around positive emotional dispositions that created parkrun 'insiders' but also 'outsiders'. Second, the chapter showed how four 'interaction rituals' (Collins, 2004) – the pre-event briefing, running or walking together, displaying milestone clothing and the post-run coffee – were key to producing a shared communal experience. Third, the analysis showed that parkrun social connection tended to be 'episodic togetherness' distinct from the social capital benefits of club-based sports. Episodic togetherness expresses a powerful but short-term feeling of community that is less about the activity itself (for example, walking, running, volunteering) and more about experiencing an 'essence of togetherness'. There were, however, a group of participants who discussed parkrun as producing more enduring, strong and trusting social bonds that strengthened bonding capital with friends and family.

While existing research has mostly focused on the health and physical benefits of parkrun, this chapter makes an important contribution to understanding how parkrun offers new opportunities for people to form and maintain a vibrant and connected social life in everyday sporting and leisure spaces. While traditional sporting clubs may be declining, new formations such as parkrun show the creative ways people continue to bond and come together to form micro-pockets of solidarity that can offer respite from headwinds of individualism, isolation and loneliness. This chapter recognizes that changing patterns of social connection in sport and leisure do not spell 'the end of community' but can produce new sites of social connection and belonging. While this is a small-scale qualitative study based on a distinctive sample – largely well-educated, middle-class and based in Tasmania – the findings suggest that parkrun may be useful as a policy intervention to improve social connection. While there is a move, particularly in Australia, for parkrun to become part of 'social prescribing' practices by GPs and health practitioners to improve health outcomes, it could also be used explicitly to address concerns about increasing isolation and loneliness. However, policy recommendations need to recognize that parkrun, like most communities, possesses 'in' and 'out' group dynamics, particularly for individuals who may not share the 'imperative of positivity'. Similarly, the finding that social connection tends to be characterized by 'episodic togetherness' marked by lighter and less obligated bonds than traditional sporting clubs is important to consider. However, this can also afford social benefits, particularly in our contemporary 'hurried' lives. Parkrun as an organization may also consider how it can help transpose the temporariness of social bonds for more lasting ones by developing and promoting opportunities for participants to socialize outside parkrun events (for example, facilitating post-run coffee, end-of-year celebrations, and so on). More generally, the international success of parkrun offers insights into alternative sporting participation models that can help promote social connection and physical activity outside traditional club-based models.

References

Ahmed, S. (2010) *The Promise of Happiness*, Duke University Press.

Bauman, Z. (2001) *Community: Seeking Safety in an Insecure World*, Polity Press.

Bauman, Z. (2005) *Liquid Life*, Polity Press.

Bennett, A. (1999) 'Subcultures or neo-tribes? Rethinking the relationship between youth, style and musical taste', *Sociology*, 33(3), 599–617.

Bowness, J., Tulle, E. and McKendrick, J. (2021) 'Understanding the parkrun community; sacred Saturdays and organic solidarity of parkrunners', *European Journal for Sport and Society*, 18(1), 44–63.

Braun, V. and Clarke, V. (2019) 'Reflecting on reflexive thematic analysis', *Qualitative Research in Sport, Exercise and Health*, 11(4), 589–597.

Byrne, D. (2022) 'A worked example of Braun and Clarke's approach to reflexive thematic analysis', *Quality and Quantity*, 56, 1391–1412.

Collins, R. (2004) *Interaction Ritual Chains*, Princeton University Press.

Davies, L.E., Taylor, P., Ramchandani, G. and Christy, E. (2021) 'Measuring the social return on investment of community sport and leisure facilities', *Managing Sport and Leisure*, 26(1–2), 93–115.

Franklin, A., Barbose Neves, B., Hookway, N., Patulny, R., Tranter, B. and Jaworski, K. (2019) 'Towards an understanding of loneliness among Australian men: gender cultures, embodied expression and the social bases of belonging', *Journal of Sociology*, 55(1), 124–143.

Hajkowicz, S., Cook, H., Wilhelmseder, L. and Boughen, N. (2013) 'The future of Australian sport: megatrends shaping the sports sector over coming decades', Consultancy report for the Australian Sports Commission.

Hindley, D. (2018) '"More than just a run in the park": an exploration of parkrun as a shared leisure space', *Leisure Sciences*, 42(1), 85–105.

Hindley, D. (2022) *parkrun: An Organised Running Revolution*, Routledge.

Hochschild, A.R. (1979) 'Emotion work, feeling rules and social structure', *The American Journal of Sociology*, 85(3), 551–575.

Jeanes, R., O'Connor, J., Penney, D., Spaaij, R., Magee, J., O'Hara, E., et al (2024) 'A mixed-method analysis of the contribution of informal sport to public health in Australia', *Health Promotion International*, 39(3), daae048. https://doi.org/10.1093/heapro/daae048

Kišjuhas, A. (2023) 'What holds society together? Emotions, social ties, and group solidarity in leisure interaction rituals', *Leisure Studies*, 43(3), 363–377.

Maffesoli, M. (1996) *The Time of the Tribes: The Decline of Individualism in Mass Society*, SAGE.

Neal, S., Pang, B., Parry, K. and Rishbeth, C. (2023) 'Informal sport and leisure, urban space and social inequalities: editors' introduction', *Leisure Studies*, 43(6), 875–886.

Oldenburg, R. (1999) *The Great Good Place: Cafes, Coffee Shops, Bookstores, Bars, Hair Salons and Other Hangouts at the Heart of a Community*, Paragon House.

Putnam, R. (2000) *Bowling Alone: The Collapse and Revival of American Community*, Simon & Schuster.

parkrun (2024) 'About'. Available at: https://www.parkrun.com/about/our-story/ (Accessed 30 May 2024).

Seippel, Ø., Breuer, C., Elmose-Osterlund, K., Feiler, S., Perenyi, S., Piatkowska, M., et al (2020) 'In troubled water? European sports clubs: their problems, capacities and opportunities', *Journal of Global Sport Management*, 8(1), 203–225.

Shipway, R., Holloway, I. and Jones, I. (2013) 'Organisations, practices, actors, and events: exploring inside the distance running social world', *International Review for the Sociology of Sport*, 48(3), 259–276.

Spaaij, R. (2009) 'The glue that holds the community together? Sport and sustainability in rural Australia', *Sport in Society*, 12(9), 1132–1146.

Thoits, P.A. (1990) 'Emotional deviance: research agendas', in T.D. Kemper (ed) *Research Agendas in the Sociology of Emotions*, State University of New York Press, pp 180–203.

Tonts, M. (2005) 'Competitive sport and social capital in rural Australia', *Journal of Rural Studies*, 21, 137–149.

Wiltshire, G. and Stevinson, C. (2018) 'Exploring the role of social capital in community-based physical activity: qualitative insights from parkrun', *Qualitative Research in Sport, Exercise and Health*, 10(1), 47–62.

Wiltshire, G., Fullagar, S. and Stevinson, C. (2018) 'Exploring parkrun as a social context for collective health practices: running with and against the moral imperatives of health responsibilisation', *Sociology of Health and Illness*, 40(1), 3–17.

9

United by Insects? Insects' Control and Development of Social Connections in a Large City

Oksana Zaporozhets and Olga Brednikova

Once, during our fieldwork, we accidentally witnessed a conversation between two neighbours – women in their 60s. The conversation took place at the entrance of an apartment building located in the centre of St. Petersburg. Built in 1902, the house had never had significant renovations. One neighbour insisted, 'Just admit it! The cockroaches are coming from your apartment!' The second woman protested, 'I don't have any! They are coming from the fifth floor, most likely from the Ivanovs. They stir up dirt all the time.'

This short dialogue highlights the basics of neighbour communication. It arose around something perceived as a shared problem – insects in their apartment building. Although the problem is recognized as shared, it does not foster a sense of shared responsibility or collective action. Instead, the conversation shifts towards assigning blame, with neighbours seeking out who might be at fault for the presence of cockroaches in the building. The issue becomes personalized and narrowed to human responsibility, ignoring other possible causes, such as poor building maintenance, substandard construction or surroundings. Ultimately, the neighbours return to their apartments without forming a plan or reaching a consensus, leaving each to address the problem independently.

This chapter focuses on specific connections – neighbour ones revolving around the presence of indoor insects. By neighbour connections, we refer to those based on spatial proximity (Abrams and Bulmer, 1986), which are inevitable for humans and non-humans. We assume that neighbouring significantly matters for urban dwellers since spatial proximity is the key characteristic of urban life, with cities being a dense concentration of people, materialities, technologies and species. Today, many urbanites could be described as *Homo Indoorus* (Dunn, 2018) since they spend most of their time at home or in other enclosed spaces. This distribution of time makes interactions that develop within indoor spaces especially significant.

In his book *Never Home Alone* (2018), Rob Dunn draws attention to often unnoticed but highly influential non-humans that inhabit our homes, such as insects, viruses and bacteria. In this chapter, we focus on connections evolving among humans, materiality and indoor insects, addressing the question of whether the presence of these species affects the possibility of neighbours to solidarize and act collectively.

One might doubt that the presence of insects in a multi-storey building could serve as grounds for the solidarity of its residents due to the perceived 'insignificance' of the problem. However, in the modern sterile city, the presence of insects indoors matters to the majority of urban dwellers: '87% of the residents [of the studied US cities] considered cockroaches (in their apartment) a serious problem' (Wood et al, 1981: 11). Dawn Biehler, in her book *Pests in the City* (2013), emphasizes the role of insects in building solidarity, referring to the case of Norwood, a mixed-income, ethnically diverse rental building in Washington, DC. In 2007, residents created an association specifically to control the spread of bedbugs, mice and mould from apartment to apartment, which promoted neighbour solidarity and helped them resist possible eviction: 'Residents united by bedbugs succeeded in their struggle to keep their homes' (Biehler, 2013: 5–6). However, the reverse is also true, as 'bedbugs divided other communities and burdened people who tried to escape them' (Biehler, 2013: 5–6).

In our exploration, we concentrate on St. Petersburg, Russia. With its 5.5 million residents, St. Petersburg is the second largest city in Russia. For us, both the city and the country exemplify international trends of growing individualization and privatization of social life as well as multiple hindrances to building solidarities caused by economic liberalization and democratic backsliding. Our chapter begins with a brief theoretical overview of neighbouring, followed by a description of neighbour relations in large Russian cities shaped by the institutional environment, particularly the state distribution system and the market. Then, we highlight the methodology of our research and delve into the neighbour connections in St. Petersburg – specifically those that emerged or failed to emerge while residents dealt with indoor insects in multi-storey and multi-apartment buildings.

Neighbour connections in cities (in Russia)

Today, spatial proximity is recognized as an 'essential and key attribute' of neighbouring (Abrams and Bulmer, 1986: 18). Defining proximity as the main characteristic of neighbouring means that the latter is no longer associated with a particular type of social relationship – a 'neighbourly' one that includes 'friendly recognition, parochial helpfulness ... and embracing ... diversity' (Kusenbach, 2006: 279). Instead, neighbouring is now defined as an ongoing process of (re)establishing connections ranging from isolation to cooperation (Crow et al, 2002). The dynamics of bonding and isolation are especially important for understanding neighbouring, where bonding and isolation are considered not opposites but concurrently present and competing tendencies. Additionally, the role of non-humans, such as materialities or species, is recognized in forming and maintaining neighbour relationships. These non-human entities are considered either important actors in neighbouring, reflecting the idea that 'social life is never reducible to the purely human alone' (Amin, 2014: 138), or crucial intermediaries in these relationships. Neighbouring, in this view, is often described as 'materially constructed relationships' where 'materials' are necessary to facilitate interactions between neighbours (Maller et al, 2016: 57). Furthermore, we consider materiality and species to be key intermediaries in neighbouring while identifying neighbours as 'people who live near one another' (Liu et al, 2023: 238). We do not deny the interpretation of non-humans as independent actors – a view supported by multi-species studies and Actor Network Theory today. Rather, we see it as a matter of emphasis, depending on the specific objectives of the research.

Neighbouring is a multidimensional and multi-scale process, making the distinction between neighbour relationships and neighbour connections an important issue. We define neighbour relationships as those developed in a specific institutional environment and, to some extent, determined by it. In recent decades, the market and governance (Power and Mee, 2020) have influenced neighbouring, including who the neighbours are and how their interactions have developed. In contrast, we consider neighbour connections as those centred around specific situations or issues. These connections may align with institutional patterns, thereby reinforcing them, or they may challenge and drive their revision and reconfiguration, at least at the local level. We assume that both relationships and connections should be considered to grasp the multidimensionality, processuality and complexity of neighbouring.

Today, neighbouring in Russia is heavily influenced by the institutional environment of the past. According to a survey, approximately 40 per cent of the inhabitants of large cities cannot afford to rent or buy a new apartment and have to remain in the ones acquired by their families decades ago (Zaporozhets and Kobyscha, 2021). This highlights the lasting influence of Soviet housing and social policies and the rapid post-Soviet marketization of real estate in the 1990s on the current situation. We identify three types of neighbouring associated with different structural conditions that existed in the USSR and Russia: neighbouring by necessity, separated neighbouring, and controlled neighbouring (Zaporozhets and Brednikova, 2022). Before unpacking these types, it is worth mentioning that neighbouring has played an especially important role because multi-storey and multi-apartment residential buildings have dominated most large Russian cities since the early 20th century. It started with 3–4 floors and has continued ever since, with an average height of 12.6 floors today (Rychagov, 2019). The number of apartments situated on the same floor of a multi-storey building has varied, usually from four to 20.

Neighbouring by necessity evolved from the distribution of housing by the Soviet state or enterprise (Zavisca, 2012), with almost no opportunity for individuals to influence the type or location of housing they were allocated or whom to neighbour. Housing was distributed by enterprises or government agencies depending on corporate affiliation, length of service, marital status of the applicant and loyalty to the state. This distribution created socially mixed urban areas: neighbours in a house or stairwell could radically differ in education, income or position, such as a director and a factory worker or a university professor and a schoolteacher. Soviet neighbours could be lifelong. Besides being neighbours, people were usually connected in various ways. For example, they were often co-workers, their children attended the same kindergarten or school, and they frequently vacationed in the same holiday resorts provided by their employers. Their lives were tightly intertwined, and the opportunity to distance themselves from their neighbours was extremely limited. This interwoven nature of lives encouraged collaboration among neighbours, as bonds formed in other contexts smoothly extended into neighbours' living spaces.

A fundamental change in neighbouring – deliberate separation (separated neighbouring) – began in the 1990s due to societal changes associated with the collapse of the Soviet Union and the marketization of housing. The mass privatization of housing and the formation of a real estate market gave people a new opportunity to choose their place of residence and, consequently, their neighbours. However, in the 1990s and early 2000s, the possibility of choosing where to live was a privilege available to few. Nevertheless, the desire to separate from the external environment and neighbours existed, and it was realized by building boundaries or the 'bunkerization' of the home – installing massive iron doors and bars on windows and enclosing balconies. These and many other measures were taken to protect apartment residents from the rapidly growing crime and shield the apartment from less immediate neighbours, who were gradually turning into strangers. The emergence of a new economy was accompanied by a crisis in Soviet enterprises, which meant that the professional and life paths of yesterday's colleagues diverged, and their income levels and lifestyles changed, which increased the demand for privacy and social distancing in places of residency.

This new separation and privacy affected the ways residents dealt with house-related issues. Almost all cooperation with neighbours was suspended. Even infrastructure challenges, such as leaking communal pipes, degrading electric cables or noise pollution, were expected to be fixed at the apartment level. The excerpt from a random online chat epitomizes the separation: 'I solve problems on my own. If I am scared of new neighbours, I install a door. If I dislike the noise outside, I install new soundproof windows and an air-conditioner.' Bunkerization revealed the growing role of materiality in producing neighbouring. For years to come, bunkerization – the use of materiality to produce desirable relations with neighbours – would become a sustainable pattern of neighbouring in large Russian cities.

The spread of mortgage programmes and the exponentially increased number of newly built houses in the 2010s made the purchase of housing more affordable for the urban middle class. The formation of a rental market has also increased the choice of housing and, with it, neighbours. Separated neighbouring is gradually being replaced by controlled neighbouring – balancing between distancing and cooperating with neighbours. This cooperation has been facilitated by creating online neighbour groups and chats. The cooperation is often based on the necessity of solving infrastructure problems (which differ for new and old buildings and various city districts) and taking care of or improving public spaces such as building hallways, courtyards, nearby parks, and so on. These actions require collective efforts and lead to interactions among residents. A more prosperous economic situation in Russia has increased trust and decreased suspicion of neighbours towards each other, making collaboration easier. However, neighbour initiatives are welcomed by the state and local authorities only when they remain small-scale, confined to the district or city level. In an authoritarian context, grassroots initiatives that attempt to scale up are seen as a threat by the state (Bederson et al, 2021).

Currently, neighbour relations in Russia are a mixture of these types.

Research methodology

How does neighbouring evolve when insects become involved? Our research was conducted in St. Petersburg from 2020 to 2023 and concentrated on residents of St. Petersburg living in various areas and encountering insects in their homes. St. Petersburg is the second largest Russian city, with a population of four million and more than 300 years of history. The research sample included urban citizens living in buildings constructed at different times, with the oldest ones built in the late 19th and early 20th centuries and the latest ones built in the last decade. The main criterion for selection was residency in a multi-apartment building with up to 20 apartments per floor. A total of 17 semi-structured interviews were conducted with residents of different ages, ranging from 20 to 78 years old. Twelve women and five men were interviewed. The gender asymmetry is because, in Russia, the home is perceived as a female sphere of responsibility (Zhelnina, 2023), so women were both more aware of their homes and more eager to share their situations with us. In addition to the interviews, we analysed online forums and chats, including the largest St. Petersburg forum, Littleone, and three local groups where encounters with insects in houses were discussed.

Controlling/fighting insects: when market and habit come into play

We began this chapter with a conversation between two neighbours who accidentally met on the stairwell of a multi-apartment building. The women were discussing the problem of cockroaches in their building, but their conversation led to nothing – each returned to their apartments to deal with the situation individually. However, a multi-apartment building is not merely a collection of individual units. All apartments are interconnected through shared materialities – common spaces, shared walls and ceilings, electrical cables, central heating, water supply, ventilation, sewage systems, and so on (Maller et al, 2016; Tkach, 2024). Unwanted insects, smells and sounds easily spread throughout the building through these shared materialities. Therefore, controlling them requires not only individual but also collective effort. Further, we will explore the strategies used by residents of multi-apartment buildings to deal with indoor insects, focusing on the connections that evolve or fail to evolve among neighbours.

Despite the immense diversity of the insect world, we will concentrate only on bedbugs and cockroaches, as research participants primarily mentioned them. St. Petersburg fits general trends in changing attitudes and policies towards indoor insects during the 20th century, which shifted from relatively peaceful coexistence to attempts at total eradication and then to recognizing the importance of friendly coexistence with insects in outdoor spaces (Biehler, 2009). A century ago, the proximity of insects to humans and their presence in urban housing was normalized. Insects were tolerated in some indoor spaces, such as cockroaches in the kitchen. Action against them was required only if a radical increase in their numbers caused significant damage. With the development of medical knowledge about the nature of infections and related epidemics, a new stage in the relationship between humans and the insects living in their homes – the stage of intensive control – began. The invention of pesticides and their intensive use since the 1950s, along with changes in construction technologies, housing maintenance and general urban hygiene policies, contributed to a significant reduction in the number of insects in cities and residential buildings worldwide (Biehler, 2013). This, in turn, reduced the attention that citizens, politicians and researchers paid to insect infestations. Today, the growing interest in indoor insects is driven by a resurgence in bedbug and cockroach infestations and the moral panics accompanying this process, especially in global megacities such as Paris and New York. Additionally, the idea of multi-species cohabitation has changed the perception of insects and sparked interest in how humans and insects share the same indoor environments.

Today, when residents of multi-storey apartment buildings in St. Petersburg encounter cockroaches or bedbugs in their apartments, they perceive it not as an everyday situation but as a significant problem or even a personal tragedy. Many interviewees mentioned intense negative emotions, ranging from shock to depression, caused by such encounters. Indoor insects are frequently perceived as invaders, occupying a space that belongs to residents. Interviewees commonly frame their experiences with insects as a war and widely use war-related metaphors. They speak of attacks and defences: 'A cockroach invasion started in the kitchen' and 'I had to defend my home from these creatures'. They also reference victories and defeats: 'We gave up and eventually moved out.' Other military analogies are equally prevalent: 'After we exterminated the cockroaches, our home looked like a battlefield.'

Framing interactions with indoor insects as war, people choose individual strategies to combat insects and try to solve the problem locally, within their apartments. The bedbugs or cockroaches could be caught and 'smeared on the wall', 'frozen' or 'trapped.' However, the most common way to eliminate unwanted insects is to use insecticides. The insecticide market in Russia is flourishing, providing a variety of options. The main criteria for choosing the toxic substance are their effectiveness and safety for people and pets. If insecticides do not work, professional exterminators are called in. To ensure that unwanted insects do not return, residents often seal their apartment's perimeter, turning them into separated boxes: cracks in the floor and walls are caulked and sealed, ventilation hatches are closed, and so on. An abundant residential renovation market offers all necessary equipment and goods. Moreover, many residents of multi-storey buildings are well-acquainted with sealing techniques or have even practised some of them, having turned their apartments into bunkers in the 1990s and 2000s. Today, as in the past, the multi-apartment building is not considered a materiality that requires collaborative care but rather a collection of sealed boxes of apartments where everyone should fight against insects on their own.

While the measures mentioned help control indoor insects, the mental health care market assists middle-class residents in dealing with situations they perceive as traumatic. One of the interviewees sought therapy to cope with her negative experience, while another considered the opportunity to seek professional help: 'I'm not joking; bedbugs can really mess with your head. It is a disaster!' Thus, developed markets and the professionalization of insect control and mental health care influence how people deal with indoor insects and, to some extent, foster individual effort, making joint actions among neighbours seem excessive or even unnecessary.

Neighbour connections: the limited possibility of collaboration

Research participants often deal with insects in their apartments independently, without involving neighbours or initiating collective actions. Strategies such as using insecticides or 'boxing' do not connect neighbours or foster communication. Instead, they connect residents to objects and materialities perceived as ideal solutions to the problem. This contributes to the isolation of neighbours and avoidance of any connections other than random conversations:

> We lived in a 60-year-old building, and there was a problem with cockroaches. That is really a problem! Apparently, neighbours took turns poisoning them, and all these cockroaches were moving throughout the house. If residents poison the cockroaches one by one, the colony will move from apartment to apartment. But I don't remember anyone showing solidarity and reaching an agreement. It was more like conversations. Someone poisoned the cockroaches, and they came to me. And then they walk in circles. But I don't remember any joint effort. I don't even know why. (Anton, 43 years old)

Online neighbour chats, along with stairwells and courtyards, were mentioned by interviewees as spaces where neighbour communication occurs and connections could potentially be established. However, chats often become places where 'distancing mechanisms' are exercised, and 'the boundaries around the matters of conversation ... with which it was appropriate for neighbours to be concerned' are set up (Crow et al, 2002: 135). Ella, a resident of a multi-storey apartment building, recalls her unsuccessful attempt to initiate collective action in her house neighbour chat:

> I wrote to the chat: 'Let's kill the bedbugs!' Neighbours replied that it was none of their concern because they had no bedbugs. But they lied! They said that they don't know anything; nothing is known at all. That's my problem. Well, I called the extermination service several times. ... There were holes in the floor around the perimeter of the room. I bought some caulk and stuck it there. (Ella, 34 years old, resident of a new housing estate)

In this instance, residents refused to acknowledge the problem publicly, distanced themselves from it and Ella and therefore withdrew from any collective actions.

So why do neighbours not act together when this could help them better control insect infestations? As previously mentioned, one reason could be the absence of solidarity and collective action patterns as a legacy of separated neighbouring. There are also other grounds that support the search for individual solutions, even though today, cooperation among neighbours is common when large-scale infrastructure problems arise, or some common spaces need to be cared for. Establishing and maintaining social and spatial distance has been a valued skill for neighbours in Russia since the 1990s, as it protects their privacy. Since bedbugs and cockroaches infiltrate the most private areas of an apartment, such as kitchens and bedrooms, their presence is perceived as particularly intimate and personal. Consequently, collective efforts that seem acceptable to neighbours when dealing with public spaces or infrastructures become unacceptable for tackling private space issues.

The refusal to act collectively and the reluctance to connect may also stem from the persistent belief that the presence of cockroaches and bedbugs is solely an individual responsibility. Interviewees often attribute infestations to specific individuals lacking personal hygiene rather than to the building's material conditions, infrastructure or surroundings. Our interviewees identify cockroaches and bedbugs as migratory creatures and a very special type of 'comers', which neither 'appear' on their own and out of nowhere nor 'live' in the building; rather, they come from somewhere and from someone: 'These were not our cockroaches; they were strangers. They came from bad neighbours, so we destroy them in every way' (Zhanna, 43 years old, resident of a 60-year-old building). This perception of insects places all responsibility for their appearance on the residents of the building. Zhanna defines the neighbours from whom the cockroaches came as 'bad'. The presence of the unwanted insects is connected to humans who are categorized socially: 'We know who they are coming from!' They are believed to be unable to maintain decent levels of cleanliness and order at home, as regular cleaning is considered the main preventative measure against unwanted insects. This is likely why the appearance of insects in buildings is associated with guilt and shame and is often accompanied by secrecy. This interpretation of insect appearances does not strengthen connections among neighbours or support collective actions. Instead, it cultivates suspicion and individual monitoring of neighbours, deepening isolation.

As previously discussed, different types of markets encourage individual strategies for coping with indoor insects. Residents search for professionals, such as exterminators or therapists, whose services seem ideal solutions to the problem. Some interviewees admitted that they found engaging in non-personalized, short-term market transactions with clear expectations easier than establishing personal connections with neighbours, which require time and commitment and do not follow a ready-made script.

Nevertheless, two cases of establishing neighbour relations and solidarity among neighbours were discovered. Natalia, a resident who has lived in her apartment for almost 50 years, told us that she and several other long-term residents collected money and called for the extermination service to help their solo-living neighbour in his 80s, who could not cope with the situation himself. She interpreted it as caring for an older adult. Natalia admitted that it was difficult for neighbours to get together despite the longevity of their living in the same apartment building. She complained: 'It used to be different – back then. Now, it feels very disconnected, very disjointed' (Natalia, 71 years old, resident of a 65-year-old building). However, Natalia confessed that other residents benefited from helping the neighbour since 'All evil came from him! He is the main reason! All cockroaches come from his apartment!' In this case, the cooperation was more a reproduction of existing hierarchies based mainly on duration of residency (but also age and gender) than a collaboration of 'equals'. In another case, cooperation was established among 'socially close' middle-class neighbours, that is, a curator of art exhibitions and a musician in a theatre orchestra. Thus, cooperation among neighbours is not inherently positive and inclusive, aiming to solve common problems. It also includes actions that reinforce social hierarchies, exclude neighbours or limit their agency, turning them into the object of care. Neither of these collective actions radically changed existing neighbour connections by making them more inclusive or long-lasting. These connections align with institutional patterns of separated or controlled neighbouring, thereby reinforcing them and existing local hierarchies.

Conclusion

This chapter examines neighbour connections around indoor insects in St. Petersburg, Russia. Based on spatial proximity, neighbouring affects the everyday life of millions. In large Russian cities, neighbour connections are especially important due to the dominance of multi-storey and multi-apartment housing. We distinguish between neighbour relations and neighbour connections, with neighbour relations being patterns influenced by the institutional environment (mainly governance and market). In contrast, neighbour connections arise from specific situations, such as encounters with indoor insects.

'Disbelief and horror' (Lynch, 2019: 393), fear and disgust are common reactions for the dwellers of sterilized cities worldwide when they encounter indoor insects. For us, both St. Petersburg and Russia reflect international trends in how these insects are perceived and dealt with. This chapter's main question is whether indoor insects' presence can drive neighbours to solidarize and act collectively. Although some instances of neighbour solidarity were observed, handling infestations is generally considered an individual task or 'personal combat'. This reliance on individual strategies is not surprising, given the market's influence through the variety of options and clear scenarios of interactions with professional services or the state's tendency to discourage collective actions that extend beyond the locality. Moreover, the lack of cooperation skills and the preference for familiar solutions, like 'boxing' (sealing apartments), reinforce individual approaches. Neighbour connections forged in response to insect infestations are fragile and short-lived, rarely leading to any radical reconfiguration of existing social ties. The strong emphasis on privacy and the use of distancing mechanisms limits solidarity among neighbours in dealing with indoor insects. While neighbours may collaborate on improving public spaces or fixing shared infrastructure, this cooperation typically stops at the threshold of their apartments. Furthermore, structures created to foster collaboration, such as house neighbour chats or alliances, can sometimes serve as tools for distancing, isolation and even exclusion.

Are there any ways to break the vicious circle of separation and individual solutions to collective problems? The realistic answer is 'no' or 'not that quickly' because it requires substantial structural changes that affect solidarities. The influence of the market or the state, the primary contributors to alienation, cannot be eliminated. However, some measures could encourage resident cooperation by developing self-governance in residential areas, enhancing skills for collaboration, and improving the infrastructure for neighbour engagement, including establishing neighbourhood centres.

In the meantime, some minor steps could be taken to alleviate the situation. These actions should undermine the widespread belief (Castillo-Neyra et al, 2023) that individuals are entirely responsible for the appearance and spread of insects indoors. A complex number of reasons cause the existence of insects. Perhaps educational programmes and media campaigns that shift the burden of responsibility away from individuals (Asshoff et al, 2022), combined with better access to information about the resurgence of indoor insects, public services and peer-to-peer support networks, could be valuable tools in addressing the issue of indoor insect infestations collaboratively.

References

Abrams, P. and Bulmer, M. (1986) *Neighbours: The Work of Philip Abrams*, Cambridge University Press.

Amin, A. (2014) 'Lively infrastructure', *Theory, Culture & Society*, 31(7–8), 137–161.

Asshoff, R., Heuckmann, B., Ryl, M. and Reinhardt, M. (2022) '"Bed bugs live in dirty places": how using live animals in teaching contributes to reducing stigma, disgust, psychological stigma, and misinformation in students', *CBE – Life Sciences Education*, 21(4), ar73.

Bederson, V., Zhelnina, A., Zaporozhets, O., Minaeva, E., Semenov, A., Tykanova, E., et al (2021) *The City of Forking Streets: The Trajectories of Urban Conflicts in Russia*, Sociology Institute Press.

Biehler, D.D. (2009) 'Permeable homes: a historical political ecology of insects and pesticides in US public housing', *Geoforum*, 40(6), 1014–1023.

Biehler, D. (2013) *Pests in the City: Flies, Bedbugs, Cockroaches, and Rats*, University of Washington Press.

Castillo-Neyra, R., Larson, A.J., Tamayo, L.D., Arevalo-Nieto, C., Brown, J., Condori-Pino, C., et al (2023) 'Perceptions of problems with household insects: qualitative and quantitative findings from peri-urban communities in Arequipa, Peru', *The American Journal of Tropical Medicine and Hygiene*, 1(aop).

Crow, G., Allan, G. and Summers, M. (2002) 'Neither busybodies nor nobodies: managing proximity and distance in neighbourly relations', *Sociology*, 36(1), 127–145.

Dunn, R. (2018) *Never Home Alone: From Microbes to Millipedes, Camel Crickets, and Honeybees, the Natural History of Where We Live*, Hachette UK.

Kusenbach, M. (2006) 'Patterns of neighboring: practicing community in the parochial realm', *Symbolic Interaction*, 29(3), 279–306.

Liu, Y., Wang, S. and Cheshire, L. (2023) 'The problems with neighbors: an examination of the influence of neighborhood context using large-scale administrative data', *Urban Affairs Review*, 59(1), 238–274.

Lynch, H. (2019) 'Toward a multispecies home', in S.A. Webb (ed) *The Routledge Handbook of Critical Social Work*, 1st edition, Routledge, pp 390–400.

Maller, C., Nicholls, L. and Strengers, Y. (2016) 'Understanding the materiality of neighbourhoods in "healthy practices": outdoor exercise practices in a new master-planned estate', *Urban Policy and Research*, 34(1), 55–72.

Power, E.R. and Mee, K.J. (2020) 'Housing: an infrastructure of care', *Housing Studies*, 35(3), 484–505.

Rychagov, M. (2019) 'How cities grow: the number of floors in Russian cities has doubled in three decades', *Forbes*, 19 January. Available at: https://www.forbes.ru/biznes/371755-kak-rastut-goroda-etazhnost-rossiyskih-gorodov-vyrosla-v-dva-raza-za-tri-desyatiletiya (Accessed 8 June 2024).

Tkach, O. (2024) 'Elastic neighboring: everyday life within the geometry and materiality of large housing estates', *Space and Culture*, 27(3), 302–318.

Wood, F.E., Robinson, W.H., Kraft, S.K. and Zungoli, P.A. (1981) 'Survey of attitudes and knowledge of public housing residents toward cockroaches', *Bulletin of the ESA*, 27(1), 9–13.

Zaporozhets, O. and Kobyscha, V. (eds) (2021) *Residential Careers of Urban Citizens in Large Cities: Life Trajectories and Spatial Mobility* (Annual Report), National Research University Higher School of Economics.

Zaporozhets, O. and Brednikova, O. (2022) 'New neighbours in new urban districts in large Russian cities: constructing scenarios of neighbouring', in L. Cheshire (ed) *Neighbours around the World: An International Look at the People Next Door*, Emerald Publishing, pp 37–54.

Zavisca, J.R. (2012) *Housing the New Russia*, Cornell University Press.

Zhelnina, A. (2023) '"Naughty," "nice," or "homo sapiens": gendered political toolkits in a housing mobilization', *Sociological Forum*, 38(1), 27–48.

PART III
Community Spaces

10

Nature-Based Social Prescribing with LGBTQIA+ Asylum Seekers and Refugees: A Feasibility Study Using 'Friends in Nature'

Nerkez Opacin, Nicholas Hill, Sarah Bekessy, Ian Seal, Jill Litt and Katherine Johnson

Introduction

Public health interest in promoting social connection as a remedy for poor health and wellbeing outcomes has grown recently, alongside recognition of the harmful mental and physical effects of loneliness (Lim, 2018; Holt-Lunstad, 2021). The human need to belong and form attachments is well established (Allen et al, 2022; Holt-Lunstad, 2022) although sustaining social bonds and communal ties is challenged by urbanization, globalization, technological advances, climate change, and local and global conflicts (O'Sullivan et al, 2021; Frontline, 2024). Population-level studies largely conducted in advanced economies suggest a global epidemic of loneliness and social isolation (O'Rourke, 2024). High rates of loneliness have been reported across various adult groups in Europe, the United States, the United Kingdom, Canada and Australia (Menec et al, 2019; Hawkley et al, 2020; Lim et al, 2022; Surkalim et al, 2022; Infurna et al, 2024), with increasing rates also observed among adolescents in Africa, Asia and the Americas (Smith et al, 2024). An expanding body of evidence links loneliness to depression, anxiety, cardiometabolic disease and cognitive decline, among other health issues (Park et al, 2020; Kang and Oremus, 2023). Recent research highlights the positive impact of nature on health, wellbeing and the reduction of loneliness (Markevych et al, 2017; Astell-Burt et al, 2022; Lavelle Sachs et al, 2024).

The need for innovative solutions to address loneliness and its harmful effects is recognized internationally. In response, governments and non-governmental organizations are promoting the benefits of communal bonds and social ties through innovative policies and programmes (Goldman et al, 2024). The World Health Organization launched the Commission on Social Connection (2024–2026) (World Health Organization, 2024) and Japan and the United Kingdom have each appointed a Minister of Loneliness (UK Government News, 2021). Public health agencies are exploring social prescription (SP) and nature-based social prescribing (NBSP) as potential strategies for decreasing the burden of disease within priority communities and geographical areas known for poor health and wellbeing outcomes (Chatterjee et al, 2018; Lavelle Sachs et al, 2024).

Unlike traditional clinical approaches that prescribe medication or refer individuals to therapies such as counselling, NBSP and SP involve health and social care professionals are prescribing social activities. These may include linking service users with community-based supports and group activities in their localities (Walker et al, 2023; Calderón-Larrañaga et al, 2024). NBSP activities, such as communal gardening, nature walks, forest therapy and birdwatching (Leavell et al, 2019), aim to enhance individual mental health and wellbeing through social connection and contact with nature (Lavelle Sachs et al, 2024; Litt et al, 2024).

In this chapter, we explore findings from a feasibility study investigating the implementation of the Friends in Nature (FIN) intervention with Lesbian, Gay, Bisexual, Transgender, Queer, Intersex and Asexual plus (LGBTQIA+) asylum seekers and refugees in Melbourne, Australia. Feasibility studies typically assess various factors, including the acceptability and appropriateness of the intervention, the feasibility of participant recruitment and retention, and the potential impact on the target population (O'Cathain et al, 2015). We briefly describe the Re-imagining Environments for Connection and Engagement: Testing Actions for Social Prescribing in Natural Spaces (RECETAS) project and the FIN intervention before introducing our observations on the issues and challenges of implementing NBSP with LGBTQIA+ asylum seekers and refugees in collaboration with Many Coloured Sky.

RECETAS

Launched in March 2021, the international, transdisciplinary RECETAS project examines the efficacy of NBSP interventions in reducing loneliness and promoting mental health and wellbeing through group activities in accessible green (forests and grasslands), blue (oceans and rivers) and grey spaces (urban gardens) where people live, work and play (for further information, see Litt et al, 2024). RECETAS aims to develop and test the effectiveness of NBSP with various populations known to be at risk of social isolation across diverse economic, geographical, political and social contexts. The RECETAS model is being tested in six cities worldwide with local teams working with different populations. In Melbourne, Australia, we are collaborating with LGBTQIA+ asylum seekers and refugees (aged 18+). Other cities and their focus groups include: Barcelona, Spain (adults aged 18+ living in socioeconomically deprived areas); Cuenca, Ecuador (older adults aged 60+ living in the community or assisted living facilities within urban areas); Helsinki, Finland (older people in assisted living facilities); Prague, Czech Republic (older adults aged 60+ identified by primary and allied healthcare practitioners as at risk of social isolation); and Marseille, France (people living in urban areas with economic and social precarity) (Litt et al, 2024).

Our partner, Many Coloured Sky, is a 'queer development agency' with national and international initiatives aimed at empowering LGBTQIA+ individuals and communities to participate fully and equally in the spaces they inhabit (Many Coloured Sky, 2018). We collaborated with Queer Refugee and Asylum Seeker Peers (QRASP), a peer-led social support group established in 2018 within the agency that regularly meets and runs activities for members in Melbourne and across Victoria.

Improving health and wellbeing through social connection

In response to the rising rates of preventable diseases globally and concerns about escalating medical costs, clinicians, public health authorities and governments are exploring alternative treatment models that leverage the places and networks where people live (Lavelle Sachs et al, 2024). Our ability to promote physical, mental and social wellbeing has been enhanced through social determinants of health models, which view health as an outcome of multiple social, systemic and structural factors. These include: (1) socioeconomic factors such as education, occupation, and income; (2) demographic markers, including age, ability, gender, sexuality, cultural and ethnic background, faith, relationship status and race; and (3) proxy and complementary indicators such as social networks, perceptions of trust and safety, housing, and access to local parks, waterways and open spaces (Lynam and Cowley, 2007; Shokouh et al, 2017). These models enable policy makers and service providers to identify populations at risk of adverse health and wellbeing outcomes and design multifactorial individual and community-level interventions (NSW Health, 2022; Reumers et al, 2022).

Social determinants of health models have been criticized for prioritizing structural factors over social indicators (Holt-Lunstad, 2022) and reinforcing beliefs about personal responsibility for health and wellbeing when diagnosing and treating at-risk individuals (Gutin, 2024). Addressing loneliness and isolation requires greater attention to the *social* within these models (Holt-Lunstad, 2022). While loneliness and social isolation are often used interchangeably, they are distinct but related concepts. Loneliness can be understood as the distress arising from a perceived mismatch between desired and actual social relationships, reflecting the quality of social interactions (Peplau and Perlman, 1982) or the subjective feeling that one's needs are unmet through the quantity or quality of social relationships (Hawkley et al, 2020). Social isolation, in contrast, is more objective and measures the actual number of relationships (Hawkley et al, 2020; Litt et al, 2024).

The way an individual experiences social connection, loneliness or social isolation can be understood through three conceptual components: structural, functional and qualitative (Holt-Lunstad, 2022: 195). The structural component refers to the interpersonal relationships an individual has across different networks and roles, including relationship status, social integration and housing situation. Functional aspects encompass both received support and perceptions of social support. Qualitative factors involve the positive and negative aspects of all social relationships, such as peer networks, familial ties, community connections and relationship status. Social isolation is measured by focusing on structural factors, whereas loneliness arises within the functional aspects of relationships. Understanding the factors involved in isolation, loneliness and inclusion-exclusion, as well as their interrelationships, facilitates the development of measures and supports the design of multifactorial interventions that enhance social connection, improve the availability and quality of support in the spaces where people live, and promote social inclusion. SP and NBSP are potential strategies to increase social connection and reduce the disease burden among groups susceptible to isolation and poor health outcomes.

Developing NBSP for LGBTQIA+ asylum seekers and refugees

LGBTIQA+ asylum seekers and refugees in Australia face numerous economic, legal, political and social challenges, including pervasive queerphobic and racially driven discrimination, exclusion and violence (Forcibly Displaced People Network, 2023). In many countries, including Australia, political, legislative, economic and welfare responses limit the ability of LGBTQIA+ asylum seekers and refugees to secure adequate housing, find employment, enrol in education, build social networks, make friends and establish a life in culturally unfamiliar environments (Yarwood et al, 2022; García Rodríguez, 2023). This precarious situation renders LGBTQIA+ asylum seekers more vulnerable to interpersonal violence and discrimination and contributes to social isolation and loneliness, unemployment, housing instability and homelessness, poor mental health and wellbeing, substance use and incarceration (Forcibly Displaced People Network, 2023; Nematy et al, 2023).

From Circle of Friends to Friends in Nature

The international RECETAS team began by developing what the research consortium termed the Friends in Nature (FIN) intervention. It is based on the Circle of Friends model developed by the Finnish Association for the Welfare of Older People (Jansson and Pitkälä, 2021). FIN was developed to meet the objectives of RECETAS and then tailored to specific cohorts in each study site where it was implemented and evaluated. FIN is a closed group intervention designed to empower members, facilitate social connections and promote contact with nature.

FIN is a 12-week programme featuring ten weeks of nature-based activities for groups of six to eight participants that has several aspects. During the first week, the group is closed, and nature activities are selected from a menu of accessible green, blue and grey spaces, while discussions about loneliness are facilitated through images. The 'nature menu' outlines potential activities, including visits to local parks, rivers, creeks, community gardens and similar sites within the metropolitan area. Participants receive an individually tailored empowerment letter in the second week based on one-on-one conversations held during the first week.

Two facilitators guide the initial activities and gradually step back as the weeks progress, allowing participants to become more empowered to make decisions and form connections, ultimately fostering a more cohesive and independent group. By identifying with and committing to the group individuals can honour their personal heritage while establishing which may improve the likelihood of sustaining social ties after the intervention concludes (Cacioppo et al, 2015). Facilitators support the group process and work towards empowering participants to build agency, gain trust, take the lead, and shape group activities and interactions over time (Jansson et al, 2018).

Methods

To explore the feasibility of NBSP, a range of methods was employed, including ethnography, focus groups, interviews and photo-elicitation, to gain insights into the programme participants and their experiences within individual activities and the intervention. Ethnographic observations were used to explore how participants engaged with the activities and interacted with other group members and the natural environment. These observations provided valuable insights into how the group navigated cultural differences and highlighted the precarious circumstances of many participants, along with the competing priorities and psychosocial challenges that prevented some from attending each week. This data was also useful for understanding barriers and challenges to uptake and retention of the intervention.

Observation data were supplemented by two focus groups held in the first and last weeks of the programme. Participants reflected on their experiences with the nature-based activities, the emotions and feelings activities and natural settings evoked, and how perceptions of place and connections with others changed throughout the programme. Photographs that participants were invited to take during each activity further enriched these reflections. The first author facilitated the intervention and conducted four semi-structured interviews with participants to gather detailed narratives about their experiences with NBSP. In the following section, we present the findings from the feasibility study and describe the four adaptations made to facilitate recruitment and adherence throughout the intervention.

Insights from the feasibility study

Ethnographic observations provided several key insights into the feasibility of the intervention for LGBTQIA+ asylum seekers and refugees. QRASP members utilized the WhatsApp platform for regular updates and events at Many Coloured Sky. During the first week of the intervention, we collectively decided that this platform would be the most effective means of communication, as participants were less responsive to emails or phone calls. The group was culturally diverse, sometimes creating challenges in connecting due to differences in communication styles, values and social norms. Many participants had limited English language skills, complicating the organization and administration of the intervention and affecting group cohesion.

Participants had been in Australia for varying lengths – from two months to ten years. While some were more settled, others faced immediate and ongoing challenges related to housing insecurity, uncertain visa status, mental health issues and racism. The limited availability of rental properties and pressure on housing and settlement services made securing affordable housing in the inner city increasingly difficult. Consequently, many participants were forced to live in the outer suburbs of Melbourne, requiring them to spend time travelling to selected nature destinations using irregular public transport. Insecure employment also impacted participation, as many sought work or engaged in casual job arrangements. Participants often had to prioritize work to avoid losing their jobs or to attend job interviews. Additionally, psychosocial challenges such as depression and anxiety frequently hindered regular attendance, with many requiring ongoing support. Facilitators often dedicated one-on-one time to ensure participants felt supported.

Based on these insights, we made several alterations to the FIN model in consultation with our partner, Many Coloured Sky. These adaptations were necessary to ensure the study's appropriateness for LGBTQIA+ asylum seekers and refugees, addressing the multiple and interlocking factors that limited engagement with the intervention. Our approach highlights the benefits of adopting an intersectional approach (Ghasemi et al, 2021) and using technology to foster connections among a diverse cohort and promote engagement with nature. In the following section, we discuss each adaptation in detail.

Adaptation 1: Duration

We decided that a 12-week programme might be too lengthy for participants, potentially leading to a high dropout rate. The intervention was shortened to six weeks for the feasibility study instead of the 12 recommended in the FIN model. Based on a review of similar interventions focused on loneliness that suggests the most effective programmes typically last between six and 16 weeks (Morrish et al, 2023), we decided the group should meet once a week for approximately three to four hours over the six weeks. This decision was made with the understanding that meaningful change could still be achieved within this timeframe while also reducing the likelihood of dropouts. The post-feasibility studies in Melbourne will run for eight weeks.

Adaptation 2: First three-week access and empowerment letter

The closed group model initially inhibited the participation of QRASP members in the intervention as it lacked the flexibility needed to accommodate the precarious circumstances faced by many LGBTQIA+ asylum seekers and refugees. To facilitate uptake, we decided to allow new participants to join the programme until week three. This adjustment increases opportunities for QRASP members to engage in the programme and ensure an appropriate group size by enabling potential participants to balance competing priorities such as housing, work and psychosocial challenges.

This change presented additional challenges related to the FIN-modelled empowerment letter based on individual conversations conducted during week one. The letter is designed to empower individuals and promote friendships by voicing their needs, desires and aspirations for the programme. To ensure fidelity to FIN and accommodate the needs of our participants, we instead developed and distributed a collective empowerment letter reflecting the shared wishes of the group during week four.

Adaptation 3: Technological engagement

Participants were actively encouraged to take pictures of nature that appealed to them. These were used to promote conversation during interviews and focus groups. Evidence suggests that activities enhancing nature connectedness through art and creativity also help individuals feel closer to nature (Arbuthnott and Sutter, 2019; Walshe et al, 2022). The activity was initially designed to inform photo-elicitation interviews, but we found that it also promoted engagement and interaction with nature.

Participants were prompted to share their pictures in the FIN WhatsApp groups. Incorporating WhatsApp into our model represented another adaptation of the FIN framework. This online platform aimed to help those unable to attend the nature-based activity days feel connected to the group. It also served as a logistical communication tool for planning meetups and discussing weather conditions. This online communication tool is essential for coordinating nature-based activities and ensuring everyone stays informed, engaged and free to express themselves.

Through these modifications, we aimed to create a supportive and connected community that thrives both in nature and online. During our interviews, some participants who could not attend all the sessions expressed their appreciation for following conversations and viewing pictures posted on the WhatsApp platform, which helped them feel closer to the group. One participant remarked, 'Thank you for keeping the WhatsApp group active and sharing pictures and conversations; it helped me feel connected to the group during my absence while unwell.' See Figure 10.1 for a post by another participant during week 2.

Adaptation 4: Intercultural reflections

The final adaptation of FIN was the incorporation of intercultural reflections throughout the intervention. This change aimed to improve communication and reduce misconceptions by raising awareness of differences in language, communication styles and cultural conventions. By fostering a deeper understanding of other cultures, participants were supported to develop authentic and lasting relationships across cultural differences by learning to connect across cultural barriers more sensitively.

This adaptation emerged from a conversation with an interviewee who shared an experience of feeling disconnected from someone who insisted they eat the food prepared for them by another participant. The interviewee felt uncomfortable and could not understand why they were being pressured to eat. The person who prepared the meal felt hurt and misunderstood when other participants did not appreciate the effort they had put into cooking for the group. Limited understanding among members of the different

Figure 10.1: A participant shared a photo of two galahs feeding in a grassy field at Darebin Parklands in a WhatsApp group, expressing gratitude for a lovely day

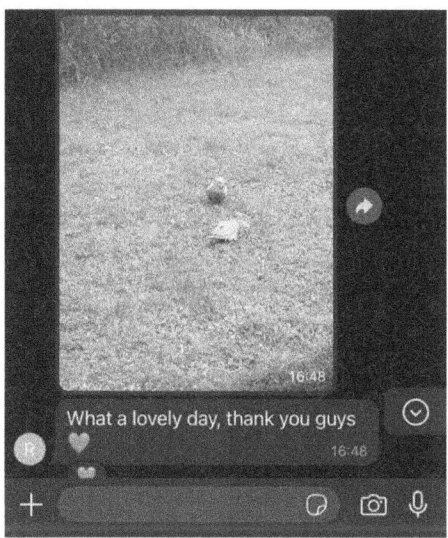

cultural conventions around sharing food inhibited social connection within this group.

The local research team facilitated intercultural reflections by sharing a meal at the beginning of each nature-based activity. This simple act prompted intercultural conversations and provided ideas for discussing topics to understand one another better. Given the cohort's cultural diversity, misunderstandings were understandable. The research team made a concerted effort to discuss culture wherever possible to avoid disconnection. Initially, the facilitator prompted these discussions, but the group began to independently initiate these conversations over time.

Food served as an excellent segue into discussions about culture and personal habits related to eating. Sharing a meal became more than just a way to fill stomachs before nature-based activities. It catalysed conversations about culture and provided an additional bonding experience. This practice helped group members connect more deeply and understand each other better, fostering a sense of community and shared experience that enriched the overall intervention.

Conclusion

The feasibility study conducted in Melbourne demonstrates the potential of an adapted FIN model for nature-based social prescribing to effectively combat loneliness and social isolation among LGBTQIA+ asylum seekers and refugees. This group, with its distinct intersectional experiences of discrimination and challenges such as language barriers, housing instability and mental health issues, necessitated adaptations to promote social connectedness and overall wellbeing through a tailored intervention. Our chapter highlights the importance of addressing both structural determinants and social connections within NBSP interventions.

This feasibility study achieved more comprehensive outcomes through close collaboration with our partner, Many Coloured Sky, and sensitive engagement with QRASP members. Qualitative methods helped to identify barriers that limited uptake of the intervention and adherence throughout the programme. Key modifications related to the duration of the intervention, technology-enhanced communication, and intercultural reflections proved essential in addressing participants' needs. We underscore the importance of customizing NBSP interventions to adapt to the unique conditions of marginalized groups.

Our insights provide a framework for future efforts to foster social inclusion and enhance mental health in diverse settings. The success of NBSP interventions depends on developing a model responsive to the target cohort's specific needs and circumstances. This approach creates new opportunities for promoting social connection through nature-based activities and social prescribing that are effectively designed for marginalized communities.

References

Allen, K.A., Gray, D.L.L., Baumeister, R.F. and Leary, M.R. (2022) 'The need to belong: a deep dive into the origins, implications, and future of a foundational construct', *Educational Psychology Review*, 34(2), 1133–1156. https://doi.org/10.1007/S10648-021-09633-6/METRICS

Arbuthnott, K.D. and Sutter, G.C. (2019) 'Songwriting for nature: increasing nature connection and well-being through musical creativity', *Environmental Education Research*, 25(9), 1300–1318. https://doi.org/10.1080/13504622.2019.1608425

Astell-Burt, T., Hartig, T., Eckermann, S., Nieuwenhuijsen, M., McMunn, A., Frumkin, H., et al (2022) 'More green, less lonely? A longitudinal cohort study', *International Journal of Epidemiology*, 51(1), 99–110. https://doi.org/10.1093/IJE/DYAB089

Cacioppo, S., Grippo, A.J., London, S., Goossens, L. and Cacioppo, J.T. (2015) 'Loneliness: clinical import and interventions', *Perspectives on Psychological Science: A Journal of the Association for Psychological Science*, 10(2), 238–249. https://doi.org/10.1177/1745691615570616

Calderón-Larrañaga, S., Greenhalgh, T., Finer, S. and Clinch, M. (2024) 'What does social prescribing look like in practice? A qualitative case study informed by practice theory', *Social Science & Medicine (1982)*, 343. https://doi.org/10.1016/J.SOCSCIMED.2024.116601

Chatterjee, H.J., Camic, P.M., Lockyer, B. and Thomson, L.J.M. (2018) 'Non-clinical community interventions: a systematised review of social prescribing schemes', *Arts & Health*, 10(2), 97–123. https://doi.org/10.1080/17533015.2017.1334002

Cochrane, B., Dixson, T. and Dixson, R. (2023) *Inhabiting Two Worlds at Once: 2023 Report into LGBTIQA+ Settlement Outcomes*, Forcibly Displaced People Network.

Frontline (2024) 'Loneliness: the hidden epidemic in low-income nations'. Available at: https://frontline.thehindu.com/news/loneliness-epidemic-third-world-countries-data-psychology-mental-health-stress/article68136000.ece (Accessed 10 October 2024).

García Rodríguez, D. (2023) 'Critiquing trends and identifying gaps in the literature on LGBTQ refugees and asylum-seekers', *Refugee Survey Quarterly*, 42(4), 518–541. https://doi.org/10.1093/RSQ/HDAD018

Ghasemi, E., Majdzadeh, R., Rajabi, F., Vedadhir, A.A., Negarandeh, R., Jamshidi, E., et al (2021) 'Applying intersectionality in designing and implementing health interventions: a scoping review', *BMC Public Health*, 21(1), 1–13. https://doi.org/10.1186/S12889-021-11449-6/TABLES/4

Goldman, N., Khanna, D., El Asmar, M.L., Qualter, P. and El-Osta, A. (2024) 'Addressing loneliness and social isolation in 52 countries: a scoping review of national policies', *BMC Public Health*, 24(1), 1–19. https://doi.org/10.1186/S12889-024-18370-8/TABLES/3

Gutin, I. (2024) 'Diagnosing social ills: theorising social determinants of health as a diagnostic category', *Sociology of Health & Illness*, 46(S1), 110–131. https://doi.org/10.1111/1467-9566.13623

Hawkley, L.C., Steptoe, A., Schumm, L.P. and Wroblewski, K. (2020) 'Comparing loneliness in England and the United States, 2014–2016: differential item functioning and risk factor prevalence and impact', *Social Science & Medicine (1982)*, 265, Article 113467. https://doi.org/10.1016/J.SOCSCIMED.2020.113467

Holt-Lunstad, J. (2021) 'Loneliness and social isolation as risk factors: the power of social connection in prevention', *American Journal of Lifestyle Medicine*, 15(5), 567–573. https://doi.org/10.1177/15598276211009454

Holt-Lunstad, J. (2022) 'Social connection as a public health issue: the evidence and a systemic framework for prioritizing the "social" in social determinants of health', *Annual Review of Public Health*, 43, 193–213. https://doi.org/10.1146/ANNUREV-PUBLHEALTH-052020-110732/CITE/REFWORKS

Infurna, F.J., Dey, N.E.Y., Avilés, T.G., Grimm, K.J., Lachman, M.E. and Gerstorf, D. (2024) 'Loneliness in midlife: historical increases and elevated levels in the United States compared with Europe', *American Psychologist*. https://doi.org/10.1037/AMP0001322

Jansson, A.H. and Pitkälä, K.H. (2021) 'Circle of friends, an encouraging intervention for alleviating loneliness', i*Journal of Nutrition, Health and Aging*, 25(6), 714–715. https://doi.org/10.1007/s12603-021-1615-5

Jansson, A.H., Savikko, N.M. and Pitkälä, K.H. (2018) 'Training professionals to implement a group model for alleviating loneliness among older people– 10-year follow-up study', *Educational Gerontology*, 44(2–3), 119–127. https://doi.org/10.1080/03601277.2017.1420005

Kang, J.W. and Oremus, M. (2023) 'Examining the combined effects of social isolation and loneliness on memory: a systematic review', *Archives of Gerontology and Geriatrics*, 104. https://doi.org/10.1016/J.ARCHGER.2022.104801

Lavelle Sachs, A., Kolster, A., Wrigley, J., Papon, V., Opacin, N., Hill, N., et al (2024) 'Connecting through nature: a systematic review of the effectiveness of nature-based social prescribing practices to combat loneliness', *Landscape and Urban Planning*, 248, Article 105071. https://doi.org/10.1016/J.LANDURBPLAN.2024.105071

Leavell, M.A., Leiferman, J.A., Gascon, M., Braddick, F., Gonzalez, J.C. and Litt, J.S. (2019) 'Nature-based social prescribing in urban settings to improve social connectedness and mental well-being: a review', *Current Environmental Health Reports*, 6(4), 297–308. https://doi.org/10.1007/S40572-019-00251-7/TABLES/1

Lim, M. (2018) 'Australian loneliness report: a survey exploring the loneliness levels of Australians and the impact on their health and wellbeing'. Available at: https://researchbank.swinburne.edu.au/file/c1d9cd16-ddbe-417f-bbc4-3d499e95bdec/1/2018-australian_loneliness_report.pdf (Accessed 15 October 2024).

Lim, M.H., Manera, K.E., Owen, K.B., Phongsavan, P. and Smith, B.J. (2022) 'Chronic and episodic loneliness and social isolation: prevalence and sociodemographic analyses from a longitudinal Australian survey'. Available at: https://doi.org/10.21203/RS.3.RS-1607036/V1 (Accessed 15 October 2024).

Litt, J.S., Coll-Planas, L., Sachs, A.L., Rochau, U., Jansson, A., Dostálová, V., et al (2024) 'Nature-based social interventions for people experiencing loneliness: the rationale and overview of the RECETAS project', *Cities & Health*, 1–14. https://doi.org/10.1080/23748834.2023.2300207

Lynam, M.J. and Cowley, S. (2007) 'Understanding marginalization as a social determinant of health', *Critical Public Health*, 17(2), 137–149. https://doi.org/10.1080/09581590601045907

Many Coloured Sky (2018) 'About'. Available at: https://www.manycolouredsky.org/about (Accessed 15 October 2024).

Markevych, I., Schoierer, J., Hartig, T., Chudnovsky, A., Hystad, P., Dzhambov, A.M., et al (2017) 'Exploring pathways linking greenspace to health: theoretical and methodological guidance', *Environmental Research*, 158, 301–317. https://doi.org/10.1016/J.ENVRES.2017.06.028

Menec, V.H., Newall, N.E., Mackenzie, C.S., Shooshtari, S. and Nowicki, S. (2019) 'Examining individual and geographic factors associated with social isolation and loneliness using Canadian Longitudinal Study on Aging (CLSA) data', *PloS One*, 14(2). https://doi.org/10.1371/JOURNAL.PONE.0211143

Morrish, N., Choudhury, S. and Medina-Lara, A. (2023) 'What works in interventions targeting loneliness: a systematic review of intervention characteristics', *BMC Public Health*, 23(1), 1–17. https://doi.org/10.1186/S12889-023-17097-2/FIGURES/2

Nematy, A., Namer, Y. and Razum, O. (2023) 'LGBTQI+ refugees' and asylum seekers' mental health: a qualitative systematic review', *Sexuality Research and Social Policy*, 20(2), 636–663. https://doi.org/10.1007/S13178-022-00705-Y/FIGURES/2

NSW Health (2022) *Social Determinants of Health: Integrated Care*. Available at: https://www.health.nsw.gov.au/integratedcare/Pages/social-determinants-of-health.aspx (Accessed 7 October 2024).

O'Cathain, A., Hoddinott, P., Lewin, S., Thomas, K.J., Young, B., Adamson, J., et al (2015) 'Maximising the impact of qualitative research in feasibility studies for randomised controlled trials: guidance for researchers', *Pilot and Feasibility Studies*, 1(1), 1–13. https://doi.org/10.1186/S40814-015-0026-Y/TABLES/2

O'Rourke, H.M. (2024) 'The global crisis of loneliness: a call for contextualised, mechanistic research', *The Lancet Healthy Longevity*, 5(4), e241–e242. https://doi.org/10.1016/S2666-7568(24)00030-8

O'Sullivan, R., Burns, A., Leavey, G., Leroi, I., Burholt, V., Lubben, J., et al (2021) 'Impact of the COVID-19 pandemic on loneliness and social isolation: a multi-country study', *International Journal of Environmental Research and Public Health*, 18(19), Article 9982. https://doi.org/10.3390/IJERPH18199982

Park, C., Majeed, A., Gill, H., Tamura, J., Ho, R.C., Mansur, R.B., et al (2020) 'The effect of loneliness on distinct health outcomes: a comprehensive review and meta-analysis', *Psychiatry Research*, 294. https://doi.org/10.1016/J.PSYCHRES.2020.113514

Peplau, L.A. and Perlman, D. (eds) (1982) *Loneliness: A Sourcebook of Current Theory, Research and Therapy*, Wiley.

Reumers, L., Bekker, M., Hilderink, H., Jansen, M., Helderman, J.K. and Ruwaard, D. (2022) 'Qualitative modelling of social determinants of health using group model building: the case of debt, poverty, and health', *International Journal for Equity in Health*, 21(1), 1–12. https://doi.org/10.1186/S12939-022-01676-7/FIGURES/5

Shokouh, S.M.H., Arab, M., Emamgholipour, S., Rashidian, A., Montazeri, A. and Zaboli, R. (2017) 'Conceptual models of social determinants of health: a narrative review', *Iranian Journal of Public Health*, 46(4), 435–446. /pmc/articles/PMC5439032/

Smith, L., López Sánchez, G.F., Pizzol, D., Yon, D.K., Oh, H., Kostev, K., et al (2024) 'Global time trends of perceived loneliness among adolescents from 28 countries in Africa, Asia, and the Americas', *Journal of Affective Disorders*, 346, 192–199. https://doi.org/10.1016/J.JAD.2023.11.032

Surkalim, D.L., Luo, M., Eres, R., Gebel, K., Van Buskirk, J., Bauman, A., et al (2022) 'The prevalence of loneliness across 113 countries: systematic review and meta-analysis', *BMJ (Clinical Research Ed.)*, 376. https://doi.org/10.1136/BMJ-2021-067068

UK Government News (2021) 'Joint message from the UK and Japanese Loneliness Ministers'. Available at: https://www.gov.uk/government/news/joint-message-from-the-uk-and-japanese-loneliness-ministers (Accessed 15 May 2023).

Walker, K., Griffiths, C., Jiang, H., Walker, K., Griffiths, C. and Jiang, H. (2023) 'Understanding the underlying mechanisms of action for successful implementation of social prescribing', *Open Journal of Preventive Medicine*, 13(2), 41–56. https://doi.org/10.4236/OJPM.2023.132004

Walshe, N., Moula, Z. and Lee, E. (2022) 'Eco-capabilities as a pathway to wellbeing and sustainability', *Sustainability*, 14(6), Article 3582. https://doi.org/10.3390/SU14063582

World Health Organization (2024) *WHO Commission on Social Connection*. Available at: https://www.who.int/groups/commission-on-social-connection (Accessed 10 June 2024).

Yarwood, V., Checchi, F., Lau, K. and Zimmerman, C. (2022) 'LGBTQI + migrants: a systematic review and conceptual framework of health, safety and wellbeing during migration', *International Journal of Environmental Research and Public Health*, 19(2). https://doi.org/10.3390/IJERPH19020869

11

Social Connectedness in Pandemic Times: A Case Study of Australia's Italian-Background Community

Simone Battiston and Damon Alexander

Introduction

Migrant communities around the world have been disproportionately affected by the COVID-19 pandemic, amplifying pre-existing health and psychosocial vulnerabilities, increasing risks of financial hardship and dislocating critical support networks (Choudhari, 2020; Bhandari et al, 2021; James et al, 2024). In Australia, asylum seekers, refugees and temporary visa holders have been particularly affected by the pandemic and the policies that were put in place to contain it. Measures that excluded these migrant groups from wage subsidies like JobKeeper and other forms of welfare support heightened their already precarious economic standing (Clibborn and Wright, 2020). At the same time, travel restrictions, extended quarantine measures and prolonged lockdowns across parts of the country disrupted support networks and social connections, contributing to heightened mental health vulnerabilities and increased social isolation (Mares et al, 2021).

Against this backdrop, the aim of this study is to explore the perceived impact of COVID-19 on one of Australia's most established migrant populations – the Italian-Australian community – and to examine how social ties were used to cope with the effects of the pandemic. This subpopulation group is of particular interest for its size and its tendency to rely on bonding ties. According to the latest Australian Bureau of Statistics Census (2021), Australia is home to 1.1 million residents who claim Italian ancestry (wholly or partly) – this is one of the largest groups in the country for ancestry responses. The behaviour of familial and bonding-oriented Italian networks (Esping-Andersen, 2009), probed in Australia by Baldassar and colleagues

(Baldassar, 2001; Baldassar et al, 2012; Baldassar and Pyke, 2014), has yet to be examined in times of crisis such as the pandemic.

Building on previous studies of migrant social networks in the Australian context (for example, Patulny, 2015), this study seeks to contribute to the literature by investigating the impact of the COVID-19 pandemic on social connectedness, bearing in mind that migrant-background communities present different characteristics of social capital to the other cohorts of the population as well as within them.

Background and literature review

Australia reported its first case of COVID-19 on 25 January 2020. Within a week, the Australian government banned entry of foreign nationals travelling from mainland China and ordered Australian citizens returning from China to self-quarantine for 14 days (Storen and Corrigan, 2020). Entry restrictions were imposed on travellers from other countries, including Italy, from 11 March, with the national border closed to all non-citizens and non-residents from 20 March 2020. Within a week, 14-day quarantine requirements were introduced for all returning travellers, along with an outward ban on Australians travelling overseas (Australian National Audit Office, 2021). Internally, a range of travel restrictions were introduced, with Tasmania, Western Australia, South Australia, Northern Territory and Queensland closing their borders to non-essential travel across March/April. Victoria and New South Wales closed their shared border in July 2020 (Storen and Corrigan, 2020). Increasingly strict social distancing measures were also introduced to minimize community transmission as part of state and federal government responses to the first wave. This included 'stay at home' orders with people only able to leave their homes for essential purposes (shopping for essential items; care giving; seeking medical treatment; or exercising); restrictions on hosting indoor and outdoor events; limits on family gatherings; a shift to remote learning for schools and universities; and the closure of non-essential services such as pubs, clubs, restaurants and places of worship (Bosely and Landis-Hanley, 2020).

While largely successful in combating the first wave of the pandemic, a resurgence of cases in Victoria in June 2020 following hotel quarantine failures led to the reintroduction of strict lockdowns with further restrictions on movement and social interaction imposed (Hurst and Taylor, 2020). Throughout the remainder of 2020 and 2021, sporadic lockdowns were enforced at state and regional levels in response to third-wave outbreaks driven by Delta and Omicron variants, with international travel and border restrictions remaining until February 2022.

While no section of Australian society escaped the effects of COVID-19 across this period, the impact of the pandemic on migrants and migrant background communities was particularly hard felt. As Mental Health Australia notes, multicultural communities rely heavily on family and social networks for support in times of crisis and 'the impact of social isolation can be magnified in comparison to the mainstream population' (Mental Health Australia, 2022: 34). In a study of culturally and linguistically diverse communities in Greater Western Sydney, Mude et al (2021) reported significant effects on income and sense of safety, with the pandemic also causing disruptions to social support group activities, access to social services, engagement with work and school, mental health and housing. Specific features of the Australian government's response to COVID-19, such as border closures and the exclusion of international students, refugees and temporary visa holders from economic assistance measures, had a particularly punitive impact on these groups, with temporary residents forced to rely on multicultural community groups, universities, churches and charities for support (O'Sullivan et al, 2020). Poor access to public health information via languages other than English also left migrant communities more vulnerable to COVID-19, increasing barriers to accessing health and support services and leaving them more open to misinformation (McCaffery et al, 2020; O'Sullivan et al, 2020; Shakespeare-Finch et al, 2020). While comparative empirical analysis is limited in the Australian context, existing research suggests that culturally and linguistically diverse communities reported greater financial impacts, higher levels of stress, and greater levels of anxiety as a result of the pandemic than those speaking English at home (Muscat et al, 2022).

Social capital and social connectedness in times of crisis

As Robert Putnam noted in his influential work *Bowling Alone* (2000: 326), 'social connectedness matters to our lives in the most profound way ... [and] ... is one of the most powerful determinants of our well-being'. Social connections generate value through the formation of social capital and provide access to critical resources (for example, emotional support, financial support and information). Social capital has also been essential in helping individuals and communities cope with crises such as disaster events and pandemics. As Dynes (2006) argues, though often overlooked, social capital is our most significant resource in responding to disaster events and crises such as terrorism. High levels of bonding social capital – ties to family and close friends – are positively linked to greater access to early disaster warnings, more immediate recovery assistance, shelter and supplies, and higher levels of disaster resilience. Bridging social capital, which refers to weaker ties with acquaintances or social groups, provides access to information and external resources critical for disaster recovery efforts. Meanwhile, linking social capital – ties between citizens and those in power – connects affected individuals to government and relief agencies (Aldrich and Meyer, 2015).

The important role of social capital and connectedness in responding to COVID-19 has been widely recognized. As Makridis and Wu (2021) have noted, social capital has proven critical in containing disease outbreaks and pandemics. High levels of social capital in communities often correlate with better health outcomes, improved access to healthcare and information, reduced exposure to disease, and greater access to political power, policy processes and accountability measures. Additionally, higher levels of trust, social norms and reciprocity lead to more widespread observance of public health measures, such as testing regimes, personal hygiene, mask-wearing, physical distancing and vaccination (see, for example, Wu et al, 2020; Alfano and Ercolano, 2021; Bartscher et al, 2021; Brodeur et al, 2021).

In Australia, research on the effects of social capital and social connectedness on individual and community resilience in the face of the pandemic remains limited. Green et al (2022) reported that a lack of social capital among vulnerable populations such as women and international students contributed to negative mental health and wellbeing outcomes during this period. Patulny and Bower (2022) noted increasing levels of isolation and loneliness resulting from lockdowns, with those possessing limited social capital among the most vulnerable. Meanwhile, Carrasco et al (2023) noted both the positive and potentially exclusionary impact of social connections within resident Horn of Africa communities in managing the impact of the pandemic, particularly during the controversial lockdown of the North Melbourne and Flemington Public Housing Towers early in the pandemic.

As Ryan et al (2015: 3) point out, migration studies have long drawn on the interlinked concepts of social networks and social capital, with social networks 'widely recognised as a key source of migrants' capital, facilitating migration and settlement as well as the maintenance of transnational lives'. Patulny (2015: 208) argues that social capital is a useful theoretical lens for exploring the diverse social connections within migrant communities and how these networks serve multiple purposes, ranging from ' "getting by" in localized, day-to-day life, or "getting ahead" in terms of improving employment, business and community engagement prospects'. In this study we employ social capital as a framework to explore how Italian-Australian migrants used social connections and the social resources embedded in networks to cope with the impact of COVID-19.

Methodology

To assess the perceived impact of the pandemic and to examine how different forms of social capital were mobilized, this study used survey data (n=483) drawn from Australia's Italian-background population. Data was collected primarily via an online survey instrument using Qualtrics (n=449) supplemented by a small number of paper-based versions of the survey distributed at community events (n=34). To facilitate responses, the questions were available in both English and Italian, removing any potential language barrier. The sample frame included self-identified Italian nationals living in Australia (temporarily or permanently) and Australian citizens of Italian origin (that is, born in Italy) or ancestry (that is, born in Australia) aged 18 years and over, with data collected between 19 November 2022 and 28 April 2023.

Survey recruitment was supported by paid nationwide advertising in Italian-language media outlets and organic social media advertising. The survey link was also distributed through Italian-Australian community organizations via Comites Melbourne (partial project funder), personal networks and chain referrals.

The survey included 36 questions exploring the perceived impact of COVID-19 (health, financial, social), access and provision of support during the pandemic, trust and reciprocity, and attitudes towards pandemic-related government policy. Demographic data covered basic characteristics such as age, gender, income, education and citizenship status. A summary of this data is provided in Table 11.1. Unfortunately, gaps remain in our understanding of the socioeconomic and demographic characteristics of the Italian-Australian community and its various sub-cohorts (Baldassar, 2005; Baldassar et al, 2012), which makes assessing the representative nature of our sample impossible. The sample itself is also heavily skewed on education (high) and income (high) variables, and despite attempts at national coverage, remains Victorian-centric.

Research suggests a strong positive correlation between social capital, social connectedness and education status (Brehm and Rahn, 1997; Putnam, 2000; Huang et al, 2009; Alexander et al 2012) so this is likely to impact the results by inflating the level of social capital reported. Similarly, the overrepresentation of Victorians in the sample may inflate the pandemic effects reported, given the more severe impact of COVID-19 in Victoria. Combined with the self-selection bias associated with online surveys (Bethlehem, 2010; Schaurer and Weiß, 2020), care should be taken in interpreting and generalizing the results reported.

Impact of COVID-19 among Italian-Australians

As a starting point, we asked respondents to self-report on the personal impact of COVID-19 across a range of areas, including financial wellbeing, physical health, mental health and sense of safety. Given the unprecedented restrictions on interpersonal contact across much of Australia during multiple lockdown phases during the pandemic and limitations on

Table 11.1: Participant characteristics

	N	Survey responses (%)	Australia (%)*
Gender			
Female	244	58.9	50.7
Male	164	39.6	49.3
Prefer not to say	6	1.4	
Age groups (years)			
18–34	46	25.1	22.7
35–64	92	50.3	38.3
65 or over	45	24.6	17.2
Not stated	300		
Educational level (bachelor degree or above)	328	80.0	26.3
Country of birth			
Italy	283	68.5	0.6
Australia	125	30.3	66.9
Other	5	1.2	

Source: * Australian Bureau of Statistics, 2021 Census

internal and external travel, we were particularly interested in exploring COVID-19's impact on social connectivity – specifically, the ability to connect to important sources of social support such as family and friends, work colleagues, community groups and associations, and faith-based organizations. A five-point Likert scale was used to measure impact across these areas, with potential responses ranging from 'no impact at all' to 'a great deal of impact'. To simplify the analysis and discussion, these responses have been converted to 'low impact', 'moderate impact' and 'high impact', with results reported in Table 11.2.

In terms of the overall impact of COVID-19, the results suggest a relatively high level of resilience across the dimensions examined, with the most significant impact reported on mental health and sense of safety. A large majority (68 per cent) reported minimal impact on financial wellbeing. This most likely reflects the overrepresentation of mid- and high-income white-collar professionals in our survey cohort, many of whom were able to transition to 'work from home' arrangements during lockdown phases of the pandemic. This is supported by the fact that 69 per cent of respondents reported minimal impact on their ability to carry out their

Table 11.2: Self-reported impact of COVID-19 across life fields

Area of impact	Low impact (%)	Moderate impact (%)	High impact (%)
Financial wellbeing	68.4	19.3	12.3
Ability to carry out usual paid work	68.7	15.1	16.2
Physical health	64.8	20.0	15.2
Sense of safety	53.8	26.7	19.5
Mental health	49.7	22.7	27.7

normal paid work. Similarly, 65 per cent reported only minimal impact on physical health, with just 15 per cent reporting high impact in this area. More significant effects were noted for the sense of safety and mental health measures, with almost half of respondents indicating moderate to high impacts on the former, and just over 50 per cent reporting moderate to high impacts on mental health.

A different picture emerges on the measures relating directly to 'social connectivity'. As Table 11.3 indicates, 49 per cent of respondents reported that COVID-19 had a high impact on their ability to connect with family and friends, with almost 40 per cent reporting a high impact on connections with community groups, clubs and associations. In contrast, relatively minimal effects were recorded for the ability to connect with religious faith (92 per cent low or moderate impact). The impact of closed national borders and restrictions on inter-state travel across periods in the pandemic is clearly evident, with 79 per cent reporting that COVID-19 had a high impact on international travel plans and 62 per cent on inter-state travel across much of Australia.

These results suggest that while our survey cohort appears to have weathered the financial impact of the pandemic reasonably successfully, the emotional and mental toll has been more challenging. Barriers to normal social interaction and the crucial support provided by family, friends and community organizations across the pandemic are likely to have exacerbated this toll.

Providing and accessing support

Table 11.4 reports on the extent to which survey respondents provided different types of economic and social support to people living outside their immediate household during the COVID-19 pandemic as well as accessing support themselves. As Table 11.4 indicates, just under 17 per cent of respondents reported providing financial support to others during the pandemic, with 24 per cent providing help for others to access medical

Table 11.3: Self-reported impact of COVID-19 on social connection

Mode of connection	Low impact (%)	Moderate impact (%)	High impact (%)
Ability to connect with family and friends	28.0	23.2	48.8
Ability to connect with community groups, clubs and associations	36.6	23.6	39.8
Ability to connect with religious faith	82.3	9.6	8.1
Travel inter-state	26.0	12.3	61.8
Travel overseas	15.1	5.7	79.1

Table 11.4: Respondent provision and access of support measures during COVID-19

Support type	Provided support (%)	Accessed support (%)
Financial support	16.8	10.5
Shopping support	46.8	19.2
Help accessing medical services	23.9	10.0
Emotional support	68.2	41.3
Information support	64.8	46.0

services. Just under half of respondents helped others with their shopping, with 68 per cent and 65 per cent providing emotional and information support, respectively. Respondents were less likely to access help across all support categories examined but reported making significant use of their social connections during the pandemic. A relatively low 10 per cent accessed financial support from those outside their household. This reflects the low number of respondents reporting a heavy financial impact due to the pandemic (12 per cent). Ten per cent drew on support to access medical services, with 19 per cent using support for shopping. Emotional and information support were the categories most frequently drawn on at 41 per cent and 46 per cent, respectively.

To explore the kinds of social resources drawn on for different tasks during the pandemic, we asked respondents to identify the nature of their relationship with those providing support across each support category used. As Table 11.5 indicates, the primary sources of financial support sought by respondents were family (32 per cent) and friends (25 per cent). However, community and Italian-Australian organizations also played a prominent role here (20 and 11 per cent, respectively). Support for practical day-to-day functions such as shopping and accessing medical services was also heavily

Table 11.5: Support network composition by support type: relationship to ego

	Financial support (%)	Shopping support (%)	Accessing medical support (%)	Emotional support (%)	Information support (%)
Family	31.8	41.1	38.0	26.7	20.5
Friends	25.0	28.2	44.0	37.8	31.3
Neighbours	4.5	15.3	8.0	10.6	6.1
Work colleagues	2.3	4.0	2.0	15.9	20.2
Religious groups	4.5	2.4	2.0	1.9	0.6
Community organizations	20.5	8.9	4.0	5.3	16.4
Italian-Australian organization	11.4	0.0	2.0	1.9	5.0
Total	100.0	100.0	100.0	100.0	100.0

skewed towards strong ties, with family and friends making up 69 per cent of shopping support ties and 82 per cent for help accessing medical services. Emotional support ties were more dispersed – family and friends remained prominent (65 per cent combined), while work colleagues (16 per cent) and neighbours (11 per cent) were also significant. Sources of information support were the most diverse reported, with friends (31 per cent), community organizations and groups (22 per cent combined), family (20 per cent), and work colleagues (20 per cent) all playing a prominent role.

Discussion

As already noted, research suggests migrant communities have been disproportionately affected by the pandemic. In Australia, migrants have faced greater barriers to accessing health and support services and information (McCaffery et al, 2020; O'Sullivan et al, 2020; Shakespeare-Finch et al, 2020); more damaging financial impacts; higher levels of stress; and greater levels of anxiety as a result of the pandemic (Muscat et al, 2022). Our findings point to similar impacts within Australia's Italian migrant-background community but also point towards a high level of resilience in the face of the pandemic's challenges. Disruptions to work and financial wellbeing during COVID-19 were minimal for a large proportion of our cohort, with health-related impacts also relatively minor for all but a few. No doubt this partially reflects the socioeconomic profile of our cohort, which is characterized by higher-than-average income and education levels – both factors that research suggests have cushioned against the economic and health impacts of the pandemic (see, for example, Australian Institute of Health and Welfare, 2021; Flavel and Baum, 2022). As one of the larger and more historically integrated non-English-speaking ancestry groups, the Italian-Australian community was also arguably better placed to withstand the worst pandemic elements than less prominent and more recently arrived populations within the broader migrant community.

Notwithstanding this resilience, and in line with other research reported in this chapter, our respondents reported significant impacts on their sense of safety during the pandemic and a marked decline in self-reported mental health. This most likely reflects the stress, uncertainty and anxiety induced by COVID-19 but also the impact of lockdowns and border restrictions in limiting access to normal social connections and supports. Importantly, nearly half of our respondents noted that these measures greatly impacted their ability to connect with family and friends, thus isolating them from important sources of support during the pandemic. Connections to community groups, clubs and associations were also negatively affected. Restrictions on domestic and international travel during the pandemic point to further disruptions to established patterns of social interaction and potential isolation from support networks. While all Australians suffered such disruptions, we can speculate that our respondents, and the migrant community more generally, were more heavily impacted due to the critical role social networks play in supporting migration and settlement and in maintaining transnational lives (Ryan et al, 2015).

The importance of social networks in coping with the impact of the pandemic is evident from our results. Respondents mobilized significant levels of network capital, providing instrumental support such as shopping, accessing pandemic-related information, obtaining medical help and offering emotional support. Within the literature on social capital and social networks, there is ongoing debate regarding the relative importance of bonding ties (connections to family and close friends) versus bridging ties (connections to acquaintances or work colleagues) in providing access to various socially embedded resources (see, for example, Granovetter, 1973; Krackhardt, 1992; Burt, 1992; 2005; Teorell, 2003).

Bonding ties may offer more secure access to resources due to the higher motivation of close connections to provide assistance. In contrast, bridging ties tend to link individuals with more diverse and socially distant groups, potentially broadening access to a wider range of resources. Thus, we might expect family and close friends to be more reliable sources of help in areas such as finance, health and emotional support, where higher levels of trust are essential. At the same time, more distant ties may play a more prominent role in providing advice or information.

The relational composition of support networks activated by our respondents largely aligns with these expected patterns, suggesting that both types of networks have been important in coping with the pandemic in different ways. Family and friends emerged as the primary source of support across all five areas measured: financial, shopping, medical, emotional and informational. Neighbours and work colleagues also played significant roles, particularly in instrumental tasks such as shopping and information-seeking, but surprisingly, they also provided emotional support. Further research will explore how the composition of these networks differs across socioeconomic categories, including gender and education, as well as by migrant status and income.

Conclusion

The burgeoning literature on the impact of COVID-19 indicates that the burden of the pandemic has been borne inequitably, highlighting the need for inclusive policies and targeted support. Migrant-background communities, already among the more socially and economically disadvantaged populations in Australia, have proven particularly vulnerable to the pandemic's effects. In a culturally and linguistically diverse country like Australia, where nearly one in two residents is either born abroad or has at least one parent born abroad (ABS, 2022), it is critical to gain a clearer understanding of the impact of large-scale disasters such as the pandemic and how to navigate such challenges successfully. This study focused on the established yet complex Italian-Australian community, examining how the pandemic impacted across multiple dimensions and how social connections were mobilized in response.

The results suggest that while members of the Italian-Australian community weathered the financial and health impacts of COVID-19 relatively well, a significant mental health and emotional toll was exacted. Sudden changes to habitual social interactions, severance of crucial support networks and the inability to travel have likely intensified the pandemic. The chapter recounts the extent to which our respondents provided different forms of economic and social support to people living outside their immediate household and how they accessed such support during the pandemic, with emotional and information support the categories most frequently provided and drawn on. The relational composition of support networks activated during the pandemic largely conformed to expected patterns. Finance, medical access and emotional support, where higher levels of trust are typically required, tended to be concentrated in family and friendship ties (strong ties). In contrast, more distant connections through community organizations, work colleagues and, to a degree, neighbours (weak ties) provided important access to information.

The exploratory nature of this study and the methodological limitations limit our interpretation of the survey data and prevent us from generalizing the research findings. However, the data points to where the impact of the pandemic was most acutely felt (that is, mental health and mobility) and the social connections activated when seeking and offering different types of support. It sheds light on how and where support is exchanged in migrant-background communities and the important role social capital plays in times of crisis.

References

Aldrich, D.P. and Meyer, M.A. (2015) 'Social capital and community resilience', *American Behavioral Scientist*, 59(2), 254–269.

Alexander, D.T., Barraket, J., Lewis, J.M. and Considine, M. (2012) 'Civic engagement and associationalism: the impact of group membership scope versus intensity of participation', *European Sociological Review*, 28(1), 43–58.

Alfano, V. and Ercolano, S. (2021) 'Social capital, quality of institutions and lockdown: evidence from Italian provinces', *Structural Change and Economic Dynamics*, 59, 31–41.

ABS (Australian Bureau of Statistics) (2022) '2021 Census: Nearly half of Australians have a parent born overseas'. Available at: https://www.abs.gov.au/media-centre/media-releases/2021-census-nearly-half-australians-have-parent-born-overseas (Accessed 15 March 2025).

Australian Institute of Health and Welfare (2021) *The First Year of COVID-19 in Australia: Direct and Indirect Health Effects*, AIHW. Available at: https://www.aihw.gov.au/reports/burden-of-disease/the-first-year-of-covid-19-in-australia/summary (Accessed 21 November 2024).

Australian National Audit Office (2021) 'Management of international travel restrictions during COVID-19'. Available at: https://www.anao.gov.au/work/performance-audit/management-international-travel-restrictions-during-covid-19 (Accessed 15 November 2023).

Baldassar, L. (2001) *Visits Home: Migration Experiences Between Italy and Australia*, Melbourne University Press.

Baldassar, L.V. (2005) 'Italians in Australia', in M. Ember, C.R. Ember and I. Skoggard (eds) *Encyclopedia of Diasporas*, Springer, pp 850–864.

Baldassar, L. and Pyke, J. (2014) 'Intra-diaspora knowledge transfer and "new" Italian migration', *International Migration*, 52(4), 128–143.

Baldassar, L., Pyke, J. and Ben-Moshe, D. (2012) *The Italian Diasporas in Australia: Current and Potential Links with the Homeland*, Centre for Citizen and Globalisation, Deakin University.

Bartscher, A.K., Seitz, S., Siegloch, S., Slotwinski, M. and Wehrhöfer, N. (2021) 'Social capital and the spread of COVID-19: insights from European countries', *Journal of Health Economics*, 80, Article 102531.

Bethlehem, J. (2010) 'Selection bias in web surveys', *International Statistical Review*, 78(2), 161–188.

Bhandari, D., Kotera, Y., Ozaki, A., Abeysinghe, S., Kosaka, M. and Tanimoto, T. (2021) 'COVID-19: challenges faced by Nepalese migrants living in Japan', *BMC Public Health*, 21, Article 752.

Boseley, M. and Landis-Hanley, J. (2020) 'Social distancing rules explained: Australia's current state by state coronavirus guidelines', *The Guardian*. Available at: https://www.theguardian.com/australia-news/2020/may/20/social-distancing-rules-australia-when-will-end-guidelines-coronavirus-laws-physical-covid-19-restrictions-signs-posters-nsw-victoria-qld-queensland-act-sa-wa-nt-tasmania (Accessed 23 May 2024).

Brehm, J. and Rahn, W. (1997) 'Individual-level evidence for the causes and consequences of social capital', *American Journal of Political Science*, 41(3), 999–1023.

Brodeur, A., Grigoryeva, I. and Kattan, L. (2021) 'Stay-at-home orders, social distancing, and trust', *Journal of Population Economics*, 34, 1321–1354.

Burt, R.S. (1992) *Structural Holes: The Social Structure of Competition*, Harvard University Press.

Burt, R.S. (2005) *Brokerage and Closure: An Introduction to Social Capital*, Oxford University Press.

Carrasco, S., Dangol, N. and Faleh, M. (2023) 'Rethinking social networks in responding to COVID-19: the case of African migrants in Melbourne's public housing', *International Journal of Disaster Risk Reduction*, 98, Article 104073.

Choudhari, R. (2020) 'COVID 19 pandemic: mental health challenges of internal migrant workers of India', *Asian Journal of Psychiatry*, 54, Article 102254.

Clibborn, S. and Wright, C.F. (2020) 'COVID-19 and the policy-induced vulnerabilities of temporary migrant workers in Australia', *Journal of Australian Political Economy*, 85, 62–70.

Dynes, R. (2006) 'Social capital: dealing with community emergencies', *Homeland Security Affairs*, 2(2), 1–26.

Esping-Andersen, G. (2009) *Incomplete Revolution: Adapting Welfare States to Women's New Roles*, John Wiley.

Flavel, J. and Baum, F. (2022) 'The influence of socio-economic conditions on the epidemiology of COVID-19 in Australia', *The Medical Journal of Australia*, 216(7), 344–345.

Granovetter, M.S. (1973) 'The strength of weak ties', *American Journal of Sociology*, 78(6), 1360–1380.

Green, H., Fernandez, R., Moxham, L. and MacPhail, C. (2022) 'Social capital and wellbeing among Australian adults during the COVID-19 pandemic: a qualitative study', *BMC Public Health*, 22, Article 2406.

Huang, J., van den Brink, H.M. and Groot, W. (2009) 'A meta-analysis of the effect of education on social capital', *Economics of Education Review*, 28(4), 454–64.

Hurst, D. and Taylor, J. (2020) 'Victoria announces stage four Coronavirus lockdown restrictions including overnight curfew', *The Guardian*. Available at: https://www.theguardian.com/australia-news/2020/aug/02/victoria-premier-daniel-andrews-stage-four-coronavirus-lockdown-restrictions-melbourne-covid-19 (Accessed 7 May 2022).

James, P.B., Gatwiri, K., Mwanri, L. and Wardle, J. (2024) 'Impacts of COVID-19 on African migrants' wellbeing, and their coping strategies in urban and regional New South Wales, Australia: a qualitative study', *Journal of Racial and Ethnic Health Disparities*, 11, 3523–3536.

Krackhardt, D. (1992) 'The strength of strong ties: the importance of philos in organizations', in N. Nohria and R.G. Eccles (eds) *Networks and Organizations*, Harvard Business School Press, pp 216–39.

Makridis, C.A. and Wu, C. (2021) 'How social capital helps communities weather the COVID-19 pandemic', *PLoS ONE*, 16(1), e0245135.

Mares, S., Jenkins, K., Lutton, S. and Newman Am, L. (2021) 'Impact of COVID-19 on the mental health needs of asylum seekers in Australia', *Australasian Psychiatry*, 29(4), 417–419.

McCaffery, K.J., Dodd, R.H., Cvejic, E., Ayrek, J., Batcup, C., Isautier, J.M.J., et al (2020) 'Health literacy and disparities in COVID-19-related knowledge, attitudes, beliefs and behaviours in Australia', *Public Health Research & Practice*, 30(4), Article e30342012.

Mental Health Australia (2022) *Mental Health During the COVID-19 Pandemic in Italian, Turkish and Vietnamese Communities*. Available at: https://embracementalhealth.org.au/service-providers/knowledge-hub/mental-health-during-covid-19-pandemic-italian-turkish-and (Accessed 20 February 2025).

Mude, W., Meru, C., Njue, C. and Fanany, R. (2021) 'A cross-sectional study of COVID-19 impacts in culturally and linguistically diverse communities in Greater Western Sydney, Australia', *BMC Public Health*, 21(1), Article 2081.

Muscat, D.M., Ayre, J., Mac, O., Batcup, C., Cvejic, E., Pickles, K., et al (2022) 'Psychological, social and financial impacts of COVID-19 on culturally and linguistically diverse communities in Sydney, Australia', *BMJ Open*, 12, e058323.

O'Sullivan, D., Rahamathulla, M. and Pawar, M. (2020) 'The impact and implications of COVID-19: an Australian perspective', *The International Journal of Community and Social Development*, 2(2), 134–151.

Patulny, R. (2015) 'A spectrum of integration: examining combinations of bonding and bridging social capital and network heterogeneity amongst Australian refugee and skilled migrants', in L. Ryan, U. Erel and A. D'Angelo (eds) *Migrant Capital: Networks, Identities and Strategies*, Palgrave Macmillan, pp 207–229.

Patulny, R. and Bower, M. (2022) 'Beware the "loneliness gap"? Examining emerging inequalities and long-term risks of loneliness and isolation emerging from COVID-19', *Australian Journal of Social Issues*, 57(3), 562–583.

Putnam, R.D. (2000) *Bowling Alone: The Collapse and Revival of American Community*, Simon & Schuster.

Ryan, L., Erel, U. and D'Angelo, A. (2015) 'Introduction: understanding "migrant capital"', in L. Ryan, U. Erel and A. D'Angelo (eds) *Migrant Capital: Networks, Identities and Strategies*, Palgrave Macmillan, pp 3–17.

Schaurer, I. and Weiß, B. (2020) 'Investigating selection bias of online surveys on Coronavirus-related behavioral outcomes', *Survey Research Methods*, 14(2), 103–108.

Shakespeare-Finch, J., Bowen-Salter, H., Cashin, M., Badawi, A., Wells, R., Rosenbaum, S., et al (2020) 'COVID-19: an Australian perspective', *Journal of Loss and Trauma*, 25(8), 662–672.

Storen, R. and Corrigan, N. (2020) 'COVID-19: a chronology of state and territory government announcements (up until 30 June 2020)', Research Paper Series, 2020–21, Department of Parliamentary Service, Parliament of Australia.

Teorell, J. (2003) 'Linking social capital to political participation: voluntary associations and networks of recruitment in Sweden', *Scandinavian Political Studies*, 26(1), 49–66.

Wu, C., Wilkes, R., Fairbrother, M. and Giordano, G. (2020) 'Social capital, trust, and state Coronavirus testing', *Contexts*. Available at: https://contexts.org/blog/healthcare-and-critical-infrastructure/#wu (Accessed 1 May 2020).

12

Local Place-Based Social Connection in Urban Fringe Areas: Learning from Resident Experiences

Jane Farmer, Tracy De Cotta, Annette Kroen and Andrew Butt

Introduction

The urban fringe local government areas of Australian capital cities have some of the fastest-growing populations in the world. Incorporating new housing developments with established urban and rural settlements, these locations are home to a diverse mix of international immigrants, long-term Australians and Indigenous Peoples.

Despite long-standing policy approaches seeking to consolidate development in Australia's inner cities, building on previously 'greenfield' urban fringe sites remains the primary location for new affordable housing. The rapid growth of these fringe suburbs is not adequately supported by social infrastructure (that is, places where people can meet, such as community hubs, leisure centres, libraries and cafés) or services focused on social wellbeing (Henderson, 2019). There are also delays in providing public transport (Kroen et al, 2023), and local employment opportunities are often limited. This results in long commutes – typically by car – to reach distant workplaces (Nicholls et al, 2018). These challenges of suburban living limit the time available for local social interactions.

Globally, newly developing areas are associated with a high risk of loneliness. The lack of 'bumping places' (social infrastructure) where locals literally bump into each other and the related lack of interaction with local 'brokers' and 'community connectors' like community development workers, librarians and baristas (Wallace et al, 2019) detract from building the web of network ties associated with local place-based communities (Kroen et al, 2022).

This chapter focuses on the idea that councils and community organizations could make the most effective use of scarce resources if they focused on fostering a social connection between local people with other local people in and with *their local places*. This contrasts with some current approaches that target social isolation without foregrounding the benefits of connecting with others living locally. Social prescribing initiatives (where lonely people are assigned to activities or supporters) are examples where connecting individuals is referenced (Consumers Health Forum of Australia, 2019). Grounding the connecting activities near where people live – helping to build connected communities of place – is often not explicitly highlighted, however. Evidence suggests a range of valuable social outcomes from connecting residents in their local locations (Aldrich and Meyer, 2015). When discussing place here, we mean the 'neighbourhood' or set of streets where people live – loosely, where you could walk in your home area in 15–20 minutes (Victoria State Government, 2021).

This chapter presents learning from how urban fringe residents currently connect (or don't) in local places. The chapter draws on data from a large Australian Research Council-funded study (2022–2025). It explores how residents currently reference the physical features of their locale and interactions with people who live around them when discussing their social connection. The chapter highlights opportunities and concludes with recommendations for policy and practice. While findings are from Melbourne, they have international relevance as rapid peri-urban growth is also widely reported for parts of Asia, North America and Europe (OECD et al, 2021).

Background

Community organizations working in Australian urban fringe suburbs often have goals to address social isolation and related challenges. For example, health organizations run positive ageing and social prescribing programmes. Similarly, councils and emergency agencies run programmes to grow social capital and resilience to cope with climate-related hazards; for example, the Red Cross' RediCommunities programme supports groups to identify and carry out collective action.

Simultaneously, there are multiple barriers to residents connecting. Evidence suggests that people moving to new suburbs are often motivated by low house prices and expect to live there for only a short time (Roggenbuck, 2019). They aspire to then move to suburbs with more amenities (Kroen and Goodman, 2022). This residential impermanence is problematic for developing connected communities, as place attachment and sense of belonging grow with the length of time residing in an area (Lewicka, 2011). To counter an expectation of impermanence, research suggests councils and community organizations should support local people to have collective social experiences that help to build memories linking people to local places, evoking a sense of rootedness over time (Matsunobu, 2018). This means that 'a place is not just tied to individuals, but also ties individuals to each other' (Wheele et al, 2023: 11).

While urban strategies often emphasize the importance of incorporating engaging features – such as pathways, playgrounds or public art – into suburban areas, there is a notable lack of guidance on how organizations can enable social connection by activating these local places in fringe suburbs. That is, there is an absence of a clear theory of change that outlines how to engage with these locations and effectively connect people with them.

In Victoria, Australia where our study was conducted, the Local Government Act requires that councils generate health, wellbeing and a shared community vision through community engagement (Victoria State Government, 2020). While connecting people *in relation to place* is implied, it is not explicitly stated. Similarly, state guidance for new urban developments (Victorian Planning Authority, 2021) emphasizes the need to provide social infrastructure. This aligns with the place-making theory that suggests 'quality places' help people to interact and make sense of their environment (Wheele et al, 2023). The urban development guidelines and Act support but don't explain how to 'create an attachment or connection between the community member and the place' (Ellery et al, 2021: 62).

Furthermore, discussions with council staff as part of our study revealed uncertainty about the parameters of council responsibility for fostering social connection when planning services in new suburbs. The ill-defined expectation that councils will step in after houses are built to somehow 'in-fill' social connections in emerging local areas suggests the need for specific guidance on this topic.

The relationships between people, other people and local places reflect evolving understandings of the concept of 'neighbourhood' over time (Drilling and Schnur, 2019). In the 1970s, there was interest in neighbourhoods as 'centres of meaning constructed out of lived experience' (Drilling and Schnur, 2019: 51) generated through daily practice. However, more recently, under the 'new mobilities paradigm' (van Kempen and Wissink, 2014), the concept of neighbourhood has lost its centrality. In this postmodern society, characterized by 'flows' enabled by digital technologies (Castells, 1999), social practices are increasingly understood as 'de-territorialised' (Drilling and Schnur, 2019: 56). While other chapters in this book focus on aspatial connection through communities of interest and modes such as social media – both significant in current society – research continues to emphasize the important role of geographical, place-based communities (Lloyd et al, 2016; Roggenbuck, 2019).

Social connection theoretical lens

We use Farmer et al's conceptual framework to understand and depict essential elements of social connection (2021; 2025). This framework was developed through a literature review and translated for practice through co-design sessions with community development workers. It intends to provide a clear and accessible explanation of social connection for councils, health organizations and community services.

The framework addresses aspects of social connection that community practitioners can influence by supporting community members as individuals or groups and influencing the built environment's design. It illustrates, first, the types of social connections individuals need to access various beneficial feelings and supports, largely based on Dunbar's work (1998). Second, it indicates key features of social connection infrastructure, including *built social infrastructure* (for example, the need for bumping spaces, mixed types of spaces), *types of activities* (for example, collaborative activities and group problem-solving), *brokering people* and *foundational aspects of the environment* (for example, safety, inclusion, accessibility), that help foster social connection. Third, the framework depicts social connection as a process that evolves over time, progressing from initial meetings to feelings of belonging (Haski-Leventhal and Bardal, 2008). This chapter primarily focuses on the second aspect of the framework concerning features of local social connection infrastructure.

Methods

Data presented in this chapter was collected as part of the Australian Research Council Project LP200301335, 'Activating social connection to address social isolation in Australia' (2022–2025). Following Ethics Committee approval, a diverse group of community participants was recruited in partnership with staff of three outer-metropolitan Melbourne councils. Using selection criteria established by the research team, the council's community development workers approached individuals from diverse backgrounds (in terms of age, socioeconomic status and cultural background) whom they believed had 'interesting stories about social connection or isolation'. This included experiences of loneliness, being well-connected, and journeys to get to know others in a new location. Those approached were given researchers' contact details and invited to reach out if they wished to volunteer to participate. The first 44 people who contacted researchers were recruited, with approximately equal numbers from each suburb. Eighty per cent self-reported as female, 18 per cent as male and one person preferred not to say. Participants ranged in age from 18 to over 85 years, 64 per cent were born overseas, and 57 per cent spoke a language other than English at home.

Each participant was interviewed over two face-to-face sessions, one to two weeks apart, with a total interview time for each participant of three to four hours (total of 88 interviews). While all interviews were conducted in English, an interpreter was present occasionally. The semi-structured interviews were guided by the social connection framework (referenced earlier) and covered types of contacts, processes of connection and local social connection infrastructure. Participants were encouraged to reflect on their experiences in relation to the geographical area where they live. Visual prompts, including pictures of locations, were used to stimulate discussion. Digital social connection was also explored (see Chapter 15, this volume). Participants received an AU$150 voucher as reimbursement for their time. Interviews were recorded with participants' informed consent, transcribed automatically using Otter.ai and then manually checked and edited by interviewers to ensure accuracy. Participant identities were safeguarded through pseudonyms, and any identifiers were removed from transcripts.

A manual thematic analysis approach (Braun and Clarke, 2006) was employed, with three researchers continuously comparing and contrasting data collected against the social connection framework following an abductive process (Timmermans and Tavory, 2022).

Findings

Despite the interview's focus on social connection in relation to *the places where they live*, residents rarely mentioned specific local locations in their discussions. Literature suggests this may be due to a sense of placelessness from living in standardized landscapes (Seamon and Sowers, 2008) or people not consciously considering where their interactions occur (Coates and Seamon, 1984). Additionally, some participants may feel a sense of impermanence, and many were migrants with (stronger) ties to their country of birth.

Given our interest in *how to connect people with others locally*, we summarize themes from our findings in three sections: first, what participants shared about their social connection to *local locations*; second, *their relationships with residents in their home locations*; and third, their *experiences that connect them to local people and locations*. We also consider digital connections and their relevance to home locations while highlighting potential opportunities to foster local, place-based connections. Illustrative quotes are given, and the participant's age group is in parentheses.

Local locations and connection

A mix of attractive, welcoming, safe and accessible local locations emerged as the most frequently mentioned features of built infrastructure that foster social connection. Participants emphasized the importance of having adequate space, tables, paving and covered areas to encourage outdoor meetings. For example, areas for cooking and socializing around park barbecues were noted as particularly inviting. Additionally, comments suggested that public building lobbies could encourage people to congregate by providing amenities such as free coffee machines and comfy seating for those waiting or after engaging in other activities. Accessible local places to meet a neighbour or friend, including cafés, were desired but often missing.

Having pleasant local places to walk was considered important for being with friends or by yourself, as being in nature was significant to reflection (connecting with yourself) and getting to know the locale. Charlotte (50s) talks about a daily walk to the beach, with a friend or by herself, as a vital ritual that makes her feel connected to a new place, but also where she reflects on connections with her old home.

> I like nature walks and the moment I made a kind of mental map of the surroundings, I felt at home. Still, there are times even now, when I'm walking along the beach or whatever, where the pine trees grow; and the wind blows through there – and I feel home. (Charlotte)

Confirming previous studies (Kroen and Goodman, 2022), the theme of feeling safe – both physically and culturally – recurred, primarily expressed by women but also mentioned by some male participants. Several participants spontaneously mentioned safety when talking about locations or looking at photos they were shown. 'Yes, I'd go there, it looks safe' or 'I would go to the train station in the day, but not at night' were the kinds of comments made consistently. Feeling safe ranged from physical safety to feeling comfortable because people look and talk like you, which is associated with experiencing a location welcoming to your culture or age group. Libraries were frequently mentioned by women across different cultures as places 'without an agenda' offering activities, help and the opportunity to encounter others – whether similar or different – while feeling safe.

Kali (20s) discussed trying locations across Melbourne to find somewhere safe. She tried the library at her university but didn't find it welcoming. She discusses a good feeling when she entered her local public library and was reassured to see other people who 'looked like her': 'I came to the library, and I see everyone looks like me. Relief. When you find people like you, you find you don't have to explain yourself anymore, like this is so comfortable.' Ira (20s) talks about a public library located in a shopping mall. When she was growing up, she went there after school and met many young people of diverse backgrounds from across her suburb. She remains friends with many of them, keeping in touch mainly via Instagram as they now live dispersed throughout the city and beyond.

These findings point to the salience of people having access to a mix of local places they find safe and attractive enough to linger in, giving more opportunities to meet neighbours or to grow feelings of being comfortable in the local area. This aligns with the findings of Bower and colleagues (Chapter 6, this volume), who point to the need for mixed infrastructure close to home that fosters relationality with locations and people.

People in home locations

Actions of other residents help people to find social connection. For example, participants mentioned being 'tapped on the shoulder' by neighbours or community development workers and asked to go along to events, clubs or activities. Charlotte talks about joining a local book group because a neighbour was 'tactfully pushy' in inviting her along. Charlotte reflected that she wasn't particularly enthusiastic about the activity itself, but it helped her meet other local people.

Reem (60s) talked about an Arabic woman community leader who holds coffee meet-ups in different shopping centre cafes in her council area. Attending these events is a valued activity for Reem as the leader is from her cultural community, and the meet-ups keep her connected to other local women who share her culture and first language: 'I meet with a special group. It's run by Amina. Amina does it. Some people coming every Tuesday ... to the group. It's for Arabic women. Iraqi, Lebanon, Syria. Every person that speaks Arabic. We have an activity, sometimes cards and when we're finished, Amina speaks.'

Adrian (60s) is an ex-council official who describes daily activities to connect local people to organize an annual multicultural event. He actively canvasses people he meets in the neighbourhood to volunteer and connects them with tasks he thinks will suit them. Diverse people meet each other by doing these activities together. Another example is Lydia (60s), who decided, on her retirement, to set up a local walking group. She made and printed leaflets and distributed them in her area. Lydia reflects that she often gets no response but feels she is doing a valuable service for others that will influence her physical health and theirs. Driving the activity also challenges her socially: 'It's not an easy process. A lot of people, they think you're selling something. A lot of them will walk off without, don't want the pamphlet – and that doesn't worry me at all, you know, I'm only trying to help them – I'm not doing anything for me.'

These stories highlight the 'shoulder-tapping' work of residents who are often self-motivated by a cause or purpose that drives them to connect with local people. Once connected, new participants identify benefits from the connecting *per se* rather than necessarily enjoyment of the topic or activity. Such 'voluntary' connectors should be supported and celebrated as they knit the shy and reticent residents into social capital networks where they and the neighbourhood benefit.

Experiences connecting people and locations

Four participants described a holistic connection with local people and places. Amal (50s) and Levi (60s) both express feeling connected with/in the locale due to working there. Amal is an immigrant from Iraq. She discusses getting a local, casual job and how this helped her get to know people and to understand and fit with the rhythms of her new neighbourhood:

> I was working as a school crossing supervisor. So, I got to know some women. Even men – ladies and men. Through my job. Even now, sometimes ... in the morning, I just pass them and bring coffee or something like that, especially in the winter. We still give each other advice. Last Saturday I met one of them – in [local shop]. I said, 'Come on, let's drink some coffee'. (Amal)

Similarly, Levi – who experiences ongoing mental ill-health – discusses a casual job delivering groceries on his bike. This led him to get to know people, their routines and the streets of the neighbourhood, causing him to feel 'not quite belonging' but a sense of comfort:

> I like it better the longer I've been here because I know a few people. I know the bloke who owns the bottle shop, I know the bloke that runs the pizza shop. I know them because I just got talking to them. I'm a friendly bloke. They come out and have a coffee and a smoke with me. It used to be my daily ritual. Not sure I feel I belong here? No – I feel accepted. (Levi)

Ira (20s), who emigrated to Australia from Eritrea as a child, says she has grown to appreciate her suburb. She is increasingly surrounded by residents, friends and acquaintances who share her cultural background. She imagines she will always live there. She likes that foodstuffs from her Eritrean culture can be purchased locally. She says she has two homes – the Australian suburb she lives in and Eritrea, her cultural home.

In contrast, about half of the participants felt disconnected from their lives in the area. This was often despite many efforts to join local groups and activities. Madeline (70s), for example, is active in several leisure activities, environmental activities and political groups, but she says she doesn't fit in. She wonders if this is because she has moved around a lot. She moved to the area in her 50s to work with refugees and didn't raise her children there. She attributes her sense of dislocation to this lack of something that binds her with the local place and people.

Of particular interest is that while Madeline, Levi, Amal and Ira share a similar suburban living context, their experiences – and the absence of certain experiences – differ in ways that influence their integration into the local social fabric without requiring an effort to connect. Madeline is trialling activities to connect with people, whereas the others focus more on discussing their environment and the people within it. These examples highlight the idea that building connections involves a process that takes time.

Digital connection and locations

Almost everyone discussed the regular use of messaging apps and social media. While this was largely to maintain contacts beyond the suburbs, sometimes digital tools were used to make and maintain local connections. Adi (60s), for example, is part of a WhatsApp group of older Indian men who meet locally. The men often travel, but they keep in touch with each other – sustaining their place-based connection over time and places:

> Friends – I can show on this one [shows phone]. How many people is coming on. This is Kabir, from India – now he's gone to Canada. From there, this is Vihaan – he is from Bombay, India. This is Hassan [suburb name], Hassan just gone to Delhi. This is Amir, the colonel he's here, a fellow member. This is [suburb name WhatsApp] Group. (Adi)

Amal (50s) used a community WhatsApp group to find local people to train with her for a marathon. She sent out a message about the training and built a new WhatsApp sub-group of running enthusiasts from those who responded. Using a different tool, Emery (20s) harnessed Bumble, primarily a dating app, to find new friends when she moved to Melbourne from another city during the COVID-19 pandemic. She found someone in her suburb and has met with her, face to face, several times.

These examples illustrate ways that digital technology can support place-based social connection. They also suggest that while people use technology to keep up with distant friends, they value local contacts and are resourceful and adaptive in using technology to meet their local social connection needs.

Opportunities

Several participants noted they often spend time outside their local area for work and expressed a desire for more opportunities to connect in local places beyond the typical 9am to 5pm hours. Some highlighted activities where social connection might be 'layered-in' on top of existing commitments; for example, they suggested the potential for connecting parents who are waiting for children during extracurricular activities. Helen (30s), for example, highlighted how new connections can be prompted:

> I go to swimming with my son and my husband. We started a few weeks ago. I don't know anyone, but we started saying like, 'Hey', you know. It's still a bit early – it's only half an hour, not too much of talking. I'll say hello, and when we'll see each other somewhere else, in familiar places, then we might like to build a relationship. (Helen)

Several participants mentioned 'wistful wants' to find others locally who might share an interest. Charlotte is interested in discussing philosophy, for example, and Emery wishes to join a group about mental health. However, they say they don't know how to find others and think their idea might be 'too niche' to find a group locally. Interestingly, both of these women are part of topic-based online groups, but they still would value some local and physical meetings.

Others commented they were unsure about acceptable social norms for meeting. Brenda deals with the dilemma of whether it's alright to invite her neighbours round by saying she would like others to invite *her*. 'It's important to know your neighbours, but people don't invite people around and this may have got worse since Covid. I'm a bit of an introvert – introducing myself to others is difficult. I can push myself to do it, but it's good when others help.' Facilitating people to hold short-term meet-up groups and campaigns encouraging people to say hi and chat to their neighbours all represent 'light-touch' activities that councils and community organizations could use to support the inclinations of currently reticent community members. However, Cheshire (2015) notes the challenges of encouraging neighbours to be friends, noting that close connection shouldn't be expected as there aren't necessarily shared interests between people who happen to live on the same street.

Discussion

This chapter explored associations between residents, local places and social connection in urban fringe areas. Our desire to link the connection between people and their living environment aligns with conclusions of a recent literature review that policy should move on from separating environments and people, instead regarding social connection as what 'emerges in the relationship between the two' (Bower et al, 2023: 12). Connecting people with other people and with place seems a particularly appropriate policy focus in the Australian context, especially in new suburbs. There have been increasing moves to embed Indigenous ways of knowing into public policy and practice. Indigenous Australians understand Country as a relational connection between all things, a tying of people to place and all that place encompasses (Tynan, 2021). Moving to understand social connection as relational ties involving people, the wider geographical area and activities lean into the way that many traditional and Indigenous cultures internationally regard the complex assembled, socio-material experience of social connection (Wheele et al, 2023).

In the research, we specifically wanted to know if and how local people connect with each other and the places where they live and if evidence from residents can give new ideas to inform strategy to connect people in place. Focusing on addressing people's social connection in relation to their local area could help councils and community organizations target strategy, effectively use limited resources and lead to a range of related social benefits. These include forming greater place attachment associated with collective efficacy, responsibility and action (Lewicka, 2011; Wheele et al, 2023).

Our findings show that people value and want social connections locally. Some brokers are working to bring their neighbours together, and community members are drawing on a range of people, built infrastructure, nature and even digital resources to create local social connections for themselves.

Aligned with the findings of Bower et al (Chapter 6, this volume), it appears that developing suburbs do not necessarily require 'big ticket', centralized social infrastructure. Instead, a mix of incidental and smaller-scale locations that are welcoming, safe and attractive may be more effective. These spaces might initially draw people in and, over time, encourage them to come together. Building a sense of belonging within the local social fabric takes time and involves elements that integrate individuals into their living environment, fostering a kind of relational collective social connection. Similarly, finding value in 'not your ideal activity' but one that brings you connection locally is significant. Finding aspects of the environment that resonate with previous places lived and cultural backgrounds can help people to bridge their cultural and geographical histories while living together in new developments.

Ideas for policy and practice

Based on our findings, we offer some ideas for urban fringe councils and community organizations aimed at facilitating social connection among residents in their local areas:

- *Create a mix of comfortable shared spaces*: The foundation for social connection in a neighbourhood lies in the ability to casually share a range of spaces where individuals feel comfortable. Initially, local social connection is not about finding 'your best friend' but rather about feeling at ease with others and finding acceptance, as expressed by Levi and Kali in this study. Neighbourhoods should have enough local locations and gathering places to provide opportunities for building social connection.

Councils should assess neighbourhoods for equitable access to social connection infrastructure.
- *Support local engagement*: Identify ways to support residents' inclinations and current activities. Implementing co-design and participatory planning opportunities at the neighbourhood level can help uncover novel opportunities while bringing local people together to meet one another. Similarly, celebrating local community connectors can recognize their hidden work connecting diverse groups and identify neighbourhoods lacking such brokers.
- *Facilitate employment and volunteering opportunities*: Providing employment opportunities, even for casual or short-term work, as well as volunteering options, can serve as a quick way to integrate newcomers into communities. This highlights the significance of finding innovative ways to generate work and volunteering prospects in new suburbs, which often struggle with limited local employment.
- *Enhance digital social connection*: Digital social connection should be recognized as a component of how residents form and maintain their circles of connection with both distant and local contacts. Supporting residents in developing the skills necessary to use digital technologies effectively is likely essential to contemporary community development.

References

Aldrich, D. and Meyer, M. (2015) 'Social capital and community resilience', *American Behavioral Scientist*, 59(2), 254–269.

Bower, M., Kent, J., Patulny, R., Green, O., McGrath, L., Teesson, L., et al (2023) 'The impact of the built environment on loneliness: a systematic review and narrative synthesis', *Health and Place*, Article 102962.

Braun, V. and Clarke, V. (2006) 'Using thematic analysis in psychology', *Qualitative Research in Psychology*, 3(2), 77–101.

Castells, M. (1999) 'Grassrooting the space of flows', *Urban Geography*, 20(4), 294–302.

Cheshire, L. (2015) '"Know your neighbours": disaster resilience and the normative practices of neighbouring in an urban context', *Environment and Planning A*, 47, 1081–1099.

Coates, G.J. and Seamon, D. (1984) 'Toward a phenomenology of place and place-making: interpreting landscape, lifeworld and aesthetics', *Oz*, 6. doi:10.4148/2378-5853.1074

Consumers Health Forum of Australia (2019) *Social Prescribing Roundtable November 2019: Report*, CHF.

Drilling, M. and Schnur, O. (2019) 'Neighbourhood research from a geographical perspective', *Journal of the Geographical Society of Berlin*, 150(2), 48–60.

Dunbar, R. (1998) 'The social brain hypothesis', *Evolutionary Anthropology*, 6, 178–190.

Ellery, P.J., Ellery, J. and Borkowsky, M. (2021) 'Toward a theoretical understanding of placemaking', *International Journal of Community Wellbeing*, 4, 55–76.

Farmer, J., De Cotta, T., Hartung, C., Knox, J., Rowe, C. and Stenta, C. (2021) *Social Connection 101*, Swinburne Social Innovation Research Institute. doi: 10.25916/sfn8-km66

Farmer, J., De Cotta, T., Savic, M., Rowe, C., Verhagen, J., Sivasubramaniam, D., et al (2025) *Social Connection 101*, revised edition, Swinburne University of Technology. https://doi.org/10.25916/sut.28415261

Haski-Leventhal, D. and Bargal, D. (2008) 'The volunteer stages and transitions model: organizational socialization of volunteers', *Human Relations*, 61(1), 67–102.

Henderson, S.R. (2019) 'Outer metropolitan areas and infrastructure deficits: policy dynamics on the edge of Melbourne, Australia', *Cities*, 90, 24–31.

Kroen, A. and Goodman, R. (2022) 'The lived transport experience of residents in Melbourne's growth areas', unpublished briefing paper, RMIT University, Melbourne.

Kroen, A., Dodson, J. and Butt, A. (2022) 'The benefits and challenges of Australian government investment in infrastructure in outer suburban growth areas', RMIT Centre for Urban Research and National Growth Areas Alliance. https://doi.org/10.25916/dpdq-qb44

Kroen, A., Pemberton, S. and De Gruyter, C. (2023) 'Measuring the timing between public transport provision and residential development in greenfield estates', *Journal of Public Transportation*, 25, Article 100068.

Lewicka, M. (2011) 'Place attachment: how far have we come in the last 40 years?', *Journal of Environmental Psychology*, 31(3), 207–230.

Lloyd, K., Fullagar, S. and Reid, S. (2016) 'Where is the "social" in constructions of "liveability"? Exploring community, social interaction and social cohesion in changing urban environments', *Urban Policy and Research*, 34(4), 343–355. doi:10.1080/08111146.2015.1118374

Matsunobu, K. (2018) 'Music making as place making: a case study of community music in Japan', *Music Education Research*, 20(4), 490–501.

Nicholls, L., Phelan, K. and Maller, C. (2018) 'A fantasy to get employment around the area: long commutes and resident health in an outer urban master-planned estate', *Urban Policy and Research*, 36(1), 48–62. doi:10.1080/08111146.2017.1308859

OECD, UN-HABITAT and UNOPS (2021) *Global State of National Urban Policy 2021: Achieving Sustainable Development Goals and Delivering Climate Action*, OECD Publishing.

Roggenbuck, C. (2019) 'Diverse lived experiences of community in masterplanned estates: a case study of Filipino and Indian migrants in Wyndham', *Urban Policy and Research*, 37(2), 185–198. doi:10.1080/08111146.2019.1578954

Seamon, D. and Sowers, J. (2008) 'Place, placelessness, Edward Relph', in P. Hubbard and R. Kitchen (eds) *Key Texts in Human Geography*, SAGE, pp 43–51.

Timmermans, S. and Tavory, I. (2022) *Data Analysis in Qualitative Research: Theorizing with Abductive Analysis*, University of Chicago Press.

Tynan, L. (2021) 'What is relationality? Indigenous knowledges, practices and responsibilities with kin', *Cultural Geographies*, 28(4), 597–610.

van Kempen, R. and Wissink, B. (2014) 'Between places and flows: towards a new agenda for neighbourhood research in an age of mobility', *Geografiska Annaler: Series B, Human Geography*, 96(2), 95–108.

Victorian Planning Authority (2021) *Precinct Structure Planning Guidelines: New Communities in Victoria*, Victorian Planning Authority.

Victoria State Government (2020) *Local Government Act 2020*, Victoria State Government.

Victoria State Government (2021) *20 Minute Neighbourhoods Plan Melbourne 2017–2050*, Victoria State Government.

Wallace, C., Farmer, J. and McCosker, A. (2019) 'Boundary spanning practices of community connectors for engaging "hardly reached" people in health services', *Social Science & Medicine*, 232, 366–373.

Wheele, T., Weber, C., Windlinger, L., Haugen, T. and Lindkvist, C. (2023) 'A narrative literature review using placemaking theories to unravel student social connectedness in hybrid university learning environments', *Buildings*, 13(2), 339.

PART IV

Digital Spaces

13

From Disruption to Digital Adaptation: Young Women's Social Connection During Lockdowns

Jessica Franks

In response to the COVID-19 pandemic, governments worldwide implemented spatial restrictions and social distancing measures that fundamentally disrupted established patterns of social connection. In Victoria and New South Wales, Australia, these disruptions were particularly profound. Between March 2020 and October 2021, Melbourne endured six lockdowns totalling 262 days, including a 112-day stretch that ranked among the world's longest continuous lockdowns (Vally and Bennett, 2021; Wahlquist, 2021). These restrictions severely limited face-to-face social interactions, with residents permitted to leave home only for essential reasons and most social gatherings prohibited (Vally and Bennett, 2021).

Social connection – the relationships and interactions individuals have with others in their social networks – encompasses emotional bonds, shared experiences and the sense of belonging that comes from these relationships. It is well documented as a fundamental human need, contributing significantly to overall wellbeing and mental health (Cacioppo and Cacioppo, 2014; Holt-Lunstad, 2021; Juvonen, 2021). Young women experienced particular challenges during this period, as the pandemic disrupted their social networks during a life stage crucial for identity formation and relationship building (Matud et al, 2020; Zhang et al, 2021).

The pandemic transformed the role of social media in young women's lives. Before COVID-19, social media was often viewed as a factor in social displacement, where time spent online potentially reduced face-to-face interactions (Twenge et al, 2019). However, during lockdowns, digital platforms became crucial tools for maintaining social connection (Ellis et al,

2020; Juvonen et al, 2021). This shift created new dynamics in how young women maintained their relationships and social networks, challenging previous understandings of digital social displacement.

This chapter charts how young women in Victoria and New South Wales navigated social connections throughout the pandemic's multiple lockdowns. Through qualitative analysis of survey data, I identify five distinct phases in their adaptation to crisis conditions: pre-pandemic social capital, network collapse, solitude, digital adaptation and the eventual emergence of a new social equilibrium. This progression reveals how social connection practices evolved in response to prolonged crisis conditions, offering insights for understanding social adaptation during public health emergencies.

The pandemic's social disruption

The COVID-19 pandemic created an unprecedented disruption to social connections, distinct from the gradual changes that typically shape social networks over time. For young women, this disruption occurred during a critical life stage where social connections play a vital role in identity formation, peer acceptance and a sense of belonging. Research has consistently shown that social connections serve as protective factors against mental health risks (Holmes et al, 2020; Loades et al, 2020), making their sudden disruption particularly concerning for this demographic.

The impact of prolonged social isolation on young women's mental health emerged as a significant concern during the pandemic. Studies documented increased rates of depression, anxiety and stress, with some young adults experiencing symptoms of post-traumatic stress disorder (Fiorillo and Gorwood, 2020; Pfefferbaum and North, 2020). With its extended lockdowns, the Victorian context intensified these challenges as young women navigated multiple waves of restrictions and social disruption.

However, amid this disruption, patterns of adaptation and resilience emerged. Digital technologies and virtual communities have become crucial mechanisms for maintaining social connections. Research by Shigeto et al (2020) revealed how young adults' coping responses varied based on factors such as perceived pandemic centrality, sense of control and individual resilience capacity. These findings highlighted the complex interplay between social connection, digital adaptation and psychological wellbeing during crises.

Through platforms like Facebook, Instagram, Tinder, TikTok and WhatsApp, young women found ways to stay connected with friends and family, share experiences, make new connections and find support during lockdowns (Pretorius and Coyle, 2021; Rosen et al, 2022). These social media platforms played a transformative role in shaping social connections and relationships during the COVID-19 pandemic (Hiebert and Kortes-Miller, 2020). In navigating the challenges of social collapse and recovery, young women demonstrated a remarkable ability to adapt and find solace in digital spaces across the pandemic period. Whether through virtual gatherings, online support networks or creative forms of expression, individuals leveraged digital platforms to mitigate the impact of social isolation and cultivate a sense of belonging (Pretorius and Coyle, 2021; Mainardi and Magaraggia, 2024).

Understanding how young women maintained and reconstructed their social connections during this period requires consideration of three key theoretical frameworks: social capital theory; resilience theory; and the convoy model of social relations. These frameworks, discussed in the following section, help explain how social networks adapt to crisis conditions and how digital platforms can support social connection during physical isolation.

Theoretical frameworks for understanding social connection in crisis

This study draws on three complementary theoretical frameworks to understand how young women's social connections adapted during the COVID-19 pandemic. Each theory offers distinct yet interconnected insights into how social networks respond to disruption, adapt under stress and reconstruct during crises.

Social capital theory

Social capital theory provides a foundation for understanding how valuable social resources are built, maintained and potentially lost during crises. Social capital, formed through network interactions, facilitates cooperation, mutual support and resource sharing (Putnam, 2000). Three primary components shape its operation: network structure; trust and reciprocity; and accessible resources. Network structure encompasses the patterns of relationships that determine information flow and social interaction opportunities (Burt, 2000; Putnam, 2000) – particularly relevant during pandemic conditions where traditional interaction patterns were disrupted. Trust and reciprocity, developed through mutual exchanges and reliable social connections (Coleman, 1988), become crucial when communities face collective challenges (Wind et al, 2011). The resource component includes both tangible and intangible assets accessible through social networks, such as emotional support, practical assistance and information sharing (Bourdieu, 1986; Lin, 2001). During the pandemic, these resources often needed to be accessed and distributed through new, primarily digital, channels.

Resilience theory

Resilience theory explains how individuals and communities adapt to and recover from significant disruptions. While originally developed to understand ecological systems (Holling, 1973), its application to social systems provides valuable insights into pandemic adaptation. Social resilience specifically addresses how individuals and groups maintain core functions while adjusting to adverse conditions (Adger, 2000; Walker et al, 2004). This concept proves particularly relevant when examining how young women maintained social connections despite physical isolation. Community resilience extends this understanding to collective adaptation, focusing on how groups leverage shared resources to navigate uncertainty (Norris et al, 2008; Magis, 2010; Supriatna et al, 2020). The Glasgow Centre for Population Health's emphasis on resilience's social nature highlights how network structures and group dynamics influence access to support resources during crises (Seaman, 2020). This framework helps explain both individual and collective adaptation strategies observed during lockdown periods.

Convoy model of social relations

The convoy model offers crucial insights into how social networks respond to sudden disruption. This model, developed by Kahn and Antonucci (1980), conceptualizes individuals as embedded within dynamic social convoys that provide support, resources and belonging. While traditionally applied to gradual life course changes, its principles become particularly relevant when examining rapid social network disruption during crises. The model's distinction between core relationships (typically stable) and peripheral connections (more fluid) helps explain the differential impacts of pandemic restrictions on various relationship types. Although originally focused on older adults' gradually evolving networks (Antonucci and Akiyama, 1987), the model's principles about relationship stability and change provide valuable insights into how young women's social networks adapted during repeated lockdowns.

Together, these theoretical frameworks inform our analysis of how young women's social connections evolved through distinct pandemic phases. Social capital theory helps explain resource access and network maintenance, resilience theory illustrates adaptation processes, and the convoy model provides insights into relationship stability and change. This theoretical integration guides our understanding of the five-stage progression detailed in the findings section.

Research approach

This study investigated young women's experiences of social connection during the COVID-19 pandemic in Victoria and New South Wales,

Australia. The focus on young women reflected their heightened vulnerability to psychological distress and social isolation (Matud et al, 2020; Zhang et al, 2021). Sixty-two women aged 16–30 were recruited through social media advertisement and snowball sampling. Participants were Victoria and New South Wales residents during the lockdowns and were offered entry into a draw for a AU$500 voucher. Demographic detail collected included 100 females, all of whom self-reported living in Victoria or New South Wales during all COVID-19 lockdowns. Sample data included age ranges 16–17 (11 per cent), 18–25 (61 per cent) and 26–30 (27 per cent). Participants' self-reported ethnicity was as follows: Australia (n=70), Asian (n=12), British (n=6), European (n=4) and Indian (n=1). One participant identified as Aboriginal and Torres Strait Islander descent.

Data collection occurred via Qualtrics online survey between December 2020 and October 2021, spanning Victoria's third through sixth lockdowns, including the state's longest 77-day lockdown (August–October 2021) and during New South Wales' second and third wave lockdowns. The survey captured retrospective reflections on pre-COVID-19 social connections and real-time experiences during lockdowns through open-ended questions about social interactions, digital media use and coping strategies. Ethics approval was obtained from the University of Melbourne Human Ethics Team (reference 2023-14515-46747-6).

Thematic analysis followed Braun and Clarke's (2006; 2019) approach, with initial themes developed through iterative reading of responses and refined through theoretical engagement. The analysis process included verification through research team collaborative sessions. While the sample size and self-selected nature of participation limit generalizability, particularly regarding internet access and digital engagement, the data revealed distinct phases in how young women navigated social connection throughout the pandemic, as presented in the findings section.

Five stages of social adaptation

Data analysis from 62 young women revealed distinct phases in how social connection was maintained and transformed throughout the pandemic, particularly in the balance between digital and face-to-face interactions. The findings are organized into five stages that chart participants' journey from pre-pandemic social capital to post-pandemic social equilibrium. Each stage illustrates how participants adapted their social connections and use of digital platforms as the pandemic progressed. The analysis shows the progression from established social capital (pre-pandemic), through experiences of shrinking networks and solitude, to the eventual reconstruction of social connections with increased digital integration.

Pre-pandemic social capital (baseline)

Survey findings established a baseline of social connections before the pandemic, revealing how young women built and maintained their social networks through regular face-to-face interactions. The network structure of their social capital was characterized by frequent in-person gatherings, with digital platforms playing only a supplementary role. Young women reported highly active social lives with frequent in-person gatherings. The regularity and variety of social interactions were evident in the participants' reflections, with one participant stating, 'I'd mostly catch up with friends at cafés or restaurants.' Another emphasized the consistent nature of social engagement, noting they were 'Very busy, consistently seeing people.' These regular interactions facilitated the development of trust and reciprocity.

Digital platforms, particularly social media, served primarily as coordination tools rather than primary communication channels. One participant said they would use platforms like Messenger to 'coordinate meetings for meals or catch up for walks, movies, and occasional day trips'. This pattern reflects how social media enhanced rather than replaced face-to-face interactions in pre-pandemic social networks, serving as a facilitator for in-person social connection rather than a substitute for it.

Social connection collapse – shrinkage of networks (pandemic phase – response)

The second phase revealed how lockdowns triggered a systematic collapse of social networks, affecting both peripheral and core relationships in ways that align with the convoy model of social relations. The collapse occurred in distinct waves, demonstrating how different layers of social capital eroded as the pandemic progressed.

Initially, the impact was most evident in peripheral social networks, those outer layers of the social convoy typically maintained through casual or opportunistic contact. One participant noted, 'Covid heavily restricted my social life between the first and second wave.' The immediate severance of these peripheral connections was evident as several friendships were 'dropping off entirely, due to being unable to meet each other in public'.

As lockdowns extended, even core relationships – those typically most stable in the convoy model – began to erode. One participant captured this progression: 'During the first few outbreaks, I went from constantly seeing friends to sometimes months in between visits. [It] drastically reduced my social life.' Another acknowledged, 'My own social networks shrunk a bit since COVID.'

By the third wave of lockdowns, this shrinkage prompted a fundamental re-evaluation of social networks. As one participant reflected, 'I haven't stayed friends with a lot of people from school, only a small handful. Covid has made me realize who my best friends are and who I can count on during tougher times.' This observation reveals how the pandemic reduced social capital quantitatively and led to a qualitative transformation of remaining social connections.

Phase of solitude (pandemic phase – response)

The third phase reveals how prolonged lockdowns transformed from a period of enforced isolation into one of complex adaptation, demonstrating elements of both vulnerability and resilience. This phase showed how young women's capacity to endure and adjust to adverse conditions evolved over time, though their experiences were notably mixed.

Initial responses to solitude varied significantly. Some participants struggled with the isolation, as evidenced by one who shared, 'I felt isolated and alone most of the time. Any social experience I had was over Zoom.' Others, however, demonstrated adaptive resilience, finding unexpected benefits in the situation: 'I actually think COVID has been a positive impact as I now know that I don't have to do something every weekend, and it doesn't matter if I miss seeing my friends and family for one weekend so I can focus on myself.'

As lockdowns persisted, the limitations of digital connection became more apparent. One participant highlighted a fundamental loss by noting, 'Losing that physical contact aspect of our relationships (e.g., hugs).' This period revealed adaptation and strain, with another participant reflecting, 'I liked the break that lockdown gave but definitely experienced lockdown fatigue.'

The extended duration of lockdowns prompted a deeper reassessment of social needs. Some participants found new ways to manage social interactions, as one explained: 'I have been able to reach out to people on my own terms rather than being forced into social situations, which makes them less overwhelming and exhausting.' However, this adaptation had limits. By the fourth and fifth lockdowns, the initial benefits of solitude were overshadowed by a growing recognition of the irreplaceable nature of physical presence. As one participant simply concluded, 'Learned to appreciate the real time I get to spend with them all now.'

This phase demonstrates how resilience operates not just as a simple ability to endure hardship, but as a dynamic process of adaptation and recognition of core social needs. While digital platforms offered some relief from isolation, they ultimately highlighted rather than resolved the fundamental human need for physical connection.

Reconstruction of networks: digital adaptation (transition phase – pre-recovery)

The fourth phase demonstrates how young women actively rebuilt their social capital through digital means, transforming their social convoys in response to prolonged isolation. This reconstruction phase showed how digital platforms evolved from supplementary tools to primary mechanisms for both maintaining existing relationships and building new ones.

The transformation was particularly evident in how participants expanded their social networks beyond traditional boundaries. As one participant explained, 'I actually made many new friends online during this time, introduced through mutual friends. As I had no work, I had time to spend on video games connecting with these people.' Others actively sought new communities, with one noting, 'I decided to engage in different platforms than what I was used to talk about important issues ... which resulted in connecting with new people online.' These experiences demonstrate how digital platforms facilitated the creation of new social convoy layers during isolation.

This digital adaptation required learning new communication practices. Previously unused technologies became essential tools for maintaining social capital, as evidenced by participants' experiences with video calling: 'I've literally never video chatted before in my life and now I do it regularly' and 'Video calling, on a handful of occasions. I'd never really used it before.'

The transition towards reopening revealed complex dynamics in this digitally reconstructed social capital. Some participants struggled with the shift back to blended interactions. One noted, 'It has been hard to transition back from social media use and finding ways to share my life experiences and connect with others when I am not doing anything noteworthy.' Another observed, 'Since they have eased, things are returning to pre-covid ways.' Notably, the pandemic temporarily relieved social pressure by creating an equal playing field where extraordinary experiences were not expected, though this equilibrium shifted as restrictions eased.

This phase reveals how social capital can be reconstructed through digital means during the crisis while highlighting the challenges of reintegrating digital and face-to-face social practices. The experience demonstrates both the adaptability of social networks and the complexity of maintaining them across virtual and physical spaces.

Post-pandemic social equilibrium (recovery)

The final phase reveals how social capital was reconstituted in a transformed landscape, demonstrating both the resilience of social networks and their capacity for permanent adaptation. After six lockdowns, participants' social convoys emerged in a hybrid form, reflecting new patterns of connection that integrated both digital and face-to-face interactions.

The re-establishment of physical interactions marked a significant shift in social capital maintenance. As one participant noted, 'Since being able to see people, it's back to as normal as I can remember,' while another observed,

'My social life has since picked up.' For some, this restoration of social capital centred around institutional routines, as evidenced by one participant who shared: 'Since we have gone back to sport and school, my social life has gone back to the same as pre-COVID.'

However, this 'return to normal' reflected a more complex reality. The social convoys that emerged post-pandemic were qualitatively different from their pre-pandemic forms, incorporating new digital practices and transformed network structures. While the core patterns of social connection resumed, they were informed by the adaptations and resilience developed during lockdowns. This new equilibrium demonstrated how crisis-driven adaptations could evolve into sustainable social practices, creating more flexible and robust social networks.

This transformation reflects broader patterns of social resilience, where systems not only recover from disruption but emerge reformed and potentially strengthened. Integrating digital and physical connection practices suggests a return to previous social capital arrangements but also the emergence of more adaptable and diverse social networks. These findings raise important questions about how theories of social capital, resilience and social convoys can help us understand crisis-driven social transformation, which are explored in the following discussion.

Understanding social connection in crisis

The five-stage progression revealed through this study demonstrates how young women's social connections were disrupted, adapted and ultimately transformed during the COVID-19 pandemic. Each theoretical framework employed offers distinct insights into this transformation process.

Social capital theory informs how network resources were maintained and reconstructed throughout the crisis. Initially, the pandemic disrupted established patterns of social capital accumulation, forcing a shift from diverse, face-to-face networks to more concentrated digital interactions. However, participants demonstrated remarkable adaptability in leveraging digital platforms to maintain their social capital. Platforms like Facebook, Instagram and WhatsApp became virtual spaces where young women could reconnect, share experiences and offer support. While this digital adaptation helped maintain social connections, it also led to denser but less diverse networks, raising questions about the quality and breadth of social capital accessible to young women in future crises.

The lens of resilience theory reveals how participants not only endured social disruption but developed new capabilities for maintaining connections. The progression through stages of collapse, solitude and reconstruction demonstrates resilience as an active process rather than a static trait. Participants showed particular resourcefulness in using digital technologies to maintain social ties, creating new forms of community engagement and emotional support. This adaptive resilience was evident in how they transformed initial isolation into opportunities for relationship reassessment and network reconstruction.

The convoy model of social relations proved especially valuable in understanding how different layers of social relationships were affected and adapted. While peripheral relationships were initially most vulnerable to disruption, core relationships demonstrated remarkable durability, though often in transformed ways. The pandemic accelerated changes in social convoy composition that might typically occur over the years, compelling rapid adaptation in how relationships were maintained. This compressed timeline of social network transformation offers unique insights into the flexibility and resilience of social convoys under pressure.

These findings have important implications for understanding how young women maintain social connection during crises. The study reveals that while digital platforms can provide crucial support for social connection during physical isolation, they work best when integrated with, rather than replacing, face-to-face interaction. The emergence of hybrid social practices suggests that future approaches to supporting social connection should consider both digital and physical dimensions of relationship maintenance.

Conclusion

The COVID-19 pandemic created unprecedented challenges for maintaining social connection, particularly among young women. This study's five-stage model demonstrates how the crisis disrupted, adapted and transformed social connection patterns. The progression from pre-pandemic social capital through collapse, solitude and reconstruction to a new equilibrium reveals both the vulnerability and resilience of social networks.

These findings suggest several key implications for policy and practice. Organizations and practitioners working with young women should anticipate and prepare for different phases of social adaptation during prolonged crises. Digital platform integration requires careful consideration – while digital tools proved vital for maintaining social connections, their effectiveness varied across different stages of the crisis. Support services should focus on helping young women develop digital resilience – the ability to use online platforms effectively while managing their limitations and potential negative impacts. This includes developing skills for maintaining diverse social networks online, managing digital fatigue, and balancing online and offline interactions.

These findings point to specific actions for practitioners and organizations supporting young women's social connection during crises:

- Develop early intervention programmes that help young women maintain diverse social networks during isolation.

- Create structured online–offline transition programmes as communities emerge from crisis periods.
- Establish peer support networks that can be activated during future crises.
- Provide practical guidance on managing digital fatigue and setting healthy online boundaries.
- Design programmes that help young women identify and maintain core relationships while developing strategies to reconnect with peripheral networks.
- Implement regular wellbeing check-ins that specifically address social connection needs at different crisis stages.

The findings also highlight the importance of supporting hybrid models of social connection. As communities emerge from crisis periods, practitioners should recognize that pre-crisis patterns of social interaction may not fully return. Instead, support should focus on helping young women integrate digital and face-to-face connections effectively, acknowledging that crisis experiences may permanently transform social networks.

These insights extend our understanding of how social connection operates during crises in several ways. They demonstrate that social adaptation during the crisis is not linear but occurs in distinct phases, each requiring different support strategies. The study also reveals how digital platforms can both support and complicate social connection, highlighting the need for nuanced approaches to digital integration in social support services.

Future research should examine how the transformed social practices identified in this study persist or evolve over time, particularly focusing on the long-term implications of hybrid social connection patterns. Additionally, investigating how different demographic groups experience similar social disruptions would provide valuable comparative insights.

The experiences documented here suggest that while crises can severely disrupt social connections, they can also catalyse new and potentially more resilient forms of social engagement. Supporting these adaptations while maintaining the essential human need for face-to-face connection remains a crucial challenge for policy and practice.

References

Adger, W.N. (2000) 'Social and ecological resilience: are they related?', *Progress in Human Geography*, 24(3), 347–364.

Antonucci, T.C. and Akiyama, H. (1987) 'Social networks in adult life and a preliminary examination of the convoy model', *Journal of Gerontology*, 42(5), 519–527. doi: 10.1093/geronj/42.5.519

Bourdieu, P. (1986) 'The forms of capital', in J.G. Richardson (ed) *Handbook of Theory and Research for the Sociology of Education*, Greenwood, pp 241–258.

Braun, V. and Clarke, V. (2006) 'Using thematic analysis in psychology', *Qualitative Research in Psychology*, 3(2), 77–101. doi: 10.1191/1478088706qp063oa.

Braun, V. and Clarke, V. (2019) 'Reflecting on reflexive thematic analysis', *Qualitative Research in Sport, Exercise and Health*, 11(4), 589–597. doi: 10.1080/2159676X.2019.1628806.

Burt, R.S. (2000) 'The network structure of social capital', *Research in Organisational Behavior*, 22, 345–423.

Cacioppo, J.T. and Cacioppo, S. (2014) 'Social relationships and health: the toxic effects of perceived social isolation', *Social and Personality Psychology Compass*, 8(2), 58–72.

Coleman, J.S. (1988) 'Social capital in the creation of human capital', *American Journal of Sociology*, 94(Supplement), S95–S120.

Ellis, W.E., Dumas, T.M. and Forbes, L.M. (2020) 'Physically isolated but socially connected: psychological adjustment and stress among adolescents during the initial COVID-19 crisis', *Canadian Journal of Behavioural Science*, 52(3), 177–187.

Fiorillo, A. and Gorwood, P. (2020) 'The consequences of the COVID-19 pandemic on mental health and implications for clinical practice', *European Psychiatry*, 63(1), e32. doi: 10.1192/j.eurpsy.2020.35.

Hiebert, A. and Kortes-Miller, K. (2021) 'Finding home in online community: exploring TikTok as a support for gender and sexual minority youth throughout COVID-19', *Journal of LGBT Youth*, 20, 800–817.

Holling, C.S. (1973) 'Resilience and stability of ecological systems', *Annual Review of Ecology and Systematics*, 4, 1–23.

Holmes, E.A., O'Connor, R.C., Perry, V.H., Tracey, I., Wessely, S., Arseneault, L., et al (2020) 'Multidisciplinary research priorities for the COVID-19 pandemic: a call for action for mental health science', *The Lancet Psychiatry*, 7(6), 547–560. doi: 10.1016/S2215-0366(20)30168-1.

Holt-Lunstad, J. (2021) 'The major health implications of social connection', *Current Directions in Psychological Science*, 30(3), 251–259. doi: 10.1177/0963721421999630.

Juvonen, J. (2021) 'Young adults' adaptability to the social challenges of the COVID-19 pandemic', *Journal of Social and Personal Relationships*, 38(8), 2371–2389.

Juvonen, J., Schacter, H.L. and Lessard, L.M. (2021) 'Connecting electronically with friends to cope with isolation during COVID-19 pandemic', *Journal of Social and Personal Relationships*, 38(6). doi: 10.1177/0265407521998459

Kahn, R.L. and Antonucci, T.C. (1980) 'Convoys over the life course: Attachment, roles, and social support', in P.B. Baltes and O.G. Grim (eds) *Life Span Development and Behavior*. Vol. 3, Academic Press, pp 253–286.

Lin, N. (2001) *Social Capital: A Theory of Social Structure and Action*, Cambridge University Press.

Loades, M.E., Chatburn, E., Higson-Sweeney, N., Reynolds, S., Shafran, R., Brigden, A., et al (2020) 'Rapid systematic review: the impact of social isolation and loneliness on the mental health of children and adolescents in the context of COVID-19', *Journal of the American Academy of Child & Adolescent Psychiatry*, 59(11), 1218–1239. doi: 10.1016/j.jaac.2020.05.009.

Magis, K. (2010) 'Community resilience: an indicator of social sustainability', *Society and Natural Resources*, 23(5), 401–416.

Mainardi, A. and Magaraggia, S. (2024) 'Young women, dating apps, and affective assemblages in the time of pandemic: no relationship is a linear transition to a fixed point', *European Journal of Women's Studies*, 31(3), 325–339.

Matud, M.P., Díaz, A., Bethencourt, J.M. and Ibáñez, I. (2020) 'Stress and psychological distress in emerging adulthood: a gender analysis', *Journal of Clinical Medicine*, 9(9), Article 2859. doi: 10.3390/jcm9092859.

Norris, F.H., Stevens, S.P., Pfefferbaum, B., Wyche, K.F. and Pfefferbaum, R.L. (2008) 'Community resilience as a metaphor, theory, set of capacities, and strategy for disaster readiness', *American Journal of Community Psychology*, 41(1–2), 127–150.

Pfefferbaum, B. and North, C.S. (2020) 'Mental health and the COVID-19 pandemic', *The New England Journal of Medicine*, 383(6), 510–512. doi: 10.1056/NEJMp2008017.

Pretorius, C. and Coyle, D. (2021) 'Young people's use of digital tools to support their mental health during COVID-19 restrictions', *Frontiers in Digital Health*, 3, 763876.

Putnam, R.D. (2000) *Bowling Alone: The Collapse and Revival of American Community*, Simon & Schuster.

Rosen, A.O., Holmes, A.L., Balluerka, N., Hidalgo, M.D., Gorostiaga, A., Gómez-Benito, J., et al (2022) 'Is social media a new type of social support? Social media use in Spain during the COVID-19 pandemic: a mixed methods study', *International Journal of Environmental Research and Public Health*, 19(7), 3952.

Seaman, P. (2020) 'Resilience for public health: supporting transformation in people and communities', Glasgow Centre for Population Health.

Shigeto, A., Laxman, D.J., Landy, J.F. and Scheier, L.M. (2021) 'Typologies of coping in young adults in the context of the COVID-19 pandemic', *Journal of General Psychology*, 148(3), 272–304. doi: 10.1080/00221309.2021.1874864

Supriatna, N., Wibowo, T.Y. and Yuniarti, K.W. (2020) 'Social resilience in the face of environmental and social threats', *Journal of Environmental Management*, 260, Article 110147. doi: 10.1016/j.jenvman.2020.110147

Twenge, J.M., Spitzberg, B.H. and Campbell, W.K. (2019) 'Less in-person social interaction with peers among U.S. adolescents in the 21st century and links to loneliness', *Journal of Social and Personal Relationships*, 36(6), 1892–1913. doi: 10.1177/0265407519836170.

Vally, H. and Bennett, C. (2021) 'COVID in Victoria: 262 days in lockdown, 3 stunning successes and 4 avoidable failures', *The Conversation*. Available at: https://theconversation.com/covid-in-victoria-262-days-in-lockdown-3-stunning-successes-and-4-avoidable-failures-172408 (Accessed 15 July 2024).

Wahlquist, C. (2021) 'How Melbourne's short, sharp COVID lockdowns became the longest in the world', *The Guardian*, 2 October. Available at: https://www.theguardian.com/australia-news/2021/oct/02/how-melbournes-short-sharp-covid-lockdowns-became-the-longest-in-the-world (Accessed 15 July 2024).

Walker, B., Holling, C.S., Carpenter, S.R. and Kinsig, A. (2004) 'Resilience, adaptability and transformability in social-ecological systems', *Ecology and Society*, 9(2), Article 5.

Wind, T.R., Fordham, M. and Komproe, I.H. (2011) 'Social capital and post-disaster mental health', *Global Health Action*, 4(1), Article 6351. doi: 10.3402/gha.v4i0.6351.

Zhang, W., Walkover, M. and Wu, Y. (2021) 'The challenge of COVID-19 for adult men and women in the United States: disparities of psychological distress by gender and age', *Public Health*, 198, 218–222.

14

Technological Bridges and Digital Ambivalences: The Role of Technology in Tackling Loneliness in Later Life

Barbara Barbosa Neves

Social connections – why they matter

In 2018, the UK made history by appointing the world's first Minister for Loneliness, followed by Japan in 2021 (Prime Minister's Office, 2018; Osaki, 2021). These political initiatives formalized the growing public concern about loneliness in industrialized countries, which has gained renewed attention with the COVID-19 pandemic (Patulny and Bower, 2022). Central to definitions of loneliness is the concept of social connections since loneliness generally relates to an absence of meaningful social relationships (Weiss, 1973; Franklin, 2009). In this vein, the UK's first strategy to tackle loneliness aimed to support, build and enhance social connections through a 'Building Connections Fund' (HM Government UK, 2018). Likewise, the Japanese government justified its establishment of a dedicated minister in response to rising suicide rates (including *kodokushi*, or 'lonely deaths', by those living alone who go unnoticed) and *hikikomori*, known as social recluses (Osaki, 2021).

Sociology has a long tradition of demonstrating the critical importance of social connections – that is, relationships that bond people – for the integration, inclusion, wellbeing and health of individuals and societies (Durkheim, 1897; Wellman and Wortley, 1990). Lack of connections harms one's health and affects educational attainment, job prospects and life satisfaction (Granovetter, 1983; Smith and Christakis, 2008; Roth and Peng, 2024). Similarly, loneliness results in adverse effects for individuals and communities – for example, prolonged loneliness increases the risk of health issues like stroke and dementia among older people (aged 65+) as well as social exclusion (Sutin et al, 2022; Neves et al, 2023a; Teshale et al, 2023). While all age groups can experience it, frail older people living in care (nursing) homes or alone in the community seem especially vulnerable to prolonged loneliness (Gardiner et al, 2020; Hawkley, 2022). This vulnerability is often linked to how these social conditions – illness, institutionalization, or being single/widowed and living alone – can affect the quantity, quality and availability of social connections (Neves et al, 2019b; Patulny and Bower, 2022).

Yet, sociologists have also shown that not all social connections are inherently positive and supportive. The academic literature suggests that to address loneliness, we must focus not just on connections but on connectedness, that is, meaningful social connections (Neves et al, 2019a; Morgan et al, 2021). As digital technologies like apps, online platforms and smart devices have the potential to create opportunities for such connectedness, they have been heralded as solutions to tackle loneliness (Hookway et al, 2019; Neves et al, 2019a). However, the effects of digital technologies in lessening loneliness depend on various factors, including age, living settings, type of technology, and how it is used (Hunt et al, 2018; Shah et al, 2021; Balki et al, 2022; Barbosa Neves et al, 2023).

Contributing to teasing out this complexity, this chapter draws on a longitudinal study of older people (aged 65+) living with prolonged loneliness to explore their uses and perceptions of digital technologies during the COVID-19 pandemic. The pandemic-related lockdowns and physical isolation policies provided a unique social context that shaped how connections could occur. This research underscores the intricate contextual nature of loneliness and the ambivalent role of technology in addressing it.

Loneliness, connectedness and technology – a relational approach

With the increasing awareness of loneliness, there has been a surge in technology-based interventions, ranging from general internet use to social robots that leverage information and communication technologies to create, maintain or reinforce social connections (Welch et al, 2023). However, the research approach to this topic often differs by age group. For teenagers and young adults, the focus is on how digital technologies, particularly social media, can intensify loneliness, as they are often saturated with online connections that many perceive as shallow or superficial (Hookway et al, 2019; Shah and Househ, 2023). In contrast, for older adults (aged 65+), who generally have fewer social contacts due to later-life circumstances (for example, retirement, widowhood), the emphasis is on how technology can alleviate loneliness, based on the belief that any digital interaction is better than limited or no contact (Hookway et al, 2019; Welch et al, 2023).

While some studies suggest that technology can reduce loneliness among older people by enhancing social connectedness (Baecker et al, 2014; Neves et al, 2019a; Shah et al, 2020), other research indicates that only in-person visits of family and friends – rather than digital contact – are associated with lower levels of loneliness (Robbins et al, 2023). Additionally, one study found that emails and videoconferencing positively impacted older people's connectedness, whereas social media had a negative influence (Balki et al, 2023). Compounding this contradictory landscape, reviews have shown the limited effects of digitally mediated interventions before and during the pandemic (Alberti, 2019; Kadowaki and Wister, 2023). Amidst this inconsistent evidence, there are calls for stronger conceptual and theoretical understandings of loneliness, as their deficiency can undermine the quality and efficacy of policy and interventions (Barbosa Neves et al, 2023).

In this chapter, I argue that advancing our understanding of loneliness requires three main steps:

1. conceptualizing loneliness as a complex personal and social issue;
2. developing a richer approach to social connectedness; and
3. viewing technologies as sociotechnical systems.

First, while public and policy discourse often suffers from definitional ambiguity – sometimes confusing loneliness with social isolation, living alone or solitude – a common definition positions it as a subjective feeling of lacking companionship and missing meaningful social connections (Weiss, 1973; Perlman and Peplau, 1981). However, social dimensions such as societal values and norms shape one's connections and their interplay. For example, contemporary Western societies often praise independence and self-sufficiency, influencing social interactions (Franklin et al, 2018; Chapter 2, this volume).

Historian Fay Alberti (2019) notes that while people have certainly felt lonely in the past, the concept of loneliness emerged around 1800 to frame a 'new' emotional state. This novel language of loneliness is attributed to socioeconomic and cultural shifts in the modern West, such as industrialization, the public/private divide, the rise of the consumer economy, decreasing religious influence, and the popularization of psycho-biological individualism (Durkheim, 1897; Alberti, 2019). Current dominant psychological approaches to loneliness tend to overemphasize an individualistic lens, treating it as a personal and pathological issue within the 'epidemic' discourse (Jeste et al, 2020). Consequently, the inherently social nature of loneliness is frequently overlooked, implying that it can be managed entirely on an individual basis.

Loneliness can be framed in various ways as both a personal and social experience; however, my approach is sociological. From this perspective, the personal encompasses emotional feelings and their consequences, while the social includes societal contexts, sociocultural norms, networks and practices that influence how loneliness is experienced and perceived (Barbosa Neves et al, 2023; Neves et al, 2023b). To connect the personal and the social, I utilize a relational framework that considers how loneliness influences and is influenced by factors such as living environments, sociocultural practices, socioeconomic status and other contextual elements. A relational sociological perspective focuses on the networks of interactions and relationships between social actors. Rather than concentrating solely on individual attributes or social structures (for example, sociocultural norms), relational sociology examines the dynamic and interconnected nature of social life, where relationships are viewed as central units of analysis (Crossley, 2010; Donati, 2010). By recognizing individuals and social structures as mutually constitutive and co-evolving, this perspective helps transcend the divide between the personal and social elements of loneliness, as well as between agency (for example, one's capacity to choose and act) and structure (for example, social systems). For instance, as I have proposed elsewhere, loneliness can be seen as a form of existential inequality: it is felt by the individual but often entails unequal social distributions of personhood, dignity and autonomy (Neves et al, 2023b). This is why loneliness can be regarded as a social injustice in policy and practice (HM Government UK, 2018).

Second, we must engage more deeply with the concept of social connectedness, which, like loneliness, appears to lack consistent definitions. It is sometimes used interchangeably with social engagement, belonging, support and social integration (Morgan et al, 2021). However, complex personal and social dimensions interplay with this concept. As noted by O'Rouke and Sidani (2017: 1), social connectedness is the 'opposite of loneliness, a subjective evaluation of the extent to which one has meaningful, close, and constructive relationships with others'. These relationships extend beyond individuals to include groups and societies as well (O'Rourke and Sidani, 2017).

Since social connectedness depends on the sociocultural contexts in which people interact, these structural dimensions are as important as personal ones (Morgan et al, 2021). Yet, when digital technologies are employed to promote social connectedness, the focus tends to be on the individual rather than broader social elements (for example, increasing one-to-one personal contact). Therefore, a relational approach to social connectedness is necessary, particularly because the interplay of structural and personal factors can sometimes exacerbate loneliness rather than alleviate it. For example, the social stigma associated with loneliness – often erroneously linked to a lack of sociability or poor social skills – can lead to internalized embarrassment, limiting people's willingness to disclose their feelings of loneliness (Neves and Petersen, 2024). Loneliness stigma appears to interact with other intersectional stigmas, particularly in later life, where being old and frail is viewed unfavourably in societies that idealize youth, ability and productivity (Neves and Petersen, 2024).

Third, viewing digital technologies and related interventions as sociotechnical systems means recognizing that technologies are developed, deployed and used at the intersection of social and technical dimensions – societal values shape technology development and vice versa (MacKenzie and Wajcman, 1999). This perspective extends beyond the physicality of devices to include social and technical aspects influencing technology's design and use. Techno-solutionist ideals, which permeate contemporary societies, illustrate how these societal values are integrated into technology, often promoting the belief that technology alone can solve all our problems (Morozov, 2013). For instance, companion robots for older people are regularly based on simplistic social views of connectedness and later life, distilled into homogeneous features like pre-defined conversation prompts (for example, 'How are you today?') and reminders (for example, medication). While these features may provide some level of engagement, they lack the depth needed to foster genuine connection or address the diverse social and emotional needs of older populations.

Thus, the role of technology in addressing loneliness must be considered within the context of these interwoven material, technical and social dimensions. Here, the relational lens is particularly useful in framing the multidimensionality required to investigate technologically mediated connectedness. In sum, I contend that through this relational approach to loneliness, connectedness and digital technologies, we can better grasp how people navigate personal connections and sociotechnical worlds, particularly during prolonged isolation, such as that experienced during the pandemic. To illustrate this relationality, I draw on a study exploring how already lonely older people perceived and coped with their loneliness during COVID-19 lockdowns.

Methods

This chapter draws on a mixed methods longitudinal study conducted with 35 older Australians (65+) living alone and reporting prolonged loneliness. Participants were recruited through municipal councils in Victoria, which experienced some of the world's longest lockdowns (University of Oxford, 2022). The selection criteria included people aged 65+ living alone, self-reporting loneliness, fluent in English and able to give informed consent. Data collection occurred during the COVID-19 pandemic and included semi-structured interviews, loneliness scales and qualitative diaries. For this chapter, I use participants' diaries from the lockdown in October 2020, along with two waves of qualitative interviews. Diaries serve as participatory tools that enable participants to narrate their feelings, actions and contexts as they see fit – acting as research partners rather than subjects (Milligan et al, 2005).

Diaries were produced by 32 participants, who recorded their daily thoughts, feelings and activities for seven days. The diary sample included 18 women and 14 men, aged 69 to 96, from various sociocultural backgrounds, with 16 participants identifying African, Asian or European heritage. Eighteen participants lived in middle-income areas (five in regional locations), seven in low-income areas and another seven in high-income areas (one in a regional location). Nineteen participants chose paper diaries, while the rest opted for digital formats like emails, texts or audio recordings. Interviews lasted, on average, 60 minutes and were conducted before and after the diaries. First, diary and interview data were thematically analysed to identify codes and themes within (individual) and across (collective) cases (Saldaña, 2021). After thoroughly reading transcripts/diaries, we developed codes and grouped them into themes. The author and a research assistant independently coded the data and then agreed on the final themes. Second, I used thematic narrative analysis to uncover 'what' was being 'told' (Riessman, 2008) about loneliness and the role of technology. While qualitative methods provide rich contextual data for in-depth exploration of any topic, they cannot be used to generalize findings to broader populations.

Results and discussion

This section presents and discusses the combined interview and diary data. Privileging narrative depth, I narrate the overall results and engage with two participants to capture general and nuanced experiences.

The complexity of loneliness

All participants experienced loneliness during the pandemic, though they had felt it at various life stages, especially in later years. They described their persistent loneliness as a profound and painful absence of people with whom to share their lives, referring to it as 'emptiness', 'disconnection' and 'despair of not having real human connection'.

Kathleen, in her early 70s, vividly exemplifies this. Originally from Poland, she made her life in Australia and became deeply involved in the local community centre, where she assists others and eases her loneliness. She has several health issues and was recovering from surgery when lockdowns began. A widow, Kathleen's son and his family live in a different state, while the rest of her relatives are overseas. Loneliness is not new to her, but like all our participants, the COVID-19 pandemic intensified it by reducing social contact and disrupting routines. Yet, as Kathleen explains, loneliness is complex:

> Loneliness makes you feel inadequate because you have nothing. You feel like you are empty. You can be lonely and have people around you. Loneliness is very, very scary because you [feel you] have nothing around you. ... Sometimes that is really hard to live with because loneliness is one of the hardest things to describe. (Kathleen)

Kathleen's words also underscore the emotional impact of loneliness, a sentiment echoed by all participants. Loneliness brought distress, rejection and devaluation. It commonly stemmed from family loss, relationship breakdowns and diminished social connections, highlighting the interplay between personal and social factors (Franklin et al, 2018; Patulny and Bower, 2022; Neves and Petersen, 2024). Some participants distinguished loneliness from living alone, noting they often felt lonelier with ex-spouses or in workplaces. Many struggled to articulate their feelings due to having loving family and friends, hiding their loneliness to avoid burdening their relations or altering how others perceived them. This relational role of social interactions and expectations in shaping emotions and responses to it was evident across all participants, underlining the complexity of loneliness (Hookway et al, 2019; Patulny and Bower, 2022; Neves et al, 2023a).

Technological bridges

Despite the immense suffering of loneliness – anguish, tears, withdrawal and suicidal ideation – participants actively sought ways to alleviate their feelings, noting that they increasingly relied on digital technology instead of pre-pandemic strategies like volunteering or outings. Everyone had a phone or a mobile phone, and they found it to be the most reliable means to stay connected.

Kathleen 'would be lost without her phone'. Her reconfigured routine centred around morning calls to check on community members' welfare and expecting family calls in the afternoon. However, once the calls ended, loneliness returned, as these social networks only occasionally engaged via digital means. Most participants felt this stark contrast between the temporary relief of digital interactions and the deepened loneliness that followed. As captured in Kathleen's diary, evenings were challenging without 'duties' (Figure 14.1).

In her post-diary interview, Kathleen emphasized how technology alleviates loneliness: 'If you're having a bit of a sore time or you're not as good that day – you know, I can sit down and have a talk, and we can all joke.' Because of the lockdown, the council lent Kathleen a new tablet,

Figure 14.1: Kathleen's handwritten diary entry reflecting on feelings of loneliness in the evening

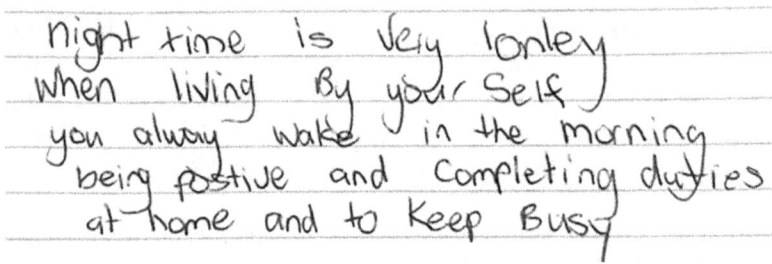

which she used more frequently. It was combined with her phone to enhance different affordances: the phone kept her in touch with friends and the local community through text messages and calls. At the same time, the tablet connected her to the world and relatives abroad through video and broader multimedia features. Her brother in England sent funny photos of his dog, brightening her days. Yet, she rarely used the tablet to communicate with friends, as most didn't 'do computers'. In her daily community calls, she noticed that older people with only landline phones were disadvantaged: 'I see why they get so lonely and cry so much.' Though varying in use and confidence, 28 participants had a tablet or computer, primarily for web browsing and social media. Most viewed these technologies as important social bridges, supporting connectedness (Baecker et al, 2014; Neves et al, 2019a; Shah et al, 2020).

Digital ambivalence(s)

While valuing digital technologies for social connectedness, participants worried about online fraud, privacy, displacement of face-to-face contact, not having assistance if the technology malfunctions, and inadequate skills due to rapid digital changes. For Bob, in his late 70s, technologies are not designed for older people, as he diarized:

> What are they going to think of next to exclude the older generation!! Advanced technology doesn't appeal to me at all in my old age; it just leaves me behind in its super race. … I find comfort in my trusty old radio (talk-back programs) to hear other human voices for connection to the outside world. (Bob)

His entry was interesting because Bob chose to produce a digital rather than paper diary for this study. He explained in interviews that he did not use his computer and phone much before the pandemic; with lockdowns, he had to rely more on them as 'life moved online'. Previously, he eased loneliness by being in a seniors' group and volunteering with an orchestra for 11 years, helping him stay connected. The pandemic halted these activities, leaving him 'cut off'.

Divorced for 36 years, Bob has minimal contact with his few remaining relatives, connecting only during funerals. After the divorce, his ex-wife took their daughter, who has Down's Syndrome, and disappeared. Although Bob has caring neighbours and friends, he has felt lonely for a long time, which depresses him. He is unsure how it started; it just 'crept' up on him. He receives a daily call from the Red Cross, which is reassuring but also a reminder of his loneliness. Bob dislikes his mobile phone, finding it too cumbersome, especially for text messages. His attempts to experiment with technology have been costly due to technical problems and a lack of support: 'How to make tech easier for older people? Make them simpler. Please. I used to say, "If I want to buy a telephone, I'll buy a telephone. If I want to buy a camera, I'll go and buy a camera".' Bob has encountered significant 'sociotechnical' ageism – digital stereotypes and marginalization that associate later life with technological ineptitude (Neves et al, 2023b). He has internalized these views and avoids seeking technological assistance to evade feelings of shame.

During lockdowns, he emailed friends and watched YouTube concerts to 'kill time' and distract from loneliness. Deteriorating eyesight forced him to give up woodworking, leaving him no hobbies. Like many participants, Bob feels ambivalent about digital technologies: they can bridge and connect social worlds, but when used for superficial interactions, they often enhance loneliness. Most participants felt that digital interactions were frequently fleeting and shallow. This helps explain the inconsistent evidence about the role of technology in connectedness and loneliness (Neves et al, 2019a; Balki et al, 2023; Kadowaki and Wister, 2023; Robbins et al, 2023). As underscored by participants, even when adequately employed for connectedness, technologies are not enough; face-to-face connections are still needed (Barbosa Neves et al, 2023; Robbins et al, 2023).

In his post-diary interview, Bob remarked that technologies 'will not wipe out the loneliness, it will just replace it temporarily – for a short time, but the loneliness is still there'. Bob sees loneliness as a symptom of being old and ill, feeling 'left for dead'. These interacting stigmas further illuminate the relational nature of loneliness and sociotechnical systems (Barbosa Neves et al, 2023; Neves and Petersen, 2024). Bob wants to befriend younger people (online and offline), not just be siloed with 'oldies', but believes that 'people don't want to have connections with older people. You know, "This old man, this silly man … We can't help him. He can't offer anything to us. We can't offer anything to him"'.

Taken together, these findings highlight the multidimensionality of loneliness in later life and the limitations of digital technologies in fully addressing it. While participants valued technology as an avenue for social connection, it regularly fell short of providing the richer, meaningful interactions they needed. All preferred close, regular face-to-face contact to alleviate their loneliness. However, even before the pandemic, many were restricted in this regard due to their living arrangements, relationship status and health conditions. The ambivalence towards digital technologies reveals the nuanced interplay between temporary relief and deeper, unresolved feelings of disconnection. The persistent nature of loneliness for this older group, compounded by societal and sociotechnical factors, highlights the need for a more critical examination of the role of digital technologies and their affordances for older people.

Conclusion

This chapter demonstrates the relational nature of loneliness by examining how interplaying personal (individual contexts) and social dimensions (stigma, ageism, ableism) affect perceptions, experiences and responses to loneliness. Participants' accounts reveal the complexity of loneliness and its persistence despite efforts to stay connected through technology. While technologies can offer social bridges, their ability to tackle loneliness fully is limited by usage type, sociotechnical circumstances, including technological access and skills, and the necessity for face-to-face connectedness in later life. This highlights the intricate relational and sociotechnical dimensions of loneliness in the broader landscape of ageing and socio-digital inclusion. It extends beyond lockdown contexts, as our participants experienced prolonged loneliness well before the COVID-19 pandemic.

These findings have significant implications for policy and interventions, emphasizing the need to destigmatize loneliness, address ageism and expand access to and literacy in digital technologies. However, they also point to the necessity of providing more comprehensive support systems beyond digital connectivity, particularly for older people who experience prolonged loneliness. This requires recognizing both the opportunities and limitations of technology in addressing the deeper emotional needs of older adults. Interventions should then consider integrated models that blend digital tools with opportunities for meaningful face-to-face interactions. These efforts must also account for the specific challenges and stigmas older people face, ensuring that interventions are inclusive and responsive to their varied experiences and needs.

References

Alberti, F.B. (2019) *A Biography of Loneliness: The History of an Emotion*, Oxford University Press.

Baecker, R., Sellen, K., Crosskey, S., Boscart, V. and Neves, B. (2014) 'Technology to reduce social isolation and loneliness', in *Proceedings of the 16th International ACM SIGACCESS Conference on Computers & Accessibility – ASSETS '14*, ACM Press, pp 27–34. Available at: http://dl.acm.org/citation.cfm?doid=2661334.2661375 (Accessed 13 October 2021).

Balki, E., Hayes, N. and Holland, C. (2022) 'Effectiveness of technology interventions in addressing social isolation, connectedness, and loneliness in older adults: systematic umbrella review', *JMIR Aging*, 5(4), e40125.

Balki, E., Holland, C. and Hayes, N. (2023) 'Use and acceptance of digital communication technology by older adults for social connectedness during the COVID-19 pandemic: mixed methods study', *Journal of Medical Internet Research*, 25, e41535.

Barbosa Neves, B., Waycott, J. and Maddox, A. (2023) 'When technologies are not enough: the challenges of digital interventions to address loneliness in later life', *Sociological Research Online*, 28(1), 150–170.

Crossley, N. (2010) *Towards Relational Sociology*, Routledge.

Donati, P. (2010) *Relational Sociology: A New Paradigm for the Social Sciences*, Routledge.

Durkheim, É. (1897) *Le suicide: étude de sociologie*, F. Alcan.

Franklin, A.S. (2009) 'On loneliness', *Geografiska Annaler: Series B, Human Geography*, 91(4), 343–354.

Franklin, A., Neves, B.B., Hookway, N., Patulny, R., Tranter, B. and Jaworski, K. (2019) 'Towards an understanding of loneliness among Australian men: gender cultures, embodied expression and the social bases of belonging', *Journal of Sociology*, 55(1), 124–143.

Gardiner, C., Laud, P., Heaton, T. and Gott, M. (2020) 'What is the prevalence of loneliness amongst older people living in residential and nursing care homes? A systematic review and meta-analysis', *Age and Ageing*, 49(5), 748–757.

Granovetter, M.S. (1983) 'The strength of weak ties: a network theory revisited', *Sociological Theory*, 1, 201–233.

Hawkley, L.C. (2022) 'Loneliness and health', *Nature Reviews Disease Primers*, 8(1), 1–2.

HM Government UK (2018) *A Connected Society: A Strategy for Tackling Loneliness – Laying the Foundations for Change*, Department for Digital, Culture, Media and Sport.

Hookway, N., Neves, B.B., Franklin, A. and Patulny, R. (2019) 'Loneliness and love in late modernity: sites of tension and resistance', in *Emotions in Late Modernity*, Routledge, pp 83–97.

Hunt, M., Marx, R., Lipson, C. and Young, J. (2018) 'No more FOMO: limiting social media decreases loneliness and depression', *Journal of Social and Clinical Psychology*, 37, 751–768.

Jeste, D.V., Lee, E.E. and Cacioppo, S. (2020) 'Battling the modern behavioral epidemic of loneliness: suggestions for research and interventions', *JAMA Psychiatry*, 77(6), 553–554.

Kadowaki, L. and Wister, A. (2023) 'Older adults and social isolation and loneliness during the COVID-19 pandemic: an integrated review of patterns, effects, and interventions', *Canadian Journal on Aging / La Revue canadienne du vieillissement*, 42(2), 199–216.

MacKenzie, D.A. and Wajcman, J. (eds) (1999) *The Social Shaping of Technology*, 2nd edition, Open University Press.

Milligan, C., Bingley, A. and Gatrell, A. (2005) 'Digging deep: using diary techniques to explore the place of health and well-being amongst older people', *Social Science & Medicine*, 61(9), 1882–1892.

Morgan, T., Wiles, J., Park, H.-J., Moeke-Maxwell, T., Dewes, O., Black S. et al (2021) 'Social connectedness: what matters to older people?', *Ageing & Society*, 41(5), 1126–1144.

Morozov, E. (2013) *To Save Everything, Click Here: The Folly of Technological Solutionism*, Public Affairs.

Neves, B.B. and Petersen, A. (2024) *The Social Stigma of Loneliness: A Sociological Approach to Understanding the Experiences of Older People*, The Sociological Review.

Neves, B.B., Franz, R., Judges, R., Beermann, C. and Baecker, R. (2019a) 'Can digital technology enhance social connectedness among older adults? A feasibility study', *Journal of Applied Gerontology*, 38(1), 49–72.

Neves, B.B., Sanders, A. and Kokanović, R. (2019b) '"It's the worst bloody feeling in the world": experiences of loneliness and social isolation among older people living in care homes', *Journal of Aging Studies*, 49, 74–84.

Neves, B.B., Colón Cabrera, D., Sanders, A. and Warren, N. (2023a) 'Pandemic diaries: lived experiences of loneliness, loss, and hope among older adults during COVID-19', *The Gerontologist*, 63(1), 120–130.

Neves, B.B., Petersen, A., Vered, M., Carter, A. and Omori, M. (2023b) 'Artificial intelligence in long-term care: technological promise, aging anxieties, and sociotechnical ageism', *Journal of Applied Gerontology*. 07334648231157370.

Neves, B.B., Sanders, A., Warren, N. and Ko, P. (2023c) *Loneliness in Later Life as Existential Inequality*, SAGE. 00380385231208649.

O'Rourke, H. and Sidani, S. (2017) 'Definition, determinants, and outcomes of social connectedness for older adults: a scoping review', *Journal of Gerontological Nursing*, 43(7), 43–52.

Osaki, T. (2021) 'As suicides rise amid the pandemic, Japan takes steps to tackle loneliness', *Japan Times*, 21 February. Available at: https://www.japantimes.co.jp/news/2021/02/21/national/japan-tackles-loneliness/ (Accessed 25 July 2022).

Patulny, R. and Bower, M. (2022) 'Beware the "loneliness gap"? Examining emerging inequalities and long-term risks of loneliness and isolation emerging from COVID-19', *Australian Journal of Social Issues*, 57(3), 562–583.

Perlman, D. and Peplau, L. (1981) 'Toward a social psychology of loneliness', *Personal Relationships in Disorder*, 3, 31–43.

Prime Minister's Office (2018) 'PM commits to government-wide drive to tackle loneliness'. Available at: https://www.gov.uk/government/news/pm-commits-to-government-wide-drive-to-tackle-loneliness (Accessed 25 July 2022).

Riessman, C.K. (2008) *Narrative Methods for the Human Sciences*, SAGE.

Robbins, R., DiClemente, R.J., Baig, N., Johnson, A., Chou, A. and Van den Bulck, J. (2023) 'Digital communications technology use and feelings of anxiety, depression, and loneliness among older adults during the COVID-19 pandemic', *Journal of Applied Gerontology*, 42(9), 1911–1920.

Roth, A.R. and Peng, S. (2024) 'Streams of interactions: social connectedness in daily life', *Social Networks*, 78, 203–211.

Saldaña, J. (2021) *The Coding Manual for Qualitative Researchers*, SAGE.

Shah, H.A. and Househ, M. (2023) 'Understanding loneliness in younger people: review of the opportunities and challenges for loneliness interventions', *Interactive Journal of Medical Research*, 12(1), e45197.

Shah, S.G.S., Nogueras, D., van Woerden, H.C. and Kiparoglou, V. (2020) 'The COVID-19 pandemic: a pandemic of lockdown loneliness and the role of digital technology', *Journal of Medical Internet Research*, 22(11), e22287.

Shah, S.G.S., Nogueras, D., van Woerden, H.C. and Kiparoglou, V. (2021) 'Evaluation of the effectiveness of digital technology interventions to reduce loneliness in older adults: systematic review and meta-analysis', *Journal of Medical Internet Research*, 23(6), e24712.

Smith, K.P. and Christakis, N.A. (2008) 'Social networks and health', *Annual Review of Sociology*, 34(1), 405–429.

Sutin, A.R., Luchetti, M., Aschwanden, D., Zhu, X., Stephan, Y. and Terracciano, A. (2022) 'Loneliness and risk of all-cause, Alzheimer's, vascular, and frontotemporal dementia: a prospective study of 492,322 individuals over 15 years', in *International Psychogeriatrics*, 35(6), 283–292.

Teshale, A.B., Htun, H.L., Hu, J., Dalli, L.L., Lim, M.H., Neves, B.B. et al (2023) 'The relationship between social isolation, social support, and loneliness with cardiovascular disease and shared risk factors: a narrative review', *Archives of Gerontology and Geriatrics*, 111, 105008.

University of Oxford (2022) *COVID-19 Government Response Tracker*, Blavatnik School of Government. Available at: https://www.bsg.ox.ac.uk/research/covid-19-government-response-tracker (Accessed 3 June 2024).

Weiss, R.S. (1973) *Loneliness: The Experience of Emotional and Social Isolation*, MIT Press.

Welch, V., Ghogomu, E.T., Barbeau, V.I., Dowling, S., Doyle, R., Beveridge, E. et al (2023) 'Digital interventions to reduce social isolation and loneliness in older adults: an evidence and gap map', *Campbell Systematic Reviews*, 19(4), e1369.

Wellman, B. and Wortley, S. (1990) 'Different strokes from different folks: community ties and social support', *American Journal of Sociology*, 96(3), 558–588.

15

Digital Pathways to Social Connection and Mental Health on the Urban Fringe

Milovan Savic and Anthony McCosker

Introduction

Like many large cities worldwide, Melbourne's rapidly expanding outer metropolitan suburbs face significant challenges, including lagging social infrastructure, transient populations and long commutes for residents. These factors contribute to heightened feelings of isolation and disconnection among residents (Layton and Latham, 2021), deepening the crisis of social connection and loneliness. Financial stress further complicates these issues, as socioeconomic status influences the impact of suburban living on loneliness (see Chapter 6, this volume). This chapter explores how residents in these areas use digital tools – including social media, messaging apps and online community forums – to foster and navigate social connection.

While social connection has long been a primary use of digital technologies, their effectiveness is increasingly uncertain (Doctorow, 2023). This chapter reveals how technology complements face-to-face interactions, helping to fill the gaps left by social isolation in urban fringe areas. We focus on case studies of three young people with psychosocial challenges, examining how they employ digital tools to navigate social connection amid rapid urban expansion and inadequate social infrastructure. We frame our analysis using the concept of a digital social connection ecosystem (Savic et al, 2025), emphasizing the dynamic and layered nature of digitally facilitated social connections. Once dominated by platforms like Facebook and simple messaging apps, this ecosystem is now fractured, with various platforms and apps catering to different interactions, from maintaining intimate relationships to engaging with the broader community.

The lifestyle typical of these suburbs – marked by long commutes and demanding work schedules (Kroen et al, 2022) – exacerbates the challenge of maintaining existing social ties and forging new ones. Many residents live among strangers, with limited opportunities for spontaneous social interactions crucial for building a sense of belonging (Layton and Latham, 2021; Ermansons et al, 2023). By examining three case studies, this chapter reveals how individuals adapt digital tools to meet their social connection needs despite the challenges posed by daily routines and the isolating nature of urban fringes.

This chapter examines the diverse uses of digital tools and their role in facilitating social connection as conceptualized in the digital social connection ecosystem model. Our case studies reveal the important role of digital social connection in creating and managing a non-judgemental safety net crucial for supporting mental health and wellbeing. Contributing to debates about the impact of digital media on sociality, we detail how some people adapt digital tools to overcome physical and social barriers, emphasizing reciprocity, frequency and intensity in close relationships while building belonging through group participation and digital cultural consumption. Our analysis employs Farmer et al's (2021; 2025) framework of social connection and identifies key implications for practice to support community connections and enhance social wellbeing.

Conceptualizing social connection

In this chapter, we conceptualize social connection as encompassing relationships within intimate, close and broader social circles, each serving specific functions such as maintaining proximity, accessing social support and fostering a sense of belonging (Farmer et al, 2021; 2024; 2025). This multifaceted concept reflects the quality and nature of relationships individuals maintain, influencing their emotional wellbeing and overall health. When these connections are lacking, various types of loneliness can arise – intimate loneliness refers to the absence of close, supportive relationships; relational loneliness reflects the lack of quality friendships or family connections; and collective loneliness pertains to disconnection from larger social groups or communities (Cacioppo and Cacioppo, 2014). Understanding these dimensions points to the necessity of balanced social connections across social connection circles, as they can mitigate feelings of isolation and loneliness and enhance overall wellbeing.

The social connection model posits that connections are maintained through the give and take of emotional and practical support, which varies depending on the closeness of the relationship (Farmer et al, 2024; 2025; Lim et al, 2024). Drawing on Robin Dunbar's (1998) social brain hypothesis, we outline the social connection ecosystem as layers or circles, each representing different types of contacts.

- *Close connections*: Individuals with whom one has intimate, proximate ties.
- *Allies*: Those relied upon for reciprocal help, support and resources.
- *Groups*: Collectives formed around shared interests, such as work, hobbies or sports.
- *Wider community*: Place-based or cultural affiliations, sustaining a sense of belonging.

Our conceptualization of social connection incorporates interdisciplinary concepts and empirical evidence on how people perceive social connection (see also Chapter 12, this volume). It highlights the importance of balanced connections across these circles, including their functional roles in providing social support and fostering community belonging. Social connection is enacted through ongoing interactions, with close relationships requiring substantial time and effort (Lim et al, 2024). As relationships extend beyond close connections, reciprocity may be more indirect and less frequent.

The literature emphasizes the role of social media in strengthening existing and fostering new connections. Social media and messaging apps create new kinds of social ties, enabling *potential connections* that have not yet been activated through interaction. This provides opportunities to access diverse networks and resources (Haythornthwaite, 2002; Ellison et al, 2007). Transient social connections are common, often forming and dissolving across social media platforms. For individuals in diaspora cultural communities, specific social media platforms and messaging apps help maintain close ties with family and friends across national borders, fostering community through shared experiences and emotional support (see Chapter 3, this volume), a concept referred to as asymmetrical mobile intimacy (Cabalquinto, 2018; Alinejad, 2019).

A digital social connection ecosystem

Research demonstrates how social media and communication technologies facilitate the development of social and emotional connections, particularly in intimate relationships, while also recognizing the potential for alienation and negative experiences. Digital media create opportunities to enhance connections across distances through asynchronous communication features that foster intimacy and support (Danielsbacka et al, 2021).

A diverse body of literature addresses this topic; indicating that digital media can help to reduce loneliness and enhance social connections through emotional exchanges and diverse relationships (Matassi et al, 2019). While these platforms can strengthen family connections (Danielsbacka et al, 2021), studies indicate that voice calls and face-to-face meetings are generally more effective than texting or social media interactions (Hall et al, 2022; Sutcliffe et al, 2023). Overall, digital communication offers valuable opportunities for connection, but it does not fully replace the benefits of in-person interactions for social wellbeing (Hall and Liu, 2022).

However, social media platforms have recently become more fragmented and unstable in their ability to support connections (Alinejad, 2019; Doctorow, 2023). Changes in algorithms, user engagement patterns and platform policies can disrupt existing relationships and limit opportunities for profound interactions. The potential drawbacks, such as isolation and superficial online interactions, have been noted for some time, indicating the need to scrutinize technology's role in human sociality (Turkle, 2011; Ryan et al, 2017). There is renewed attention to their role in contributing to young people's mental ill-health (Haidt, 2024), despite strong criticism of these claims. Dating and hookup apps specialize in connecting people in proximate locations, for both intimate relationships and friendships. However, research shows that women, LGBTQIA+ and other marginalized groups often develop strategies to navigate safety and wellbeing on these platforms (Albury et al, 2019; Byron, 2020; Duguay, 2022).

This chapter emphasizes the dynamic nature of the digital social connection ecosystem, with social media platforms and apps supporting different types of social connection, from intimate relationships to broader communities (Savic et al, 2025). Our case studies explore how digital tools are used to manage social connection within this ecosystem. Importantly, our approach is platform- and device-agnostic, recognizing people use various digital tools for different layers of social connection.

Notes on the methodology

This chapter draws on data from the Australian Research Council-funded study 'Activating Social Connection in Australia', which explores social connection and isolation among residents in three outer metropolitan areas of Melbourne, Australia. It complements the methodological details provided in Chapter 12 by Farmer et al, focusing on the elements pertinent to the analysis presented here.

The study employed a qualitative methodology, utilizing in-depth interviews centred on three case studies of participants experiencing mental health challenges. These individuals were recruited through a partner organization – a mental health service provider whose services they received. The three case studies presented in this chapter were selected for their unique ability to adapt digital tools to overcome physical and social barriers, emphasizing reciprocity, frequency and intensity in their relationships. While the larger study included interviews with 44 participants, this chapter focuses on three case studies for their skilled engagement with digital tools for social connection. Their experiences offer valuable insights into how digital interactions can create a non-judgemental safety net, crucial for supporting mental health and wellbeing, and highlight lessons that can improve the way social connection is fostered in local communities.

Each participant engaged in two face-to-face interviews, lasting 60 to 120 minutes, conducted one to two weeks apart. This interval between the interviews allowed participants to reflect more deeply on their social connections. The semi-structured interviews followed a predetermined topic schedule and were held in local community centres. To better facilitate discussions, we used a visual social connection model to prompt reflections across different layers of social connection. The first interview broadly explored social connection in place, while the second focused on digital media use. Participants received an AU$150 voucher as compensation for their involvement. Interviews were audio-recorded, transcribed using OtterAI, and reviewed for accuracy.

Data analysis employed the circles of social connection model to identify patterns in digital media use. An abductive approach was taken (Timmermans and Tavory, 2022), moving between interview data, the conceptual model, and existing literature on social connection and digital media. The findings from these case studies contribute to a better understanding of how digital tools can enhance social connections among individuals facing mental health challenges.

Findings: navigating social connectivity in digital spaces

Findings indicate that participants did not distinguish between in-person and digitally mediated connections; their experiences showed that digital elements are integral to social interactions. This illustrates how digital and face-to-face interactions are amalgamated into everyday sociality. The three case studies that follow show how digital tools are adapted to manage and enhance social connection within the context of mental health challenges and the isolating environment of outer urban fringes.

Digital lifelines: Emery's social connection journey

Emery, a 24-year-old woman, moved from another Australian state to the northern suburbs of Melbourne just before the COVID-19 lockdowns. As a newcomer, she faced challenges in building local social connections, compounded by mental health challenges, including agoraphobia, which made leaving the house difficult. Emery used Instagram, BeReal (a spontaneous photo-sharing app) and Bumble (a proximity-based dating and friendship app) to balance intimate contact with friends and access new in-person connections to navigate these barriers.

Although Emery prefers face-to-face interactions, the pandemic pushed her to explore social media to help meet her social needs. This adaptability allowed her to expand her local network despite physical and mental health challenges. For example, she used Bumble BFF[1] to connect with others in her area: 'I got an app called Bumble BFF. Bumble's like a dating app, but you can switch it to make friends. I made a profile and asked, "Hey, anxious girl, are you looking for a new friend? is anyone local?" So, I met a girl who's now a good friend.'

Emery's use of Bumble BFF helped her navigate the difficulties of being new to the area and lockdown restrictions. The app's geolocative feature allowed her to connect with others within a five-kilometre movement radius during lockdowns. Finding common ground eased her initial hesitation to meet new people: 'I sent her a message, which was scary. I've never used a dating app or talked to a stranger like that before. I focused on our shared interests, like *The Office* and our dogs, which gave me something to talk about.' Through Bumble BFF, Emery found opportunities for connection and lessened the anxiety of reaching out. The app's features, such as shared interests and location-based matching, made her feel more comfortable.

Emery primarily uses Instagram to learn about local events and places, following accounts that recommend art shows, cafés and restaurants: 'I follow accounts that do recommendations, like, "Check out this place; They do great cupcakes." So, I watch videos like that.' Instagram serves a dual purpose for Emery: it connects her to the wider community and helps her build a sense of place and belonging. She engages passively by viewing stories, allowing her to stay updated without the pressure of intense conversation: 'I follow people to keep up with what's happening in their lives, and I engage by liking and commenting. I follow my best friend; she posts about her cats. ... I can like the pictures and comment without needing a deep conversation.'

Emery's engagement with BeReal also offers regular intimate contact with close friends. BeReal is more than another social media app in her digital arsenal; it's a carefully curated, intimate space where she shares spontaneous life moments exclusively with a select group of closest connections: 'BeReal is for closer relationships. Instagram is more about presenting the best version of myself. BeReal requires you to show your real life. I even posted from the bath once, hiding behind bubbles. It's just for people I'm okay seeing me in my everyday life.' The app's design encourages unfiltered snapshots, countering the polished performances on social media. Emery noted that BeReal deepens her connections with friends and enhances her self-assuredness in her social identity through simple sharing.

Emery's social media use exemplifies the digital social connection ecosystem, balancing intimate bonds and broader community ties. The three apps offer different ways to manage social connection: Instagram for light-touch interactions and local belonging; BeReal for intimate exchanges with close friends; and Bumble BFF to meet new people locally. This balance is crucial for her wellbeing and sense of belonging, especially given her mental health challenges.

Digital emotional support and friendships: Cristina's Discord community

In her early 20s, Cristina recently moved out of her family home, where she lived with her mother, stepfather and three stepsiblings. Although she remains in touch with them, she does not receive the strong support she desires. Faced with complex mental health issues and a lack of close, intimate connections in her immediate surroundings, Cristina navigates geographically dispersed online digital communities to find allies who provide judgement-free social support. Her journey reveals the benefits of cultivating digital connections across circles of connection.

As an avid and tech-savvy user, Cristina strategically sought interest-based online communities through Discord,[2] building close relationships that she lacks in her immediate environment. Initially introduced to Discord by school friends, she began exploring its many communities:

> I can't remember exactly how I found Discord. But one night, I was browsing the App Store and came across it. I thought, 'Oh, yeah, I'll download this.' Because some of my friends from school were using it. So, I downloaded it, and we started talking through Discord. Then, I decided to join a few servers, and that's how I discovered my passion for voice acting.

By joining these communities (that is, Discord servers), Cristina expands her passion for voice acting within a highly supportive environment. Discord has become her primary tool for daily interaction, transcending geographical barriers and time zone differences to facilitate connections within the group's circle of connection: 'We always check up on each other. We know how to make each other laugh. ... My friends are good listeners, so if I'm having a bad day, they're always there for me. And I'll do the same for them.'

Cristina's routine of checking in with her online friends involves nurturing emotionally supportive relationships across diverse locations. These friends form an essential layer of her social connections, providing reciprocal support that aligns with the *allies'* circle of connection. The asynchronous nature of their communication fosters a sense of ambient co-presence (Madinaou, 2016), making members of the Discord server feel continuously connected even when not actively communicating.

Cristina emphasizes that aligned personalities are the connecting thread that brought her group together, enabling close friendships on a platform often perceived as niche (Floegel, 2021). Her regular interactions and emotional reliance on her Discord friends reflect the depth of these bonds, which Cristina described as comparable to those found in physical proximity.

Another aspect of Cristina's digital media use is her avoidance of public-facing platforms like Twitter (X), Facebook or Instagram, seeking spaces that offer sanctuary and allow her to express herself without fear of judgement. This safe, non-judgemental environment is crucial, as she found this lacking at home, exacerbating her mental health issues: 'I would go to them before I would go to my mom. With moms, they kind of judge you on whatever you tell them. But my friends don't judge me; they listen.'

Cristina's choice to confide in her online friends rather than her mother exemplifies the emotional safety net these digital connections can provide, fulfilling her need for support within the *close connections* circle. Finding non-judgemental support has been challenging in her family and local social life, and she has worked hard to find digital tools that offer a buffer against the stigma and misunderstanding often encountered in her family relationships.

> I use Bumble to find friends. I went on a few dates, but that wasn't really what I was looking for, so I started using it more for the friends side of it. It's good because you can talk to people there, and it's easier to start a conversation since you're not talking directly to their face. For me, it's just a lot easier to make friends that way.

Cristina's strategic use of Bumble for friendships aligns with her comfort in initiating conversations online rather than face-to-face. The app's features lower the barriers to social interaction and alleviate her anxiety about in-person meetings. 'No, we text Bumble ... whenever I can; it's just easier. ... I tend to lose track of people. So, talking on Bumble is easier than scrolling down to find their name.' This aspect of the app helps her organize and regulate her connections, allowing her to maintain distance while exploring new friendships. In this way, dating and friendship apps serve as emotional sanctuaries and practical tools for building local connections.

For Cristina, Discord and Bumble meet her emotional and social needs despite physical isolation and mental health challenges by facilitating interactions based on shared interests and regular check-ins. Her experiences exemplify the importance of digital literacy and personalized approaches to selecting the right apps, as her strategic use of these platforms allows her to cultivate supportive connections and navigate social interactions that align with her mental health and social connection needs.

Social connectivity in the face of complex family relationships: Maeve's digital ties

Maeve, a young non-binary person from a low socioeconomic background, navigates multiple challenges, including anxiety, Asperger's and complex family dynamics within a multi-family household. Employed in a low-skilled job, Maeve feels their queer identity adds another layer of complexity to their social interactions.

While harbouring a clear preference for face-to-face interactions, Maeve's life circumstances necessitate an innovative approach to socialization, combining both digital and physical environments. Due to the limitations imposed by their socioeconomic situation and fractured family relationships, Maeve has adopted strategies for using Facebook, Instagram and Snapchat as digitally augmented geographical spaces, enabling localized social connection. However, managing these digital tools for social connection requires masking or context-switching as they move between professional, personal and interest-based groups and connections.

Maeve reflects on how mobile devices and social media platforms give young people instant access to and opportunities for digital social connection: 'Just the interface – many kids have their phones with them anyway, and they're growing up learning how to use this stuff. If I go here – on the homepage – I'm already connected with hundreds of people I might know. And it's just two button presses away.' Despite this digital connectivity at their fingertips, Maeve also felt strongly about the need to connect with people in their local area. In traditional settings, the physical environment creates 'bumping spaces' (Bagnall et al, 2017) that facilitate spontaneous interactions and friendships. Maeve's reliance on digital platforms suggests that, similar to bumping spaces, the opportunities for connection can be cultivated online. This ease of developing and nurturing relationships, without the constraint of geographical location, helps Maeve expand their social circle: 'If it weren't for social media, I wouldn't have met half the people I know today. It's so easy to connect with someone, even for someone like me, who has, you know, anxiety, depression, ADHD, Asperger's. … It's easy for me to go online and make a new friend.'

Maeve estimates that approximately half of their social connections are formed through digital platforms, reflecting the important role social media plays in providing accessible avenues for interaction despite the limitations imposed by their mental health conditions. These connections include social allies and more casual connections, representing a diverse network spanning various circles of connection. Maeve maintains two Facebook accounts – one personal and one professional – and talks about the need for context-switching or adapting their behaviour and presentation depending on the platform, as well as 'masking', which involves concealing aspects of their identity to fit in with different social groups:

I don't need it as much as I used to, but it was a massive part of my life for a while. I'd come home, see what my friends are doing and then post about what I did on the weekend.

Then, you know, Instagram is for sharing what I do on the weekends or cool events I attend.

Snapchat is ... still very much about communicating through text or this and that, but Snapchat adds an extra visual representation to it.

Digital environments can lower interaction barriers, making them effective socialization platforms, particularly for those facing various obstacles. This highlights the diverse ways individuals can establish and maintain social ties across different circles of connection.

Maintaining a sense of place is important to Maeve. Given their frequent relocations and complicated family dynamics, they use social media to remain linked to the local community. Maeve uses Facebook's features, such as pages and groups, to stay informed about local events and interest groups. In this sense, Maeve's 'digital tethering' to their hometown points to the role of digital platforms in fostering a sense of connection to one's broader community. Even after relocating, Maeve sustains a quiet yet profound connection to their previous local area through Facebook groups. This passive engagement offers comfort and awareness of the community's pulse without requiring active participation: 'I'm still a part of the [old hometown] Facebook groups and stuff. So, I feel like I'm still in that community, even though I don't live there anymore. ... If I left those Facebook groups, I'd feel cut off. There's no reason for me to engage with them otherwise.'

This connection to the broader community is vital for Maeve's wellbeing. Online circles act as a low-demand bridge back to their roots, subtly linking them to the wider community of their previous locality. While unobtrusive, this silent companionship is deeply grounding – allowing them to stay informed and connected without constant pressure to interact. For Maeve, these digital spaces are critical for social continuity, offering a lifeline of familiarity and belonging that aligns with their lifestyle and comfort level. In the context of their family difficulties, Maeve's experiences reflect a form of emotional loneliness characterized by the absence of close, supportive relationships. Their reliance on digital platforms provides an avenue to seek connections that fulfil this emotional need, compensating for the complexities of their family dynamics.

Conclusion

This chapter explored how young people facing mental health challenges and isolation in urban fringes use digital tools to bridge connectivity gaps across their social circles. Central to the three cases is the adaptive and skilled use of various platforms and apps to create and maintain localized connections that offer social support and emotional safety. Each case illustrates the effort in tailoring digital tools to meet specific social connection goals. In close connections, reciprocity, frequency and intensity of interactions are key. Emery's use of BeReal for spontaneous sharing fosters intimacy, while Cristina's daily interactions on Discord provide depth and support routines through regular checking-in. In groups, interactions shift to lighter, less frequent engagements; for instance, Emery's light-touch Instagram maintains a social presence with minimal commitment. Finally, for the broader community, Maeve utilizes Facebook to stay connected to her hometown, creating a sense of belonging despite physical distance. They navigate the digital social connection ecosystem to overcome their unique barriers and mental health challenges, demonstrating how tailored digital interactions can effectively address their distinctive needs for connection.

These findings have implications for service providers and local government. Specifically, integrating targeted digital capabilities into community programmes can foster local connections and reduce isolation, as demonstrated by Emery's and Cristina's effective use of digital tools to navigate their social needs. We propose that local governments promote and support local online community groups through platforms like Facebook and WhatsApp – as well as other digital tools that facilitate group dynamics – ensuring that those who are less digitally skilled have more opportunities to connect.

Additionally, digital literacy workshops can explore and support the kind of strategic uses of digital tools for intimate and close connections we have described in our case studies. The case studies illustrate that these skills are essential for socially isolated individuals, as seen in Cristina's reliance on Discord for emotional support and community engagement. By addressing this often-overlooked aspect of digital social connection, services can enhance local belonging and support structures for improving wellbeing, ultimately contributing to stronger, more connected communities.

Discussions around digital engagements are often polarized: some studies highlight benefits; others cite increased isolation and adverse implications for mental health. Despite growing criticism regarding the potential harm of excessive social media use, it is evident that digital environments can lower interaction barriers, making them effective socialization platforms for those facing obstacles. This chapter illustrated how people actively curate and tailor their digitally mediated interactions to achieve social connection goals and mitigate feelings of isolation and loneliness. By investing time and effort, our case studies showed how individuals cultivate, manage and sustain connection across various layers of social connection despite contextual challenges such as time and distance constraints, emotional difficulties and varying levels of digital dexterity. While not a panacea, digital tools should not be dismissed. Tailored programmes to enhance digital literacy can help people harness the benefits of digital connectivity while mitigating its pitfalls.

Notes

1. Bumble BFF is a feature within the Bumble app designed for users to find and form platonic friendships.
2. Discord is a platform that allows users to chat via text, voice and video on dedicated servers that function as distinct communities. Originally popular among gamers, it has expanded to accommodate a wide range of communities, including those focused on hobbies, education and professional networking.

References

Albury, K., Byron, P., McCosker, A., Pym, T., Walshe, J., Race, K., et al (2019) *Safety, Risk and Wellbeing on Dating Apps: Final Report*, Swinburne University of Technology.

Alinejad, D. (2019) 'Careful co-presence: the transnational mediation of emotional intimacy', *Social Media + Society*, 5(2).

Bagnall, A., South, J., Di Martino, S., Mitchell, B., Pilkington, G. and Newton, R. (2017) *Systematic Scoping Review of Reviews of the Evidence for 'What Works to Boost Social Relations' and its Relationship to Community Wellbeing*, What Works Well Centre for Wellbeing.

Byron, P. (2020) *Digital Media, Friendship and Cultures of Care*, Routledge.

Cabalquinto, E.C.B. (2018) '"We're not only here but we're there in spirit": asymmetrical mobile intimacy and the transnational Filipino family', *Mobile Media & Communication*, 6(1), 37–52.

Cacioppo, J.T. and Cacioppo, S. (2014) 'Social relationships and health: the toxic effects of perceived social isolation', *Social and Personality Psychology Compass*, 8(2), 58–72.

Danielsbacka, M., Tammisalo, K. and Tanskanen, A.O. (2021) 'Digital and traditional communication with kin: displacement or reinforcement?', *Journal of Family Studies*, 29, 1270–1291.

Doctorow, C. (2023) 'The "enshittification" of TikTok: or how, exactly, platforms die', *Wired*, January. Available at: https://www.wired.com/story/tiktok-platforms-cory-doctorow/ (Accessed 15 February 2025).

Duguay, S. (2022) *Personal but not Private: Queer Women, Sexuality, and Identity Modulation on Digital Platforms*, Oxford University Press.

Dunbar, R. (1998) 'The social brain hypothesis', *Evolutionary Anthropology: Issues, News, and Reviews*, 6(5), 178–190.

Ellison, N.B., Steinfield, C. and Lampe, C. (2007) 'The benefits of Facebook "friends": social capital and college students' use of online social network sites', *Journal of Computer-Mediated Communication*, 12, 1143–1168.

Ermansons, G., Kienzler, H., Asif, Z. and Schofield, P. (2023) 'Refugee mental health and the role of place in the Global North countries: a scoping review', *Health & Place*, 79, 102964.

Farmer, J., De Cotta, T., Hartung, C., Knox, J., Roew, C. and Stenta, C. (2021) *Social Connection 101* [Guide], Social Innovation Research Institute.

Farmer, J., Rowe, C., De Cotta, T. and Savic, M. (2024) *Social Connection Guide for Activity Planning*, Swinburne University of Technology.

Farmer, J., De Cotta, T., Savic, M., Rowe, C., Verhagen, J., Sivasubramaniam, D., et al (2025) *Social Connection 101*, revised edition, Swinburne University of Technology. https://doi.org/10.25916/sut.28415261

Floegel, D. (2021) 'Porn bans, purges, and rebirths: the biopolitics of platform death in queer fandoms', *Internet Histories*, 6, 90–112.

Haidt, J. (2024) *The Anxious Generation: How the Great Rewiring of Childhood is Causing an Epidemic of Mental Illness*, Random House.

Hall, J.A. and Liu, D. (2022) 'Social media use, social displacement, and well-being', *Current Opinion in Psychology*, 46, Article 101339.

Hall, J.A., Pennington, N. and Merolla, A.J. (2022) 'Which mediated social interactions satisfy the need to belong?', *Journal of Computer-Mediated Communication*, 28(1), 1–12.

Haythornthwaite, C. (2002) 'Strong, weak, and latent ties and the impact of new media', *The Information Society*, 18(5), 385–401.

Kroen, A., Dodson, J. and Butt, A. (2022) *The Benefits and Challenges of Australian Government Investment in Infrastructure in Outer Suburban Growth Areas: Final Report*, RMIT Centre for Urban Research and National Growth Areas Alliance.

Layton, J. and Latham, A. (2021) 'Social infrastructure and public life – notes on Finsbury Park, London', *Urban Geography*, 43, 755–776.

Lim, M.S.C., Davis, A.C., Rowe, C. and Douglass, C.H. (2024) 'Mild structure, low pressure: how might we increase young people's social connection in the COVID-19 era', *International Journal of Adolescence and Youth*, 29(1), Article 2387096. doi: 10.1080/02673843.2024.2387096

Madianou, M. (2016) 'Ambient co-presence: transnational family practices in polymedia environments', *Global Networks*, 16, 183–201.

Matassi, M., Boczkowski, P.J. and Mitchelstein, E. (2019) 'Domesticating WhatsApp: family, friends, work, and study in everyday communication', *New Media & Society*, 21(10), 2183–2200.

Ryan, T., Allen, K.A., Gray, D.L.L. and McInerney, D.M. (2017) 'How social are social media? A review of online social behaviour and connectedness', *Journal of Relationships Research*, 8, e8.

Savic, M., McCosker, A. and Farmer, J. (2025, in press) 'Navigating isolation: mobilising a digital social connection ecosystem on the urban fringe', *Information, Communication & Society*. doi: 10.1080/1369118X.2025.2502646

Sutcliffe, A., Dunbar, R. and El-Jarn, H. (2023) 'Investigating the use of social media in intimate social relationships', *Behavior & Information Technology*, 42(4), 379–391.

Timmermans, S. and Tavory, I. (2022) *Data Analysis in Qualitative Research: Theorizing with Abductive Analysis*, University of Chicago Press.

Turkle, S. (2011) *Alone Together: Why We Expect More from Technology and Less from Each Other*, Basic Books.

16

Improving Social Connection in Everyday Spaces: Some Guidelines for Everyday Policy and Practice

Roger Patulny, Milovan Savic and Jane Farmer

What is social connection? Concept, challenges and opportunities

Social connection is a complex, interdisciplinary and multifaceted phenomenon. It is revealed in everyday interactions, situations and contexts, and it is inherently relational. This book has provided many examples showing that social connection cannot be reduced just to pathologized patterns of loneliness, solvable through medicalized treatments tailored to individuals and that social context and meaning are paramount for understanding and treating social disconnection.

Population ageing in Australia and around the world has created an increased demand for carers without sufficient resources to meet this demand, resulting in rising loneliness among elderly Australians, particularly those in aged care facilities (Neves et al, 2019). *Changing work practices* – increasingly flexible, mobile, precarious and virtual – disrupt the formation and stability of local networks (Glavin et al, 2019) and long-term retirement transitions (Patulny, 2009). *Cost of living* pressures render socializing a luxury and transform long-term unemployment into a stigmatized purgatory of isolation (Peterie et al, 2019). *Unsocial urban environments*, comprising inadequate, unaffordable and unprotected housing and urban sprawl (that is, 'exopolis'; Soja, 2000) or high-rises (Cheung et al, 2017), combined with poor public transport and few social amenities, erode community connections (Bower et al, 2024. A rush to digital-first communication becomes problematic when it entirely replaces face-to-face connections (Nowland et al, 2018; Patulny, 2020; Chapter 15, this volume), eroding institutions that perform important social functions like clubs, societies and trade unions (Leigh and Terrel, 2020).

Cultural changes also significantly impact social connection. *Family structures* are shifting towards single-person households and individualized culture (Hookway et al, 2019), placing more pressure on nuclear families and mothers to maintain communities (Franklin et al, 2019; Patulny, 2024). Gender role changes bring distinct challenges for *men's social connection*, as many struggle with the transition from primary breadwinner to sharing care work. Traditional and hegemonic masculinity norms that eschew vulnerability lead to instrumental rather than emotionally supportive relationships (Patulny, 2024), increasing men's loneliness (Botha and Bower, 2024).

Immigration presents its challenges, as immigrants face scapegoating (Hsu, 2021) while navigating challenges to connect in new countries (Patulny, 2015). The shift to algorithmically siloed digital connection has fuelled a rise in intolerance and 'dark-side social capital' (Patulny and Svendsen, 2007), particularly challenging for young people embedded in toxic online communities (Nilan et al, 2023), threatening social cohesion and acceptance of diversity.

So, what do we do about the 'problem' of social connection? Do we now have a clear sense of what it is? Can we improve it in the context of complexity and multiple meanings? Should we ask more critical questions, such as: Who are we improving it for? Who is being left behind? And are there some for whom we might even be making things worse?

While it was not the purpose of this book to generate a comprehensive review of evidence on causes, interventions and 'what works', or provide detailed policy prescriptions to address these issues, the studies contained here provide abundant insights for moving forward. Taken together, the observations and recommendations can serve as a set of guidelines about what we should and shouldn't do when trying to improve everyday social connection across various spaces. Critically, the studies provide important *contextualized* hints about how we might proceed, who might benefit, and who might be left behind or suffer. We have organized these ideas into themes that offer solutions to the social connection problem in the context of the various spaces analysed in this collection – personal, physical, community and digital. We also offer our perspective on universal themes that span these contexts, gaps in the research, and potential challenges and solutions for these gaps.

Addressing disconnection in personal spaces

The focus of the first section of the book was on how social connection operates within everyday personal and intimate spaces. This section makes the point that structural, cultural and institutionalized forces shape how people become embedded within communities and networks (Grzymala-Kazlowska and Ryan, 2022), and strongly impact even the most private, intimate and (seemingly) individualized relationships. Patulny notes the impact of gender, masculinity and nuclear family norms and institutions on men's connections (Chapter 2). Cabalquinto (Chapter 3) traces how digital connective capacities and cultural modes of communication shape lines of connection between transnational families. Knox and Komu (Chapter 4) point out how social connections among the elderly are nurtured and supported by the type of institutional care they receive. And Bennetts and colleagues (Chapter 5) emphasize the importance of human–animal relationships and demonstrate how they picked up the 'connectivity slack' during (human/government-instituted) COVID-19 lockdowns. These findings accord with the need to support interventions encouraging cultural change and a better 'care culture', perhaps particularly among men in their personal (Pointon et al, 2020; Patulny, 2024) and working relationships (Hookway and Cruickshank, 2024).

Several key policy and intervention recommendations arise from this section. The first set advocates for *educational campaigns encouraging more respectful and diverse personal relationships*. Patulny asserts the importance of educational campaigns to promote respectful attitudes, emotional disclosure, assistance and reciprocity among boys and men while supporting initiatives that help men develop more diverse friendship groups. Bennetts and colleagues similarly argue for improving understanding among public and professional practitioners (potentially including GPs and those involved in social prescribing) of pets' role in providing comfort, purpose, meaning and social connection.

The second set of recommendations is to *critically assess how everyday social institutions (for example, migrant, family, care networks) support personal social interaction or encourage dependency, inequality and exploitation*. Cabalquinto shows how migrants from different cultural, transnational and digital-literacy backgrounds connect unequally and asymmetrically. He argues that mutual and intercultural care practices require recognition of these distinctions. Patulny highlights men's social dependency on women and the nuclear family domicile. Bearing in mind the fragility of the notion of 'home' as a haven of autonomy and status (Cheshire et al, 2021), Patulny argues that such dependency on women as social connectors creates risks both for men's isolation and for ongoing gender inequality and exploitation. Knox and Komu advocate for uniform quality standards in care facilities to counteract health and aged care inequalities, including supported accommodation that is safe, barrier-free, high quality, home-like and tailored to individual needs.

The third set of recommendations encourages *the expansion and diversification of personal connections and networks*. Cabalquinto emphasizes how government policies must consider transnational digital and local connections to shape positive ageing. Patulny advocates for initiatives encouraging men to broaden their intimate networks. Knox and Komu argue for greater recognition of older people's social needs, ensuring care services help maintain meaningful social interactions. Bennetts et al recommend organizing social connection around pets as 'talking points' for broader engagement.

Addressing disconnection in physical spaces

The second section of the book focused on how social connection is constrained and enabled by housing, as well as physical and urban environmental qualities beyond the household. Bower and colleagues (Chapter 6) showed that housing quality and neighbourhood amenities impact social connection through localized interrelations between communities, cultures, available resources and their environments. Sung (Chapter 7) demonstrated how the urban environment shapes the mental health outcomes of elderly Koreans, pointing to the importance of networks beyond the immediate family. Hookway and Dwyer (Chapter 8) captured the relationality between urban spaces and communities through third spaces like public parks, pointing to new types of communities like parkrun as potential antidotes to declining traditional sports organizations. Zaporozhets and Brednikova (Chapter 9) showed how urban problems can unite or divide communities, dependent upon pre-existing trust norms and regulatory capacities.

These studies offer further policy and practice recommendations for promoting social connection in physical spaces. The most common recommendation was for *clearer, stronger and more just government regulations on urban design and amenities, focusing on encouraging social connection*. Government regulation can shape homemaking (Cheshire et al, 2021), and Bower et al argue that housing and urban design should produce affordable, high-quality, safe, secure homes within communities, with space for guests and access to public amenities, particularly for those of low socioeconomic status and public housing residents. They argue that minimum housing standards could be changed and better enforced to ensure that intermittent maintenance and improvements are applied consistently to all forms of housing, including public housing. Zaporozhets and Brednikova emphasize supporting housing resident cooperation in Russia through self-governance rules and infrastructure development, aligning with calls for social cities built around connective, accessible transport (Bower et al, 2024).

A related recommendation was for *greater government investment in physical housing and social amenities*. Bower and colleagues advocate for equitable access to social infrastructure, particularly for isolated populations. Sung suggests policy makers should focus on residents whose social networks are restricted to immediate family, designing amenities to encourage broader engagement. However, as Zaporozhets and Brednikova note, securing such investments faces real-world challenges, particularly in authoritarian states resistant to supporting independent community development.

A further recommendation was that policy and interventions should *embrace a flexible and personalized approach to providing housing, amenities and community activities*. Bower et al recommend mandatory 'personalization of space' clauses in rental agreements to enhance belonging. Hookway and Dwyer advocate for flexible 'pop-up' communities such as parkrun as a solution for healthy social exercise.

A final recommendation concerning physical spaces is to *design cooperatives, interventions and programmes to value-add opportunities for flexible, incidental and collectivized interactions in physical spaces*. While neighbourliness arises from the intertwining of the lives of people living in close enough proximity (Cheshire, 2022), incidental interactions and challenges can come from beyond the immediate locale. Hookway and Dwyer note how digitally organized neo-tribal communities such as parkrun generate social 'interaction-rituals' that promote extensive incidental interaction. This offers new insight into the importance of featuring 'incidental extra' local rituals and practices to add value when designing interventions promoting social connection.

Zaporozhets and Brednikova argue that pervasive beliefs in individual responsibility for environments lead to rising collective problems, such as insects appearing and spreading throughout shared residential accommodation. Such beliefs ignore the negotiated, escalated process of forming neighbourly (or unneighbourly) connections, and how formal disputes rapidly rise out of breakdowns in quiet 'everyday' agreements around mundane practices (Cheshire et al, 2021). Zaporozhets and Brednikova suggest that identifying how issues around materiality and infrastructure are common to all may begin to push back against this overly individualized ethos, leading to improved neighbourliness and collectivized action.

Addressing disconnection in community spaces

The third section of the book examined social connection among different kinds of communities, and the forms of interventions, strategies and pitfalls that help and hinder such connections. Opacin and colleagues (Chapter 10) examined nature-based social prescribing for LGBTQIA+ refugee and asylum-seeker communities, finding that referring people to nature-based group activities could help prevent loneliness. Battiston and Alexander (Chapter 11) investigated how the Italian-Australian community managed the COVID-19 pandemic and the kinds of ties they drew upon to cope with lockdown and isolation. Farmer and colleagues (Chapter 12) examined social connection in urban fringe communities of place, showing how meaningful interactions can be supported in rapidly changing areas through appropriate community engagement and social infrastructure investment. These chapters produced several recommendations for promoting social connection in community spaces, oriented around promoting culturally appropriate connective strategies and building effective social infrastructure.

The first recommendation is that *interventions to improve community connections need to be customized and tailored to fit the cultural and identity needs of different communities*. Opacin et al note the need to customize interventions and evaluations to account for multiple intersecting forms of social exclusions within unique settings, particularly when considering risks of discrimination and violence among groups like LGBTQIA+ asylum seekers. Battiston and Alexander find that migrants turn to trusted family and close friends rather than governments for support, suggesting services should be built around culturally trusted sources rather than regular government pathways.

The second recommendation is that *interventions should have a flexible design and purposefully look for ways to encourage community engagement*. Opacin et al's adaptative approach includes shorter intervention duration, weaving nature-based activities throughout programmes, and allowing flexible group entry times. Farmer and colleagues advocate that providers should optimize all spaces and activities for social connection, making areas congenial to waiting and interaction, ensuring safety and accessibility for different languages and presentations, and building social interactions into events.

A third recommendation is to *focus specifically on where people get support from and connect them to the right people in the community rather than just any people or institutions*. Opacin et al emphasize digital as well as physical engagement, such as sharing nature pictures through social media for intercultural reflection. Battiston and Alexander recommend examining how support flows through migrant communities' bonding and bridging ties. Farmer et al highlight the importance of connecting people with each other and their local area, as social connection emerges through relationships that encourage place attachments and local identity.

A final community theme is to *consider the interplay between personal, organizational and digital means of promoting social connection*. Farmer et al consider multiple methods: encouraging neighbour interaction, supporting short-term meet-up groups, empowering 'super-connectors', studying successful connecting organizations, using digital communication and optimizing local employment opportunities. This accords with calls for better working conditions for culturally relevant care workers (Zhao et al, 2023) and new ways to support community volunteering (Leigh and Terrel, 2020).

Addressing disconnection in digital spaces

The final section examined the role of digital technologies in contemporary social connection, and how such connective technologies operate best when integrated with everyday physical practices and interactions. Franks (Chapter 13) traced how young women adapted their social connections during COVID-19 lockdowns, revealing distinct phases from network collapse to digital adaptation and new social equilibriums. Barbosa Neves (Chapter 14) looked at the stigma of loneliness among older people in aged care facilities, noting the need for more comprehensive support systems and the opportunities and limitations of digital interactive technology. Savic and McCosker (Chapter 15) examined how digital platforms can foster connections among urban youth in Melbourne, highlighting how digital literacy and the digital divide shape connection potentials.

These studies produced recommendations for encouraging digital-physical social interaction. The first recommendation was *to use digital tools to create safe and de-stigmatized digital spaces that facilitate adaptation and resilience*. Franks demonstrated how digital can evolve from supplementary tools to primary mechanisms for maintaining social capital during crisis, emphasizing the need for frameworks that support network adaptation and recovery. Barbosa Neves argued for the need to destigmatize loneliness and address ageism through expanded access to and literacy in digital technologies among older people while ensuring interventions remain responsive to their varied experiences and needs.

A second recommendation is *to actively use social media platforms to foster positive interactions and network reconstruction*. Franks shows how social media can support the emergence of new social equilibriums, highlighting the importance of understanding how networks respond to and recover from disruption. Savic and McCosker suggest that digital tools and skills in intimate and close connection can be fostered through digital literacy workshops and programmes, noting that while services often avoid this aspect of social connection, digital connection can make a significant difference for socially isolated people.

A third set of recommendations is to *critically realize and work with the positive and negative aspects of digital technologies, and the need to integrate them with physical activities and interactions*. Barbosa Neves advocates for comprehensive support systems that recognize both the potential and limitations of digital connection for older people experiencing loneliness. She emphasizes the importance of blending digital tools with face-to-face interactions. Savic and McCosker recommend local governments promote and support local online community groups while acknowledging that digital environments can lower interaction barriers despite concerns about constant social media engagement. These works accord with calls for using the digital connection and social media as supportive tools that complement rather than substitute for face-to-face connection (Nowland et al, 2018; Patulny, 2020).

Themes, gaps and solutions across everyday spaces

Several overarching themes emerged across the book to transcend the various spatial dimensions we have focused on. Each is in keeping with our structural-relational approach to understanding social connection.

Many studies raised *the importance of resourcing and inequality*. The resources required to produce supportive aged care facilities include appropriately trained and remunerated care and health staff and high quality, barrier-free, individually tailored housing (Chapter 4, this volume). If such requirements are left to the private market, it has great potential to open social connective inequalities between wealthier and poorer retirees. Similarly, geographically concentrated economic deprivation can erode neighbourhood connections, with a lack of resources hindering the development of third spaces and accessible, high-quality social infrastructure (Chapter 6, this volume), as well as reducing neighbourliness and increasing neighbour annoyance (Cheshire, 2022). And digital inequalities and the digital divide reduce the capacity of those left behind to engage with online social contacts (Chapter 15, this volume). The digital divide has now taken on international dimensions, mirroring globalized, asymmetric cultural divides and economic migration structures (Chapter 3, this volume).

The studies here also reveal that *interventions should be cognizant that socioeconomic conditions and demographic intersections strongly influence social connection*. These include socioeconomic intersections with gender and partner status (Chapter 2), older age (Chapter 14), urban residence (Chapter 6), and migrant status (Chapter 3 and Chapter 11). This aligns, for example, with calls for elder-centred community planning, where technological solutions can help (for example, companion robots, chatbots, online engagement; Neves et al, 2023), but it should be built around the need for work to encourage, and not hinder, socializing either at or outside of work. Structural inequalities must also be recognized in determining appropriate interventions for social disconnection. Social prescribing and related services may need to be assessed and overhauled for how well they account for socioeconomic differences and resources in sourcing and referring lonely 'patients' into appropriate, sustainable interventions. They should also be cognizant that 'differentiated embedding', comprised of graduated and multi-layered levels of connection, trust and reciprocity, affords different resources to different groups (for example, migrants) in different circumstances (Grzymala-Kazlowska and Ryan, 2022).

A third theme relates to *the role of stigma in compounding loneliness*. This was noted in multiple studies, including men's reluctance to admit to loneliness and isolation (Chapter 2), how stigmatized persons considered dirty and unclean were subject to greater isolation and loneliness in Russian housing blocks (Chapter 9), the stigma faced by LGBTQIA+ asylum seekers and refugees (Chapter 10) and the compounding impact of stigma on the isolation of older people (Chapter 14). These findings align with other studies that have identified the significant impact of stigma on isolation in other areas, such as unemployment (Peterie et al, 2019). More research and experimentation in interventions are needed to reduce both the stigma associated with loneliness and the compounding effects of other stigmas that *increase* loneliness.

A fourth theme common to all spaces is *the need to look beyond conventional institutions and networks in seeking new forms of connection.* Exclusive focus on nuclear families in Australia (Chapter 2) or child-centred families among elderly Koreans (Chapter 7) have been identified as constraining the development of wider networks. Concentrating on local migrant networks of Filipinos misses the extent to which such networks are now highly globalized and digitally organized and supported (Chapter 3). The parkrun phenomenon shows how new pop-up activity forms replace more conventional sports associations (Chapter 8).

Complementing all these themes is a final one of great importance: despite socioeconomic and other structural constraints, *people have agency in making connections, which can be helped through tailoring programmes.* As with all social circumstances, there is a balance between determining structures and the capacity of agents to make choices, work around, shape these structures (in the long term) and exercise agency. Patulny (Chapter 2) notes how men can develop more inclusive attitudes and engage in different connection practices through deliberate investment in education and interactive skills (that is, emotional capital) to change the internal structures that shape their interactions. Cabalquinto (Chapter 3) notes that when governments and organizations tailor culturally and digitally nuanced policies and interventions to engage with affective experiences, they transcend support in encouraging migrant's active social engagement and thus 'propel generative ways of ageing in a digital world'. Farmer et al (Chapter 12) advocate identifying, appreciating and celebrating community connectors, and developing ways to grow more of these helpful people. It should be recognized, however, that capacities for the agency will be constrained by real-world political situations and government regimes that actively discourage the formation of local solidarity movements and active agency (Chapter 9). And Savic and McCosker (Chapter 15) argue that providers should create tailored programmes to enhance digital literacy, helping people harness benefits and avoid the pitfalls of digital connectivity.

Conclusion: Where to for social connection?

The chapters in this collection provide international, qualitative and quantitative evidence to shape guidelines for nurturing social connection across different everyday spaces. In personal spaces, the evidence points to the need for educational campaigns that encourage more respectful and diverse relationships, particularly among men (Chapter 2). These initiatives should critically examine how everyday social institutions – from migrant networks to family structures to care facilities – either support or potentially hinder meaningful social interaction. As shown throughout the collection, expanding and diversifying personal networks is crucial, whether for elderly residents in care facilities (Chapter 4) or transnational families maintaining connections across borders (Chapter 3).

For physical spaces, the studies advocate for stronger government regulation and investment in urban design and amenities that prioritize social connection. This includes ensuring housing is affordable, high quality and conducive to hosting social gatherings (Chapter 6). The evidence suggests taking a flexible, personalized approach to providing housing and community facilities while designing programmes that create opportunities for incidental interactions, as demonstrated by the success of initiatives like parkrun (Chapter 8).

In community spaces, successful interventions require careful customization to fit diverse cultural and identity needs, particularly for marginalized groups (Chapter 10). Programmes should maintain flexible designs that actively encourage community engagement while focusing on connecting people to appropriate support networks rather than generic social opportunities. As Farmer and colleagues (Chapter 12) demonstrate, this requires considering the interplay between personal, organizational and digital means of fostering connection.

Digital spaces, while presenting their own challenges, offer important opportunities when thoughtfully integrated with physical interaction. The evidence suggests using digital tools to create safe, destigmatized spaces (Chapter 13) while fostering positive online interactions and resilience. However, as several chapters emphasize, the digital connection works best when it complements rather than replaces face-to-face interaction (Chapter 14 and Chapter 15).

Critically, these spatial dimensions of social connection are deeply interconnected and shaped by broader structural forces. Future research and interventions must address how macro social and urban processes shape community and neighbourhood interactions (Cheshire, 2022). It should focus on issues of resourcing and inequality, recognize the influence of socioeconomic conditions and demographic intersections, and account for how stigma compounds disconnection. While conventional institutions and networks remain important, new forms of connection are emerging that deserve attention. Throughout all spaces, people maintain agency in making connections, though this can be enhanced through carefully tailored programmes that recognize social connection as fundamentally relational rather than purely individual.

While providing new conceptualization and contextual understandings of social connection in personal, physical, community and digital spaces, there are still, nonetheless, gaps worthy of future research. A central part of this book – and the focus of our opening chapter – was about highlighting a need to properly scrutinize what is meant by those discussing and studying social connection and to more appropriately capture, describe and define it in a manner that has been elusive thus far. This elusiveness stems partly from the absence of a unified social connection theory, with researchers instead drawing upon and synthesizing theoretical frameworks from adjacent concepts such as social capital, social networks and belonging.

In our opening chapter, we charted some perspectives that drive researchers' understandings of social connection and where it is situated in disciplines of knowledge. We developed the idea that social connection is fundamentally *relational* (Crossley, 2010), representing simultaneously an individual's subjective evaluation of how their relationships make them feel and the functions of their relationships. These aspects may be related to the quality of a person's relationships and their own structural position within broader social circles and contexts. The synthesized conceptualization we outline in Chapter 1 indicates social connection as a phenomenon that interconnects people through social, cultural and structural relationships and networks rather than something reducible to individual skills or responsibilities (Patulny and Olson, 2019). This synthesis reflects the need to draw together diverse theoretical strands to fully capture the complexity of social connection.

Looking at the chapters through the lens of this synthesized model, we can see varied levels of engagement with these different circles of connection and their dimensions of connection. Several chapters examine close connections: Patulny (Chapter 2) reveals how masculinity norms affect men's capacity for intimate bonds, while Bennetts and colleagues (Chapter 5) extend this to human–animal relationships. The role of social allies is evident in Battiston and Alexander's (Chapter 11) analysis of how Italian-Australians mobilized support networks during the pandemic and in Cabalquinto's (Chapter 3) examination of how older Filipina Australians maintain transnational connections through digital means.

Group connections are explored through various lenses: Hookway and Dwyer (Chapter 8) show how parkrun creates 'episodic togetherness' through shared rituals, while Opacin and colleagues (Chapter 10) demonstrate how nature-based activities can foster group belonging among LGBTQIA+ refugees. Wider community belonging is examined in several contexts: Farmer and colleagues (Chapter 12) reveal how social infrastructure supports community connection in urban fringe areas. Knox and Komu (Chapter 4) show how care facility design can nurture broader social engagement among older adults.

The structural dimensions of connection are particularly evident in studies of physical spaces, such as Bower and colleagues' (Chapter 6) analysis of housing environments and Sung's (Chapter 7) examination of urban–rural disparities in South Korean networks. The quality dimension emerges strongly in studies of digital connection, with Franks (Chapter 13), Barbosa Neves (Chapter 14) and Savic and McCosker (Chapter 15) all exploring how digital platforms can support or hinder meaningful interaction across different age groups and contexts.

Despite this rich engagement with different aspects of social connection, several research gaps remain. Mapping the patterns and networks across individuals and social groups circles of connection, their complexity, and outcomes requires further attention. While some studies, like Sung's examination of elder networks and Patulny's analysis of men's connections, begin this work, we need a more systematic investigation of how different circles of connection interact with sociodemographic characteristics and structural conditions. The role of economic resources and social capital in enabling or constraining both initial connection to diverse social contacts and maintenance of networks also deserves deeper examination. This may be particularly so in relation to work and employment. Work can be a significant place to make connection, but a long-hours work culture and irregular shift work are detrimental to making and keeping local neighbourhood connections. Given recent findings that unemployment significantly impacts loneliness and isolation (Peterie et al, 2019; Botha and Bower, 2024), understanding how aspects of workplaces like different rules and cultures, changing between workplaces and periods of unemployment, affect social connection, is important. Social connection or disconnection might also affect satisfaction with work, affecting retention and productivity, and so intersections between satisfaction with work and work-related opportunities to connect, at and outside workplaces, are crucial.

Digital connection presents its own research challenges. As Frank's analysis of young women's pandemic experiences shows, we need to better understand how personal social networks adapt to and recover from major disruptions and how digital platforms can support this resilience. Similarly, the role of digital platforms in social connection for people with chronic conditions affecting mobility, decline in mobility due to ageing, and mental health conditions affecting social anxiety and stigma, would benefit from further research. This includes examining how digital spaces interact with physical ones during periods of change and adaptation. The intersection of digital literacy, social inequality, and social connection outcomes also requires further investigation, as highlighted by Savic and McCosker's work with urban youth.

Ultimately, this collection demonstrates that improving social connection requires attention to both structural conditions and individual agency across multiple spaces. While personal choices and actions matter, they operate within broader social, cultural, political, economic and technological contexts that shape connection opportunities. Therefore, future research and interventions must work at multiple levels – from supporting individual capacity for meaningful connection to addressing the structural barriers that limit connection opportunities. Only by understanding social connection as fundamentally relational rather than purely individual can we develop effective strategies for fostering it across all spaces of everyday life.

Looking ahead: challenges and opportunities

The challenges ahead are significant. We have to ask ourselves why social (dis)connection is such a prominent problem right now? Certainly, our susceptibility, awareness and even fear of disconnection may be heightened by our recent – literally isolating – experiences of a pandemic. However, unlike COVID-19, social disconnection is not a sudden emergent disease that we can treat with tried and tested interventions. We might understand the decline of social connection as a bit of a societal slow burn influenced by forces including changing political ideology from welfarism to individualism – influencing our capacity to care about others or seeing relating as valuable. Coupled with prioritizing techno-determinism as acceptable for driving work culture, we are where we are. Potentially deeply entrenched in social atomization.

However, before we give up and creep to our computers to seek solace in watching Netflix on our own, we need to look for the rays of hope. Very recently, there has been a move, reflected in this book, from focusing solely on loneliness, measuring loneliness and competing about which suburb or country is most lonely to talking about social connection. While social connection is something of an umbrella term, as we've discussed, this may be beneficial. This means there can be a range of interventions, practitioner and organizational roles, types of policies, and structural and individual-oriented actions to address the issue. As we've noted, this is precisely what is needed as social connection is relational. It needs a supportive policy context, built environment, service inputs and changing peoples' attitudes to hosting, kindness and reciprocity. It will be hard to change structural issues of work to value and support social connection among workers. It will be hard to see social media as for support and care rather than angry shouting. However, social connection is now widely discussed – particularly in public health policy – with its structural determinants acknowledged. Perhaps this means bold moves to bolster interventions and roles to nurture solidarity are just around the corner. This book contains useful insights about where to start.

References

Botha, F. and Bower, M. (2024) 'Predictors of male loneliness across life stages: an Australian study of longitudinal data', *BMC Public Health*, 24, Article 1285.

Bower, M., Smout, S., Johnson, S., Costello, A., Andres, L., Donohoe-Bales, A. et al (2024) *Placing social connection at the heart of public policy in the United Kingdom and Australia*, UCL Policy Lab & The Matilda Centre for Research in Mental Health and Substance Use. https://doi.org/10.25910/3eb2-6h89

Cheshire, L. (2022) *Neighbours around the World: An International Look at the People Next Door*, Emerald Publishing.

Cheshire, L., Easthope, H. and ten Have, C. (2021) 'Unneighbourliness and the unmaking of home', *Housing, Theory and Society*, 38(2), 133–151.

Cheung, L.T.O., Fung, I.H.H., Wong, J.Y.H. and Yip, P.S.F. (2017) 'High-rise living and social interaction: a study of residents in Hong Kong', *Habitat International*, 63, 94–103.

Crossley, N. (2010) *Towards Relational Sociology*, Routledge.

Franklin, A., Barbosa Neves, B., Hookway, N., Patulny, R., Tranter, B. and Jaworski, K. (2019) 'Towards an understanding of loneliness among Australian men: gender cultures, embodied expression and the social bases of belonging', *Journal of Sociology*, 55(1), 124–143.

Glavin, P., Bierman, A. and Schieman, S. (2019) 'Workers in the gig economy feel lonely and powerless', *The Conversation*. Available at: https://theconversation.com/workers-in-the-gig-economy-feel-lonely-and-powerless-127188 (Accessed 15 March 2025).

Grzymala-Kazlowska, A. and Ryan, L. (2022) 'Bringing anchoring and embedding together: theorising migrants' lives over-time', *Comparative Migration Studies*, 10, 46.

Hookway, N. and Cruickshank, V. (2024) 'Changing masculinities? Using caring masculinity to analyse social media responses to the decline of men in Australian primary school teaching', *Journal of Sociology*, 60(1), 229–247.

Hookway, N., Barbosa Neves, B., Franklin, A. and Patulny, R. (2019) 'Loneliness and love in late modernity: sites of tension and resistance', in R. Patulny, A. Bellocchi, R.E. Olson, S. Khorana, J. McKenzie and M. Peterie (eds) *Emotions in Late Modernity*, Routledge, pp 83–97.

Hsu, J. (2021) *Being Chinese in Australia*, Lowy Institute.

Leigh, A. and Terrel, N. (2020) *Reconnected: A Community Builders Handbook*, La Trobe University Press.

Neves, B.B., Sanders, A. and Kokanović, R. (2019) '"It's the worst bloody feeling in the world": experiences of loneliness and social isolation among older people living in care homes', *Journal of Aging Studies*, 49, 74–84.

Neves, B.B., Petersen, A., Vered, M., Carter, A. and Omori, M. (2023) 'Artificial intelligence in long-term care: technological promise, aging anxieties, and sociotechnical ageism', *Journal of Applied Gerontology*, 42(6), 1274–1282.

Nilan, P., Roose, J., Peucker, M. and Turner, B. (2023) 'Young masculinities and right-wing populism in Australia', *Youth*, 3, 285–299.

Nowland, R., Necka, E. and Cacioppo, J. (2018) 'Loneliness and social internet use: pathways to reconnection in a digital world?', *Perspectives on Psychological Science*, 13(1), 70–87.

Patulny, R. (2009) 'The golden years? Social contact amongst retired men and women in Australia', *Family Matters*, 83, 39–47.

Patulny, R. (2015) 'A spectrum of integration: examining combinations of bonding and bridging social capital and network heterogeneity amongst Australian refugee and skilled migrants', in L. Ryan (ed) *Migrant Capital: Networks, Identities and Strategies*, Palgrave Macmillan, pp 207–229.

Patulny, R. (2020) 'Does social media make us more or less lonely depends on how you use it', *The Conversation*, 22 January. Available at: https://theconversation.com/does-social-media-make-us-more-or-less-lonely-depends-on-how-you-use-it-128468 (Accessed 15 March 2025).

Patulny, R. (2024) '"Happy wives, happy social lives?" Men are more emotionally disconnected than women – what can be done about it?', *The Conversation*, 1 October. Available at: https://theconversation.com/happy-wives-happy-social-lives-men-are-more-emotionally-disconnected-than-women-what-can-be-done-about-it-239194 (Accessed 15 March 2025).

Patulny, R. and Svendsen, G. (2007) 'The social capital grid: bonding, bridging, qualitative, quantitative', *International Journal of Sociology and Social Policy*, 27(1/2), 32–51.

Patulny, R. and Olson, R. (2019) 'Emotions in late modernity' in R. Patulny, A. Bellocchi, R. Olson, S. Khorana, J. McKenzie and M. Peterie (eds) *Emotions in Late Modernity*, Routledge, pp 8–24.

Peterie, M., Ramia, G., Marston, G. and Patulny, R. (2019) 'Social isolation as stigma-management: explaining long-term unemployed people's "failure" to network', *Sociology*, 53(6), 1043–1060.

Pointon, D., Hughes, B. and Cook, L. (2020) *The Men's Table: A Model of Care*, National Mental Health Commission.

Soja, E. (2000) *Postmetropolis: Critical Studies of Cities and Regions*, Blackwell Publishers.

Zhao, I.Y., Holroyd, E., Garrett, N., Wright-St Clair, V.A. and Neville, S. (2023) 'Chinese late-life immigrants' loneliness and social isolation in host countries: an integrative review', *Journal of Clinical Nursing*, 32, 1615–1624.

Index

References to figures appear in *italic* type; those in **bold** type refer to tables.
References to endnotes show both the page number and the note number (230n1).

A

aesthetic communities 119, 120
affordable housing 93, 96, 97, 123, 150, 174, 235
ageing population 42, 61, 103, 232
agency 3, 4–5, 44, 240
Alberti, F. 207
allies 12, 221, 225, 227, 242
Alone Together Study 94–95
animals *see* human-animal interactions; insect control; pet ownership
anthrozoology 72–73
anxiety 73, 76, 77, 145, 150, 192
art and craft 64–65
asylum seekers *see* LGBTQIA+ asylum seekers and refugees
Australia
  COVID-19 pandemic 160–161
  loneliness 89
  long-term care 57
  pet ownership 71–72
  stay-at-home orders 94–97
  urban fringe areas 174, 175–176
  see also Italian-Australian community; older Filipino Australians
Australian Housing Conditions Dataset 95
Australian Red Cross 12
Australian Social Attitudes Survey (AUSSA) 25

B

Baldassar, L. 44
Bauman, Z. 119
belonging 121, 122, 123–124, 184, 229
BeReal 224, 225, 229
Biehler, D. 131
bifocality 44
bonding social capital 8–9, 161
  Parkrun 125, 126, 127
bonding ties 168

Bourdieu, P. 8
Bowling Alone (Putnam) 161
bridging social capital 8–9, 31, 161
bridging ties 168
built environment 4, 6
  and loneliness 90–98
  long-term care 59, 62–63, 65–67
  see also housing; physical spaces
built infrastructure 177, 178–179
Bumble 226
Bumble BFF 224, 225, 230n1
bunkerization 133, 134
Burkitt, I. 52

C

care practices 44, 48–51
care staff 59, 62, 65
Carrasco, S. 162
Cheshire, L. 37
children
  caring for 44
  men's relationship towards 28, 31
  older adults living with 106, 109, 112
  Parkrun 126
  and pets 72, 74, 76, 77, 79–80
  see also grandchildren
Chinese networks 10
close connections 12, **13**, 168, 221, 242
  with neighbours 183
  through digital technologies 226, 229, 238
co-housing 93
collective loneliness 220
Collins, R. 120
Commission on Social Connection, WHO 1, 146
community 6
  see also aesthetic communities; local community
community activities 180
  see also social activities

247

community development perspectives 9–10
community engagement 237
community spaces 6, 8, 9, 79, 236–237, 241
convoy model of social relations *see* social convoy model
cooking 47–48
cost of living 232
COVID-19 pandemic
  Australia 160–161
  and community connections 4
  and digital technology 5, 191–193, 223–224
  impact on Italian-Australian community 162–170
  impact on migrant communities 159, 160–161
  and loneliness 210–211, 212–213
  older adults' social network profiles 102–113
  and pet ownership 71, 73–81
  and social capital 162
  stay-at-home orders 94–97
  young women's social connections during 191–201
  five stages of social adaptation 195–199
  social disruption 192–192
cultural differences 152–153
cultural frameworks 10
culture shift 62

D

deinstitutionalization 61
depression 73, 145, 150, 192
depressive symptoms **111**, 112
diabetes 47
digital ambivalence(s) 212–214
digital communication 232–233
digital connection 4–5, 243
  during COVID-19 pandemic 191–193, 197–198
  pre-COVID-19 196
  in urban fringe areas 182, 185, 219–229
digital divides 5
digital emotional support 225–226, 229
digital knitting 44
digital literacy workshops 229
digital media practices
  older Filipino Australians 42–54
    as care practices 48–51
    challenges 51–53
    as self-care 46–48
digital platforms 7, 9
  see also digital technologies; social media platforms
digital social connection ecosystem 221–222
digital spaces 8, 237–238, 241
digital technologies
  and community development 9–10
  and cultural norms 10

and loneliness 205–214
men 33, 37–38
and temporal dimensions of social connection 11
see also social media; social media platforms
Discord 225–226, 229, 230n2
Dunbar, R. 12, 220
Dunn, R. 131

E

economic inequality 3
economic resources 243
educational campaigns 234
emails 106, 113, 207, 213
emotional ambivalence 52
emotional loneliness 89
emotional support 225–226, 229
emotions 120, 122
employment 185, 243
episodic togetherness 124–125, 127, 128
exercise *see* Parkrun
external structures 7, 24

F

Facebook 46, 47–48, 49, 53, 226, 227–228, 229
Facebook Messenger 50–51, 52
family
  importance to Italian-Australian community 167, 168, 169
  importance to men 29, 31, 36, 37
  importance to older adults 102
  lack of support from 225, 226
  and Parkrun 126
family relationships 227–228
family structures 233
Farmer, J. 44, 177
feelings 33, *34*
  see also emotions
Filipino Australians *see* older Filipino Australians
financial wellbeing 164–165
Finland
  ageing population 61
  long-term care 57–58, 60–68
Finnish Elderly Care Act 61–62
Foundation for Social Connection 90
Friends in Nature (FIN) intervention 149–154
friendships
  on digital platforms 224, 226
  men 28, 29, 35, 37, 125
  Parkrun 125–126
  time investment 11

G

gender *see* male social connectivity; non-binary persons; young women's social connections
gender differences in norms and attitudes 27

INDEX

gender differences in social networks and support 30
gender differences in social practices, interactions and activities 32
gender differences in socially oriented feelings 34
gender roles 233
government regulation 235
grandchildren 44, 49–50
Green, H. 162
group connections 242
guanxi networks 10

H

Hall, J.A. 11
health and wellbeing 145, 147–148
  see also mental health; nature-based social prescribing (NBSP); social prescribing (SP)
health information 46–47
health outcomes 23
hegemonic cultures 36
hegemonic masculinity 26, 35, 233
Hindley, D. 122, 124
housing 91–98, 133–134, 235–236
  affordable 93, 96, 97, 123, 150, 174, 235
  see also built environment
housing disrepair 92
housing tenure 94, 96
housing types 92–93, 95
human-animal interactions 72–73
  see also insect control; pet ownership

I

identity needs 237
  see also queer identity; social identity
immigration 233
  see also Italian-Australian community; migrants; older Filipino Australians
Indigenous Australians 183
individual agency 3, 4–5, 44, 240
individual-centred interventions 4
  see also social prescribing (SP)
inequality 3, 239
insect control 130, 131, 134–140
Instagram 179, 192, 199, 223–225, 226, 227, 229
institutionalization 59
  see also deinstitutionalization
interaction rituals 120, 123–124
intercultural reflections 152–153
internal structures 7–8, 24
internet connectivity 51–52
intimate loneliness 220
Italian-Australian community 159–160
  impact of COVID-19 on 162–170

J

Japan 1, 146
job satisfaction 62

K

Kahn, R.L. and Antonucci, T.C. 194
kindness 26, 29, 31, 35
Kišjuhas, A. 122

L

Lass-Hennemann, J. 80
latent class analysis (LCA) 105
leisure rituals 122, 123–124
LGBTQIA+ asylum seekers and refugees 147, 148–149
  nature-based social prescribing (NBSP) 149–154
life course theory 10–11
lived environment 93–94, 95
local community 60, 67
local engagement 185
local social connection 174–185
  connection to locale 181–182
  digital connection 182
  local locations and connection 178–180
  opportunities for connection 182–183
  social activities 180
loneliness 3, 90, 205–206
  among men 125
  in Australia 89
  and built environment 90–98
  and digital technology 205–214
  and health 23, 145
  and stigma 239–240
  through COVID-19 lockdowns 162
  types of 220
  urban fringe areas 174
long-term care
  Finish case study 57–58, 60–68
  social connection in 58–59

M

Maffesoli, M. 120
Makridis, C.A. and Wu, C. 162
male social connectivity 23–24
  and masculinity norms 26–28
  policy and research recommendations 36–38
  social disconnection 35–36
  social networks and support 28–31
  social practices, interactions and activities 31–33
  socially oriented feelings 33, *34*
Many Coloured Sky 147, 150
marginalized groups 3, 5, 222
masculinity norms 26–28, 37, 233
mental health
  and COVID-19 73, 76, 80, 94–95, 165
  older Koreans 109
  Parkrun 126
  and social capital 162

and social media platforms 222, 225
  see also anxiety; depression;
    depressive symptoms
migrants 6–7, 42
  impact of COVID-19 on 159, 160–161
  social capital 162
  see also Italian-Australian community;
    older Filipino Australians
Migration Data Portal 42
Mude, W. 161
multicultural events 180

N

nature 179
nature-based social prescribing (NBSP) 146–147
  LGBTQIA+ asylum seekers and
    refugees 149–154
neighbour connections 130, 132,
  137–139, 140
neighbour relationships 132, 183
neighbourhood communication 130, 135
neighbourhoods 175, 176
  see also local social connection
neighbouring 131–134
  and insect control 134–140
neo-tribalism 120
network structure 193
Never Home Alone (Dunn) 131
non-binary persons 227–228

O

older Filipino Australians
  digital media practices 42–54
    as care practices 48–51
    challenges 51–53
    as self-care 46–48
older Koreans' social network
  profiles 102–113
older migrants 42
older people
  and loneliness 3, 206–209
    complexity of loneliness 210–211
    digital ambivalence(s) 212–214
    technological bridges 211–212
  see also long-term care; older
    Filipino Australians
Organization for Economic Co-operation
  and Development (OECD) 5
O'Rourke, H. and Sidani, S. 207

P

Pahl, R. 12
Parents, Pets & Pandemic Survey 74
Parkrun 118–128
  episodic togetherness 124–125, 127, 128
  friendships 125–126
  rituals 123–124
  social connection 119–120, 121–123

Patulny, R. and Bower, M. 162
personal connections 3
personal spaces 6, 8, 233–235, 241
Pests in the City (Biehler) 131
pet ownership 71–81
  benefits and challenges 77–80
  pet attachment and pet-related activities 76
photo elicitation 45, 46
physical spaces 8, 36–28, 235–236,
  241, 243
  see also built environment
physical-structural constraints 4
place-based social connection 174–185
  connection to locale 181–182
  digital connection 182
  local locations and connection 178–180
  opportunities for connection 182–183
  social activities 180
Polish migrants 6–7
population ageing 42, 61, 103, 232
positivity 122
process, social connection as 24–25
psychological intervention 4
  see also social prescribing (SP)
public spaces 4, 124, 178–180, 184–185
Putnam, R. 119, 161

Q

queer identity 227
  see also LGBTQIA+ asylum seekers
    and refugees
Queer Refugee and Asylum Seeker Peers
  (QRASP) 147, 150, 151

R

Ratcliffe, J. 26, 29, 31
Re-imagining Environments for Connection
  and Engagement (RECTAS) 146–147, 149
reciprocity 193
refugees *see* LGBTQIA+ asylum seekers
  and refugees
relational approaches 7–8
relational loneliness 220
relationship formation 11
resilience 197
resilience theory 194, 199–200
resourcing 239
Rezes Acosta, C. 7
rituals 120, 122, 123–124
Russia 131–134
  see also St. Petersburg
Ryan, L. 6, 35, 162

S

safety, sense of 168, 179
shared places 184–185
  see also public spaces
Shigeto, A. 192

INDEX

social activities 177, 180, 236
  long-term care 59, 64–65, 67
  men 31–33, 35
  older adults 113
social adaptation 195–199, 201
social allies 12, 221, 225, 227, 242
social brain hypothesis 12
social capital 8–9, 161–162, 168, 196, 198, 243
  see also bonding social capital; bridging social capital
social capital theory 193, 194, 199
social connection 1–2, 89–90, 161, 220–221, 232–233
  challenges and opportunities 243
  community development perspectives 9–10
  community/societal connectedness 6
  cultural dimensions 10
  functional dimensions 5–6
  future research 241–242
  importance of 205–206
  in long-term care 58–59
    challenges to 59–60
  at Parkrun 119–120, 121–124
  pragmatic synthesised models 11–14, 242
  as process 24–25
  quality dimensions 6
  relational approaches 7–8, 242
  research gaps 243–244
  and social capital 8–9
  social network perspectives 6–7
  structural constraints 3–5
  structural dimensions 5
  temporal dimensions 10–11
  see also local social connection; male social connectivity
social connection collapse 196–197
social connection ecosystem 219, 220, 221
social convoy model 11, 194, 200
social convoys 194, 196, 197–199, 200
social determinants of health models 147–148
social disruption 192–193
  five stages of social adaptation 195–199
social identity 96
social infrastructure 4, 97–98, 174, 177, 235
social institutions 234
social isolation 23, 162, 192, 197
social loneliness 89
social manners 28
social media 207
social media platforms 8, 191–192, 222, 223–225, 226, 227, 229, 238
  see also individual platforms
social network profiles 102–113
social network theory 6–7
social networks 24, 102, 234–235

Italian-Australian community **167**, 168–169
  men 28–31, 35, 37
  migrants 162
social prescribing (SP) 4, 90, 127, 146, 175, 239
  see also nature-based social prescribing (NBSP)
social resilience 194
socially oriented feelings 33, *34*
societal connectedness 6
socioeconomic conditions 239
socioeconomic status 93, 167–168
solitude 197
South Korea
  ageing population 103
  older adults' social network profiles 103–113
Soviet Union 133–134
sports *see* Parkrun
St. Petersburg 131
  neighbouring and insect control 134–140
staff development 65
stay-at-home orders 94–97, 160
stigma 239–240
Stones, R. 7, 24
structural constraints 3–5
structural inequalities 239
structured environment 92–93, 95–96
support networks 237

T

third spaces 4, 124
togetherness, episodic 124–125, 127, 128
transactional relational norms 28, 35
transport 4, 174
travel restrictions 106, 159, 160, 165, 168
trust 26, 35, 193
Twitter (X) 226

U

unemployment 243
United Kingdom 1
  Loneliness Strategy 90
  Minister of Loneliness 146
  pet ownership 72
United Nations 42
United States
  Foundation for Social Connection 90
  pet ownership 72, 73
urban environments 232
urban fringe areas 174–185
  connection to locale 181–182
  digital connection 182, 185, 219–229
  ideas for policy and practice 184–185
  local locations and connection 178–180
  opportunities for connection 182–183
  social activities 180

251

V

videoconferencing 207
volunteering 185

W

WhatsApp 150, 152, *153*, 182, 229
work 243
work practices 232
World Health Organization, Commission on Social Connection 1, 146

Y

young women's social connection 191–201
   five stages of social adaptation 195–199
   recommendations for practitioners 200–201
   social disruption 192–193
YouTube 46–47, 213

Z

Zontini, E. 44

www.ingramcontent.com/pod-product-compliance
Lightning Source LLC
Chambersburg PA
CBHW051533020426
42333CB00016B/1912